SERENDIPITY

The genealogy of Tomes, Steel, Raymaley and Schaeffer families

JAMES STEEL TOMES

authorHOUSE®

AuthorHouse™
1663 Liberty Drive
Bloomington, IN 47403
www.authorhouse.com
Phone: 1-800-839-8640

Published by AuthorHouse 01/21/2015

ISBN: 978-1-4969-3842-8 (sc)
ISBN: 978-1-4969-3841-1 (e)

SERENDIPITY

The genealogy of Tomes, Steel, Raymaley and Schaeffer families

James Steel Tomes

CONTENTS

ACKNOWLEDGEMENTS

I could not have written this book without help from family members, our "English Cousins" namely retired Major Ian M. Tomes, of Somerset, England, the late Colonel L.T. Tomes, Lord Edward Baldwin of Oxford, and my American cousins, Arthur C. Tomes, Arthur Tomes Lewry and his wife Lolly, Mary Tomes Prinz, Francis Phillip Tomes, Joanna Gunderson, and the late Alexander Hadden Tomes and Gordon Fairburn; Tom Drysdale, and Sylvia Hague (Raymaley) Duncan as well as the many other Tomes, Steel and Raymaley cousins and friends here in the United States; my college roommate and now late Professor of Sociology and author of many books, our close friend Dr. Robert Dentler and his wife Helen; my good friend and published author, Steven Lewis; fellow Caxtonians, Edward Quattrocchi, John Blew, Kim Coventry, and Hayward Blake and long time friends, Dick and Jackie Higgins, and Bob and Nancy Gunn, Robin Goldsmith and my good friend and long-time religious teacher, Reverend Philip Blackwell; Jack Simpson, the remarkably skilled and very patient curator of the genealogy and local history sections of the Newberry Library. Professional editing help has been given generously by our good friend, Virginia Steele Wood, a published author and Reference Specialist in Naval & Maritime History, and Genealogy, at the Library of Congress in Washington, D.C.

Many thanks also to John Rosenheim, a long time friend, with his wife Audrey, and helpful business consultant, who provided significant production assistance to the publication of my essay "Where Are The Christians".

And last, but certainly never least, my wife, Josie who has heard all these stories many times over. Thank you, one and all.

Josie and I also want to acknowledge the help and knowledge we have gained during our lives from the many, many other friends we have made during our lives. I have only been able to mention a few here and in the body of this book – there are simply too many to list but they are all remembered, appreciated and acknowledged.

Since I live in Chicago, I have organized my comments about genealogy around the resources of The Newberry Library. It has one of America's outstanding collections of genealogical resources, and a uniquely well-qualified and helpful staff. Its Friends of Genealogy (FOG) conduct frequent workshops and other genealogy programs. It is "one of America's best kept secrets" that I invite everyone to learn more about and use, by visiting in person or via their website. (www.newberry.org), or by mail to:

The Newberry Library
60 West Walton Street
Chicago, Illinois 60010
Telephone: (312) 255- 3510

I have found my own genealogical search most rewarding in surprisingly meaningful ways, and want to share the experience and knowledge with others. As with the writing of many family stories, a major incentive is to make a record for one's family of cousins, children, grandchildren and friends.

The Appendix of this book is a summary of the journals, letters, memoirs, articles, books and pedigrees that I discovered during my long search.

James S. Tomes

DEDICATION

This book is dedicated to the memory of our ancestors, but mainly to our children and grandchildren, and their descendants. To our ancestors for their legacy of hard work, integrity, tenacity and adventurous spirit. And to our descendants in the hope that they will find these stories of interest, inspiration and help as they find their own ways in this increasingly complicated and difficult world.

When we discovered the treasure trove of manuscripts, books and records left by our ancestors we decided that we should pass on their stories and the stories of our own lives, and hopefully stimulate our descendants to do the same for their descendants. Some of our grandchildren are quite young so we will probably not get to know them as full grown adults, but by passing on our family history and our memoirs they will at least be able read about who we think we are and what we think of the times we live in.*

So, this book is part family history, part memoir, and part commentary on the scientific and religious lessons of genealogy. Those lessons are, namely; that we are all mortals with but a limited time here on earth; that we are brothers and sisters with all the other humans on this earth; that we must do our best to live beneficial lives; and take good care of the earth, its creatures and natural beauty, for as long as we are its guests and caretakers.

Jim and Josie Tomes,
Chicago, Illinois, 2008

*This book should be read in tandem with "The Private Travel Journals of Francis Tomes (1780-1869), "Our Great-Grandfather" (correspondence between Mary Elizabeth Tomes Burckhardt and her father Francis Tomes (1840-1868, with photographs), "The Private Memoirs of Robert Tomes" (1817-1882), and Robert Tomes's many books and articles.

"Gee, Dad, we seem to come from a long line of people who have all died!"

PREFACE

Serendipity

The first public telling of part of this story, which is now this book, was a short luncheon talk I gave at the Newberry Library for the Caxton Club in April, 2000, eight years ago. My good friend, Ed Quattrocchi, Renaissance scholar and fellow Caxtonian, told me that I "owed it to the club to do a luncheon talk", and he was right. The short talk was well received and I was encouraged to follow it up with an article for the Caxtonian. When I started to write the full story I realized that it would be far too long for an article. I therefore began to write the book, which has since morphed into two related books of over two hundred pages, now virtually finished, to be published later this year. Then, Tony Batko was also right when he told me I should present it as a paper to the Chicago Literary Club, and he "volunteered" me to present it on April 3rd, 2006. So, I give thanks to both Ed and Tony for spurring me on.

This first book, "Serendipity", is about discovering our family's genealogies. The second book, "The Meanings of Genealogy", is about the religious and scientific views of the history of mankind, and the relationship between genealogy, science and religion.

Introduction

Why bother with genealogies at all? Who cares? Isn't it just an impractical hobby? Well, yes, it is certainly impractical, but it can also be a source of profound knowledge. Knowing, and being able to tell your children and grandchildren about the heroics, tragedies, successes and failures of their ancestors is a very personal way to relate their lives to history. Also, if you are as lucky as we have been, finding memoirs and journals and books written by our ancestors, they come alive as real people. To read what they thought over 150 years ago, in their own handwriting, is quite moving.

It is also profound in the sense that seeing your own ancestral tree is a personal reminder that none of us lives forever. Seeing your own name near the bottom of a long genealogical chart makes it very clear that we are each marching in an inexorable column of mortal human beings.

As our youngest daughter said, after seeing her place in a ten-generation family tree:

"Gee, Dad, we seem to come from a long line of people who have all died!"

Very true, and a dramatic way of teaching the lesson of every human being's mortality.

One of the not-so-obvious conceits of genealogy is the choice we all usually make to trace only one or two lines of ancestry that carry out paternal or maternal surnames. Tomes or Steel for me and Schaeffer or Raymaley, for Josie. The conceit is however, necessary because the geometric expansion of the number of each of our ancestors would quickly make our searches impossibly unwieldy if we didn't limit them.

For example; since we all have two parents, and each of them have two parents, etc., the arithmetic illustrates the problem in just ten generations. The geometric progression of 2, 4, 8, 16, 32, 64, 128, 256, 512, and 1,024, shows that each of us has 1,024 ances-

tors in just ten generations! An impossibly huge chart. It is however very important to remember that if we trace one surname back ten generations we are only seeing 1/1,024th of our genetic heritage at the tenth generation. We are each the product of an enormous gene pool. The recent developments in the science of population genetics, using DNA science, show how all mankind is closely related and has left a traceable trail of its migrations covering the earth.

Counting generations backwards in history is also instructive. If each generation takes twenty years, ten generations should take 200 years. But my Tomes family's ancestry has actually averaged thirty-five years per generation for ten generations, so our direct ancestry goes back 350 years to the 1600's. Our indirect, collateral, Tomes ancestry goes back to the 1400's in England, another five generations, totaling fifteen, give or take a few. Since surnames were rarely used by ordinary people before the 1400's it is extremely rare to find genealogies that go back further in time.

But, for a scientific and historical perspective, if you count backwards in time to the emergence of Upright Man (Homo Erectus) 1,500,000 years ago from Africa, you get 100,000 generations at 15 yrs/gen. Or, if you count backwards 200,000 years ago to the emergence of Homo Sapiens in Africa, you get 13,300 generations, or 60,000 years ago to the first emigration out of Africa of Homo Sapiens, our common ancestor, you get 4,000 generations, at 15 yrs/gen. (In this remote sense we are all "African-Americans") Or, if you count back to the magnificent cave art at Chauvet, in the Ardeche, France, 33,000 years ago, you get 2,200 generations; or to the cave art at Lascaux, 18,000 years ago, you get 1,200 generations. Or, from 5000 BCE when writing first appeared in Sumer, you get 460 generations, and from the beginning of the Egyptian Dynasties in 3,950 BCE, you get 290 generations. So, ten, or fifteen, or even twenty-five, generations doesn't get us very far back in history!

Also, for a Biblical perspective, the New Testament shows two separate and very different genealogies for Jesus, one in Matthew and one in Luke. Matthew traces 14 generations from Abraham to King David, then 28 more generations from David to Jesus, totaling 42. Luke traces backwards in time to David in 43 generations, then on to Abraham in 15 more generations, totaling 58 generations, a difference of 16 generations between Luke and Matthew. Luke then proceeds to list 20 more generations from Abraham to Adam, totaling 78 generations from Jesus to Adam. A comparison of the two genealogies also shows almost no similarity between the names, as well as the number of

generations. It is obvious that Matthew and Luke didn't coordinate their genealogies, but it is also obvious that they each thought it was of great importance to link Jesus to the Old Testament Hebrew heritage of Abraham and David, as foretold in Isaiah. And the Old Testament genealogies in Genesis and Chronicles tell an incredibly creative story of the lives of the Prophets whose average life span in Genesis is well over 500 years! So much for Biblical genealogy. Most other religions have equally creative genealogies. But, the main points are: First, the fact of our inevitable mortality; Second; the personal stories of our ancestors; Third, the historical and religious significance of genealogies; and Fourth, our close genetic relationship with all other human beings.

The Search

The search is the story of a forty-year-long genealogical search that ultimately reunited my long separated family of Tomes ancestors and cousins, and the story of Josie's ancestors. The search also enabled me to find and collect the many 19th century books and magazine articles written by my great-grandfather, Dr. Robert Tomes, and also a treasure-trove of his and his father Francis's unpublished journals, letters, and memoirs. Most of these manuscripts have now been restored, transcribed and published privately, and are now in the special collections of the Newberry Library. It also enabled us to restore Josie's family farm and cemetery.

The search is called "Serendipitous" because of the repeated accidental good fortune that propelled the search forward, albeit after many long interruptions. While our results were unusually successful, many other amateur genealogists have told me of similar experiences. The main lesson of this search for other amateur genealogists is to follow up every lead and never give up. Some serendipitous events will probably happen to keep your search alive.

The word "Serendipitous" was in fact coined by the English novelist, historian, book collector, and founder of the Strawberry Hill Press, Horace Walpole (1717-1797). It was based upon an Indian fable, "Three Princes of Serendip", the ancient name for Ceylon, now Sri Lanka. The fable tells the story of three princes who left Serendip and traveled the ancient world, repeatedly making accidental, but fortuitous discoveries. The fable thus perfectly describes my own experiences.

The book contains a number of short biographical sketches of my wife Josie's and my ancestors. My father's family surname is Tomes (English) and my mother's is Steel and Wilson (Scottish). My collateral Tomes ancestors started coming to America in the late 1600's. My direct ancestor, Francis Tomes, came to America in 1815.

The Tomes family group is still quite small, now numbering only about 900 families world wide, mostly in the United States and England, but with some in Canada, Australia, New Zealand and South Africa. The majority are from England, the Cotswolds area (Gloucester and Warwickshire) as well as Buckinghamshire and Dorset. There are also scatterings of families in mainland Europe, including Hungary, the former Czechoslovakia and the Ukraine. Some of these families have acquired the Tomes spelling of their name after their European name, such as "Tomescz" has been anglicized to "Tomes".

Josie's family is all Pennsylvania "Dutch", meaning "Deutsch" - German speaking from the southern Rhine valley - now Alsace in France, and the Palatinate - now north of Strasbourg in Germany, and western Switzerland. On Josie's mother's side were Schaeffers, Urichs and Witmeyers. On her father's side were Raymaleys, Nahligs, Schumachers and Burgers. Her Schumacher ancestor was with the Mennonite group led by Pastorious who settled Germantown near Philadelphia in 1683. The others followed soon after in the 1700's.

These family stories are not the epic sagas of famous people, but they are the true and often heroic stories of the lives of extended families of real, ordinary people. Most of them emigrated to America beginning in its early days, took great risks and worked hard to live good lives and, mostly, succeeded. Such stories are shared by many American families.

They crossed the Atlantic Ocean from England, Scotland and the Rhineland to Virginia, Pennsylvania and New York on small, dangerous, disease-prone sailing ships. Some worked off their contracts of servitude and homesteaded frontier farms; others started businesses and traveled throughout frontier America on horseback, stagecoach, wagons, and riverboats. They and their children fought as Yankees in the Revolutionary War and on both the Union and Confederate sides of the Civil War. Later on, others served during World Wars I and II, the Korean War, Vietnam and Iraq. They became farmers, soldiers, businessmen and businesswomen, doctors, writers, artists, lawyers, teachers and ministers. It is, in short, a very personal history of America. Some of these people are best described by their own journals memoirs and books, all available at the Newberry Library.

The book also includes brief biographical sketches of some contemporary Tomeses in England whom we call "Our English Cousins", because we have become quite friendly with them, staying at their homes and welcoming them to our homes here in Wilmette and Chicago. Chief among them is retired Major Ian M.

Tomes, who has provided the key genealogical information to solve the puzzle that stumped us here for over 35 years. More about "Our English Cousins" later.

In Chicago, we are most fortunate to have on our doorstep one of the best genealogical resource libraries in America, The Newberry Library. In addition to its great humanities collections, The Newberry has a very extensive genealogy collection, and an excellent staff ready to help the novice and the professional in starting and developing their searches.

And we also have some other great institutions here in Chicago for exploring other aspects of the history of mankind: The Field Museum, with its magnificent and just reopened permanent exhibit on the Evolving Planet showing the four billion year history of all life on earth; The Lutheran School of Theology, with its continuing annual, free to the public, course on the Epic of Creation, comparing the theological and scientific views of life on earth; the Oriental Institute, with its extraordinary displays of mankind's earliest history, from prehistoric times through the cultures of Mesopotamia in the middle east; the Adler Planetarium, with its astronomical view of the universe; The Pritzker Military Library; and the University of Chicago, with its great library and faculty resource, particularly in comparative religion.

... the first book came to me, serendipitously, from a neighbor, Tom Cullen, in Wilmette who called me to say that he had a three-volume history of the Civil War, "The War With The South", by a Robert Tomes ...

THE BEGINNING

The Story Of The Search

The story of the search began at the Newberry Library in 1959 where I learned for the first time about the existence of my great-grandfather Dr. Robert Tomes, in the National Encyclopedia of American Biography. My father had never told me about his grandfather Robert, whom I discovered from his brief biography was a medical doctor who wrote many histories and other books, as well as articles for Harper's Monthly Magazine, and who traveled extensively in Europe and America in the 1800's.

My father had rarely even talked about his own father who was also a medical doctor, but who died in 1920 before I was born. My father's parents had been divorced when he was just 14 years old and my father was given in custody to his father, who carelessly let him drop out of high school, thereby ending his formal education. The trauma of the divorce and his careless father probably made my father not want to know more about his ancestry. But my personal curiosity had led me to the Newberry. When I reported finding Robert's biography to my father he casually acknowledged his identity and then told me he thought his grandfather was buried in a family cemetery plot at Trinity Church in New York City.

I wrote to Trinity and learned that Robert, his mother Maria Roberts Tomes, and my grandfather, Dr. William Tomes, and many other family members were actually buried in the Trinity Cemetery Annex at 153rd Street and Riverside Drive, just south of the George Washington Bridge. The original Trinity Cemetery in lower Manhattan had been closed in 1845 and Robert's father, Francis Tomes, had bought the family plot in the Annex in 1852. The Annex had been donated to the church by John James Audubon, the ornithologist, who was also a member of Trinity Church and who owned a farm along the Hudson River. The Annex land is a steep, twenty-six acre hill that descends toward the river from what is now Broadway, to Riverside Drive, between 153rd and 155th Streets. Audubon and many other early New York City families are also buried there.

The discovery of Robert's biography started me on a search for copies of his books, but that was before the Internet and my occasional searching in bookstores for his books proved fruitless. However, the first book came to me, serendipitously, from a neighbor, Tom Cullen, in Wilmette who called me to say that he had a three-volume history of the Civil War, "The War With The South", by a Robert Tomes and did I want it? I of course said yes and offered to pay him, but he refused payment and generously gave the set to me. Over the years since then I have been able to acquire multiple copies of all of Robert's books and articles, mainly via the Internet.

However, in 1959 I was still unable to trace Robert's father Francis who was described in the cemetery records only as "Francis Tomes from England", the purchaser of the plot, but he was not buried there. Since I was then a very busy young lawyer and husband about to become a father, I couldn't spend much time on genealogy. So the search for Francis Tomes did not produce any results beyond that 1959 dead-end for the next thirty-five years. The intervening years were nevertheless filled with many interesting serendipitous experiences that ultimately led to success.

The next serendipitous event was that in 1961 a business associate and scientist friend, Dr. Arthur Cox, gave me a copy of a biography of "Sir John Tomes (1815-1895), The Father of British Dentistry". I read the book and learned quickly that Sir John was not a direct ancestor, but his ancestral home was at Weston-on-Avon in the Cotswolds, just south of Stratford-on-Avon.

Then, beginning in 1965, my business travels took me to London frequently and, since I particularly enjoyed the Cotswolds, I visited the church in Weston-on-Avon during a weekend in England. I will never forget that cold and wet November afternoon when genealogy became a very personal experience for me. I was standing alone in the church cemetery searching for names on gravestones when looked down at a very old, flat black grave-stone lying in the grass and saw my own name "James Tomes" inscribed! I truly shivered, thought sympathetically of old Scrooge in Dickens' Christmas Carol, and sought the churchwarden. He told me that there were no Tomeses living then in Weston, but directed me to the nearby village of Long-Marston where he said there was still an old manor house owned by a Tomes.

I drove the few miles to Long-Marston and, after inquiring first with the post-mistress I found the sexton of the village's ancient Norman church, St. James's. It turned out that the church stood off the road adjacent to "The King's Lodge", the 16th century ancestral Tomes manor house. It was then owned by retired Brigadier Clement Tomes, who was then living in Dorset, but has since died.

St. James' sexton, Harold Newman, his wife Irene, and their daughter Linda, and son Mark, lived across the road from the church and couldn't have been more hospitable. They invited me into their thatched cottage for tea and a chat. Irene was the head of the local Women's Institute, which had recently produced a manuscript history of Long-Marston, including a brief genealogy of the local Tomeses. I also learned, and noted for future reference to Josie, that Linda was enrolled as a student in a "Nanny College". (more serendipity)

The Tomes manor house was called "The King's Lodge" because in the year 1651, its owner, a "John Tomes, yeoman", had provided a night's refuge to the Prince of Wales, the future King Charles II when he was fleeing Oliver Cromwell after losing the battle of Worcester, a few miles west of Long-Marston. Prince Charles's escape to France via the Boscobel tree and various other overnight refuges is a very exciting, romantic and true story. In 1660 Prince Charles was restored to the throne as King Charles II and, it turned out,

Ancestral home "King's Lodge" in Long Marston

didn't forget John Tomes, whose half-sister, Alice Tomes, married Thomas Welles, a 17th century colonial governor of what is now Connecticut, by granting that colony special constitutional autonomy and a unique form of representative government. Connecticut still calls itself, "The Constitution State".

So, I had found an English Tomes family with a dramatic claim to an exciting bit of English history, in a picturesque and friendly village in the Cotswolds. Even though neither Sir John Tomes or John Tomes, yeoman, or Brigadier Clement Tomes were direct ancestors, they were part of the small Tomes clan, and would have to do, very well indeed, until we found the real ones.

Since I was traveling to England frequently during those years, Josie and I returned to Long-Marston on occasion becoming acquainted with the Newmans. In the early 1970's we employed Linda as a nanny for our four young children at our home in Wilmette. Linda is an exceptionally bright and caring person and she became a close friend with whom we are still in touch. She now has four grown children of her own, one a doctor, one a lawyer, one an accomplished artist at the Royal Academy and one still in university. A few years later

we stayed at The King's Lodge which had by then been sold by the Tomeses and become a bed and breakfast.

While visiting the Lodge I found a book by Thomas Blount, The Royal Miracle, the story of Charles II's escape, in which I found a paragraph referring to a number of other Tomeses who had lived in Gloucestershire. Some of them had immigrated to America. One of those men was a Francis Tomes, described as "a Quaker" residing near Albemarle Sound, North Carolina, in 1672. I copied the paragraph and brought it home with me for future use in the continuing search for my ancestor, Francis Tomes.

I would not have a chance to follow up this lead until 1990 when I met a learned historian and genealogist, Virginia Steele Wood, ("Ginny") of the Library of Congress in Washington, DC who introduced me to its Quaker records. Meeting Ginny was another in the long series of serendipitous events. She and I were dinner guests in Washington of mutual friends, Donald and Mary Petrie, of Wainscot, New York. Donald and I were business associates and Donald was then in the throes of writing The Prize Game (1999), an excellent book of sea stories illustrating the doctrine and practice of prize law in the days of sail. Ginny is the Naval and Maritime

History Specialist, and a genealogy specialist, at the Library of Congress, so she was able to be very helpful to Donald, and then also to me. Ginny is also an accomplished author in her own right, and has become a good friend of ours.

During the course of our dinner conversation I mentioned my involvement in a long search for my family's genealogy and had recently learned that a possible ancestor was an early American Quaker. Ginny quickly said, "You are lucky if you have a Quaker in your ancestry. The "Meetings" kept detailed family information." I made a date to meet Ginny the next week at the Local History and Genealogy Reading Room at the Library of Congress. When I arrived she directed me to the section on Quakers and I was able to hit pay dirt very quickly, finding on the first page of Hinshaw's American Encyclopedia of American Quaker Genealogy that the first Meeting of the Perquimans County Quakers was held at the home of Francis Tomes! I yelped "Eureka" loudly and was quickly shushed by other patrons of the library.

As it turned out, the Quaker Francis Tomes was not a direct ancestor, but he was a part of the Tomes clan from the Cotswolds, and was influential in early North Carolina. I will return to the story of the Quaker Francis

Tomes at a later point in this book. Hinshaw's Encyclopedia is marvelous to read through, whether or not your ancestors are Quakers. In detailed records of their meetings it provides much information about the early Quaker settlers; who was married to whom, children born, Quakers "dismissed" for owning firearms or slaves, etc.

Dick had been a British Army captain serving with the infantry in Belgium and France at the beginning of WW II in 1939-1940. He had in fact been one of the Warwickshire Regiment soldiers ordered to "fight to the last man and the last round" in defense of the perimeter south of Dunkirk in May of 1940.

OUR ENGLISH COUSINS

Ultimately, the Newmans told retired Colonel L.T. "Dick" Tomes, one of the sons of the late Brigadier Tomes, that they knew us as American Tomeses who were interested in family history. Colonel Dick Tomes then wrote to me in 1991 offering to put me in touch with his nephew, Major Ian Tomes, their family's amateur genealogist, who was then serving with the British Army in Zimbabwe, Africa. I sent Colonel Tomes what information I had about our ancestry, which only went back to Francis Tomes, about whom we knew only that he had emigrated from England to America in the early 19th century. Dick promised to pass the information on to his nephew Ian when he returned to England.

In 1992 Josie and I visited Dick and his wife Jane at their home in Dorset and became good friends. As we became acquainted with them we learned that Dick had been a British Army captain serving with the infantry in Belgium and France at the beginning of WW II in 1939-1940.

He had in fact been one of the Warwickshire Regiment soldiers ordered to "fight to the last man and the last round" in defense of the perimeter south of Dunkirk in May of 1940. He did so, was wounded firing an anti-tank gun against oncoming German SS tanks, was captured, and spent the rest of the war in prisoner of war camps. He actually escaped twice, but was recaptured each time and was finally liberated by American forces at the end of the war. Dick wrote a classically modest memoir of his World

Captain "Dick" Tomes and A. Schonfield in Trieste, 1946

War II experiences, which is available at the Newberry Library.*

Jane had enlisted in the British Army Auxiliary Territorial Service (A.T.S.) forces at age 17 in 1940 and served as an ambulance driver in Italy and Austria during the war. Dick and Jane met after the war in Trieste, were married and have two children. Dick stayed in the Army; serving as an intelligence officer in Europe and Washington, DC, eventually became a Brigadier and retired as a Colonel to Dorset where they opened a bookshop in Axminster, nearby their retirement home in Hawkchurch. Dick sadly died at age 87 in 2003. There is a memorial to him at the church in Hawkchurch, where Jane is still the leader of the church bell ringers. In December, 2005 we stayed with Jane at her home, met her most interesting son Michael, and enjoyed their intelligent cheerful company. Dick and Jane will always exemplify the quiet, modest courage and decency of the English people.

*(For the complete story of the Dunkirk evacuation in May and June of 1940, see "Dunkirk, Fight To The Last Man", by Hugh Sebag-Montefiore (2006). The book includes references to Dick Tomes' memoir and his diary entries as Adjutant recording the actual words of the order sent to his Second Battalion, the Royal Warwickshire Regiment, "You will hold your present position at all costs to the last man and last round. This is essential in order that a vitally important operation may take place." They did, at the town of Wormhout south of Dunkirk. The author states, "The men who fought at Wormhout deserve to be remembered, like those who did the same at other strong-points, for standing their ground and thereby holding up the Germans for just long enough to allow the British Expeditionary Force to retreat up the secure corridor behind them to Dunkirk." Compounding the tragedy of losing 80% of the Battalion in the Wormhout battle, approximately 90 of the survivors who couldn't escape were murdered by the Nazi SS Unit who captured them. They were herded into a small barn and gunned down, one of the war crimes for which the SS commander, Captain Fritz Knoechlein, was tried, convicted and hanged after the war.)

Dick's older brother, retired Air Commodore John Tomes Royal Air Force (RAF) is a 1933 graduate of Oxford where he also was a reserve pilot in the RAF. After Oxford he was posted on active duty to Cairo where he met his wife to be, Joanne Maxwell, whom he taught to fly while they were in Egypt. We have a wonderful 1938 picture of Joanne in her flying suit with helmet and goggles. During the war John was a bomber squadron commander in the RAF flying missions over Europe and also a member of the RAF staff. John also stayed in military service after the war and was posted to various command positions in Europe and England. After retiring

Joanne Tomes in Cairo, Egypt 1938.

as an Air Commodore (Brigadier) he served as a consultant in Paris for seven years and then retired to Bath, England where he and Joanne still live in a spacious apartment overlooking the Avon River. John continues to write travel guides and histories and Joanne still knits beautiful sweaters for all of her grand children and great-grand children, including our grand-children. We were happy to celebrate John and Joanne's 93rd birthdays with them in Bath in December, 2005.

Col. Dick and Cdre. John's father, the late Brigadier Clement Tomes (1882-1972), was also a professional soldier, serving first in India and then as an infantry officer in Belgium (Mons and Ypres) and France throughout World War I. He was wounded and deco-rated for valor and stayed in military service until retiring as a Brigadier after World War II. Clements's brother, Geoffrey (1884-1915) also served as an infantry officer, first in India and then at Gallipoli in World War I where he was decorated for valor and then killed leading a company of Gurkha soldiers. (Incidentally, my father also served, at Ypres in 1918 in the American army)

One of Cdre. John's sons, retired Major Ian Tomes (born 1940), is a graduate of Sandhurst and served as an infantry officer in Northern Ireland, Germany, Hong Kong, West Berlin, Nigeria, Ghana, Kenya and Zimbabwe. He too was decorated for valor receiving the Military Cross for combat service. He met and married his Swiss wife Verena while she was serving as a nurse in Africa. They have two sons, Sasha, born in 1969, and Kieran, born in 1973. Sasha is now a Major in the British Army, serving in the Household Cavalry (an armored reconnaissance Regiment). He is currently stationed in Kenya, having previously been at Windsor and Bosnia and Iraq. Kieran is in the fashion business in Somerset.

Thus, we are collaterally related to a remarkable family of "English Tomes Cousins" with whom we have become good friends during the past ten years.

Top Right: Colonel (Retired) "Dick" Tomes.

Below: Jim Tomes with Dick and Jane Tomes in Hawkchurch, Dorset 1995.

Above: Dick and Jane with Jim and Josie at a Pub.

Right: The Tomes Bookshop in Axminster, from left to right, Julia, Jane, Michael, and Dick.

Top left: John and Joanne Maxwell Tomes on their wedding day.

Top right: A young couple John and Joanne and below the couple later in life.

Bottom: Jim Tomes with Air Cdre (Retired) John Tomes, his wife Joanne, and Josie Tomes in 1995.

Air Cdre John Tomes died at age 95 in Bath, England on September 16, 2008. He was an extraordinary man, a rare combination of bravery, thoughtfulness, and modesty about his accomplishments. We were privileged to meet and spend some time with him and lovely wife Joanne during the years before he passed away.

Wedding of Lieutenant C. T. Tomes and Edith Gladys Newall, Colaba, India, July, 1912.

THE WEDDING OF LIEUT. C. T. TOMES.

On Tuesday, the 16th of April, at the Afghan Memorial Church, Colaba, there took place the wedding of Lieutenant and Adjutant C. T. Tomes with Miss Newall, only daughter of the late Lieut.-Colonel W. P. Newall, 2nd K. E. O. Gurkhas.

The bride was well-known to the battalion when staying with her brother, Lieut. C. L. N. Newall (then in the regiment, now in his father's old regiment, the 2nd K. E. O. Gurkhas) in Peshawar during 1909, and the announcement of her engagement in the next year to our then popular Adjutant-to-be was received with great pleasure.

The ceremony took place at noon and by that time, although by the wish of the bride the wedding was a very quiet one and few guests outside the regiment were invited, the Church was full of Officers, N.-C. O.s and men anxious to wish the happy pair the best of luck in their entry into the Holy state. There were present: Mrs. Vaughan, Mrs. Besant, Major Elkington, Captains Besant, Sinnott (from Kirkee) and Waterworth, Lieutenants Bannerman, Knight-Bruce, Haliley, Macky (from Kirkee), Bamber, Johnson, Onslow, Walker and Harwood.

Colonel Vaughan was at Matheran and unfortunately could not be present.

The Groom, with his best man (his brother Lieutenant G. Tomes, of our old friends the Third Sikhs) were there a few minutes before

the hour and a little after the bride (wearing, (so we have been advised by an expert) a dress of white crepe-de-chine, trimmed with Honiton lace and pearl edging, surmounted by a wreath of orange blossom and a long tulle veil and carrying a beautiful bouquet), appeared and took her place by the Chancel.

She was given away by her brother and the ceremony went off without a hitch.

At its conclusion the bride and groom walked through a lane of swords formed by officers of the Corps to their carriage, from which the horses had been unharnessed and which was dragged amidst cheers to the Officers' Mess by Sergeants of the Battalion.

In the Mess the health of the happy pair was proposed by Major Elkington and drunk with great enthusiasm. After lunch Mr. and Mrs. Tomes left for Matheran where they stayed for a week and then went to Ceylon.

We all wish them the best of good luck and prosperity in their new life.

TOMES OF LONG MARSTON - MAIN LINE OF DESCENT

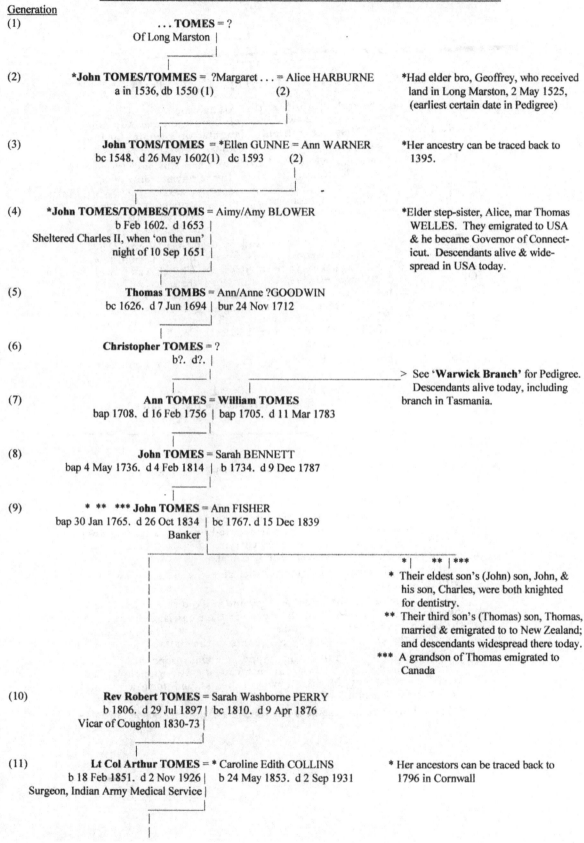

Generation

(1)   ... **TOMES** = ?
           Of Long Marston |

(2)   ***John TOMES/TOMMES** = ?Margaret ... = Alice HARBURNE
        a in 1536, db 1550 (1)   (2)

       *Had elder bro, Geoffrey, who received
       land in Long Marston, 2 May 1525,
       (earliest certain date in Pedigree)

(3)   **John TOMS/TOMES** = *Ellen GUNNE = Ann WARNER
      bc 1548. d 26 May 1602(1)   dc 1593   (2)

       *Her ancestry can be traced back to
       1395.

(4)   ***John TOMES/TOMBES/TOMS** = Aimy/Amy BLOWER
         b Feb 1602. d 1653 |
   Sheltered Charles II, when 'on the run' |
       night of 10 Sep 1651 |

       *Elder step-sister, Alice, mar Thomas
       WELLES. They emigrated to USA
       & he became Governor of Connect-
       icut. Descendants alive & wide-
       spread in USA today.

(5)   **Thomas TOMBS** = Ann/Anne ?GOODWIN
     bc 1626. d 7 Jun 1694 | bur 24 Nov 1712

(6)   **Christopher TOMES** = ?
          b?. d?. |

      > See '**Warwick Branch**' for Pedigree.
      Descendants alive today, including
(7)   **Ann TOMES** = **William TOMES**   branch in Tasmania.
    bap 1708. d 16 Feb 1756 | bap 1705. d 11 Mar 1783

(8)   **John TOMES** = Sarah BENNETT
    bap 4 May 1736. d 4 Feb 1814 | b 1734. d 9 Dec 1787

(9)   *** ** *** John TOMES** = Ann FISHER
    bap 30 Jan 1765. d 26 Oct 1834 | bc 1767. d 15 Dec 1839
          Banker |

        * | ** | ***
      * Their eldest son's (John) son, John, &
       his son, Charles, were both knighted
       for dentistry.
     ** Their third son's (Thomas) son, Thomas,
       married & emigrated to to New Zealand;
       and descendants widespread there today.
   *** A grandson of Thomas emigrated to
       Canada

(10)   **Rev Robert TOMES** = Sarah Washborne PERRY
      b 1806. d 29 Jul 1897 | bc 1810. d 9 Apr 1876
       Vicar of Coughton 1830-73 |

(11)   **Lt Col Arthur TOMES** = * Caroline Edith COLLINS
     b 18 Feb 1851. d 2 Nov 1926 | b 24 May 1853. d 2 Sep 1931
  Surgeon, Indian Army Medical Service |

       * Her ancestors can be traced back to
       1796 in Cornwall

(12)   **Brig Clement Thurston** = *Edith Gladys NEWALL = Alexandra Clare CAMPBELL   *Her bother was
        TOMES CBE DSO MC (1) b 21 Mar 1883   (2) b 8 Sep 1886   Chief of the Air
        b 28 Aug 1882. d 6 Oct 1962 | d 26 Jun 1947   d 2 Apr 1976   Staff during 1940
        Served in Royal Warwickshire Regt, | (mar Clement, 1948, after 'Battle of Britain'
        1901-42, including World War 1. | death of Edith)

                |

(13)**Air Cdre John Newall TOMES CBE** = *Joan ('Joanne') MAXWELL   * Her ancestors can be traced back to
           b 7 Feb 1913 | b 28 Sep 1913   c 1395 in Scotland & include the
      Served in Royal Air Force 1935-63, | Marquess of Aberdeen line
         including bomber pilot, WW2 |

                |

(14)   **Major Ian Maxwell** = * Verena MEYER   * Her ancestors can be traced back to
        TOMES MBE MC | b 5 Sep 1941   1619 in Switzerland
        b 8 Jan 1940_ | Swiss
      Served Royal Warwickshire Regt/ |
      Royal Regt of Fusiliers, 1958-95 |

                |

(15) **Major Sacha Christopher TOMES** = * Countess Louisa Isabelle = Emma   * Her ancestors were Austrian & Polish
        b 10 Oct 1969, West Berlin (1) Zofia RICHTER VON (2) PUGH
        Serving in Household Cavalry | MORGENSTERN   b 27 May 1969
                | b 22 Dec 1969

                |

(16)   **Harvey Maximilian Roman TOMES**
            b 8 Jan 1997

Coat of Arms

Ancestral home' King's Lodge' in Long Marston

11TH GENERATION

[PAGE (G10) 1]   **[PAGE (G10) 1. ANNEX A]**

Lt Col Arthur = Caroline Edith
TOMES   COLLINS
WAR   b 24 May 1853,
       St. Columb Major, CON
       d 2 Sep 1931,
       Lynwood, Douglas Ave, Exmouth
       (W) Est: £7,603 3s 8d

Caroline Edith COLLINS

[PAGE (G10) 1]

b 18 Feb, bap 25 May, 1851, both at Coughton, WAR
Surgeon in Indian Army Medical Service, joining in 1876.
Spent all career in India, of which "a great deal was spent
in a swampy and unwholesome part of Bengal."
Retired as a Lt Col & then lived at Abbot's Leigh House,
near Bristol. Moved then to Exmouth, DEV, in about
1915 & in that year was "drilling regularly as a private
in the Devonshire Training Corps."

d 2 Nov 1926, Lynwood, Douglas Ave, Exmouth,
       (W) Est: £22,036 2s 5d

(m 8 Nov 1877, ?India)

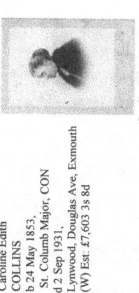

Arthur Tomes

[PAGE (G10) 1. ANNEX B]

Mary Dorothy
b 6 Jul 1886, 7 Cromwell Grove,
Hammersmith, London
dum 30 Jul 1968, 12 Portland Ave,
Exmouth, DEV
(W) Est: £38,238

Ella Ogilvy BELL

Capt Geoffrey = Ella Ogilvy
           BELL MA
b 6 Oct 1884, Midnapore, India   b 21 Sep 1887
Commissioned 1905 into Queen's (West Surrey) Regt   One of the earliest
& one year later transferred to 53rd Sikhs (Punjab   female graduates
Frontier Force). Went with Regt to Egypt at start of   at Oxford (St.
World War 1. In Jul 1915 joined 1/5 Gurkha Rifles   Hilda's). Later
and was kia on 10 Aug 1915 at Chanak Bair,   Librarian at
Gallipoli, just after taking command of 1/6 Gurkha   Bodleian Library,
Rifles whose officers had all been killed or wounded.   Oxford.
No known grave but name (with over 20,000 others)   d 10 May 1976,
on Helles Memorial on the tip of Gallipoli Peninsula   East Terr, Budleigh
(Panel Ref: 269 to 272 293 to 295). Memorial also in   Salterton, DEV
Long Marston Church.   (W) Est: £2,540 7s 4d   Est: £12,700

(m 27 Jan 1914, Ealing, MDX)

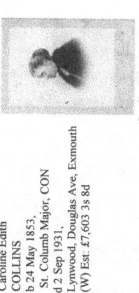

Geoffrey TOMES

(G11) 1

Brig Clement Thurstan
TOMES CBE DSO MC
b 28 Aug 1882

[PAGE (G12) 1]

George
Arthur
b 1880,
d 1882

Maud
TOMES
b 1878,
d 1880
[Assumed both were
born in & died in
India]

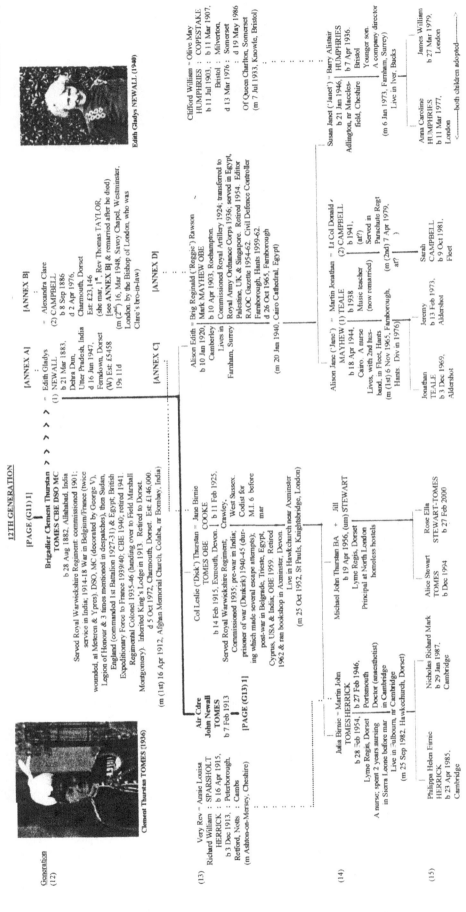

Edith Gladys NEWALL (1940)

Clement Thurstan TOMES (1936)

12TH GENERATION

Generation
(12)

[PAGE (G11) 1]

Brigadier Clement Thurstan TOMES CBE DSO MC
b 28 Aug 1882, Allahabad, India
Served Royal Warwickshire Regiment; commissioned 1901; service in India; 1914-18 War in Belgium/France (twice wounded, at Meteren & Ypres). DSO, MC (decorated by George V), Legion of Honour & 3 times mentioned in despatches), then Sudan, England (commanded 1st Battalion 1927-31) & Egypt; British Expeditionary Force to France 1939/40; CBE 1940; retired 1941. Regimental Colonel 1935-46 (handing over to Field Marshall Montgomery). Inherited King's Lodge in 1913. Retired to Dorset.
d 5 Oct 1972, Charmouth, Dorset. Est. £146,000.
(m (1st) 16 Apr 1912, Afghan Memorial Church, Colaba, nr Bombay, India)

[ANNEX A]
= Edith Gladys (1) NEWALL.
b 21 Mar 1883, Dehra Dun, Utter Pradesh, India
d 16 Jun 1947, Ferndown, Dorset (W) Est £5458 19s 11d

[ANNEX B]
= Alexandra Clare (2) CAMPBELL.
b 8 Sep 1886
d 2 Apr 1976, Charmouth, Dorset
Est. £23,146 (she mar, 1st, Rev Thomas TAYLOR, [see ANNEX B] & remarried after he died) (m (2nd) 16, Mar 1948, Savoy Chapel, Westminster, London, by the Bishop of London, who was Clare's bro-in-law)

[ANNEX C]

[ANNEX D]

Clifford William = Olive May COPESTAKE.
HUMPHRIES :
b 11 Jul 1903, : b 11 Mar 1907,
Bristol : Milverton,
d 13 Mar 1976 : Somerset
: d 19 May 1986
Of Queen Charlton, Somerset
(m 7 Jul 1933, Knowle, Bristol)

Susan Janet ('Janet') = Barry Alistair
b 21 Jan 1946, : HUMPHRIES
Adlington, nr Maccles- : b 7 Apr 1936.
field, Cheshire : Bristol
: Younger son.
: A company director
(m 6 Jan 1973, Farnham, Surrey)
Live in Iver, Bucks

Anna Caroline : James William
HUMPHRIES : b 27 Mar 1979,
b 11 Mar 1977, : London
London
—both children adopted——

Alison Edith = Brig Reginald ('Reggie') Rawson
b 10 Jan 1920, Mark MAYHEW OBE
Camberley b 10 Apr 1903, Roehampton.
Lives in Commissioned Royal Artillery, 1924; transferred to
Farnham, Surrey Royal Army Ordnance Corps 1936; served in Egypt, Palestine, UK & Singapore. Retired 1954. Editor RAOC Gazette 1954-62. Civil Defence Controller Farnborough, Hants 1959-62.
d 26 Oct 1965, Farnborough
(m 20 Jan 1940, Cairo Cathedral, Egypt)

Alison Jane ('Jane') = Martin Jonathan = Lt Col Donald
MAYHEW (1) TEALE (2) CAMPBELL
b 18 Apr 1944, b 1938 b 1941,
Cairo. A nurse. Music teacher (at?)
Lives, with 2nd hus- (now remarried) Served in
band, in Fleet, Hants Parachute Regt
(m (1st) 6 Nov 1965, Farnborough, (m (2nd) 7 Apr 1979,
Hants Div in 1976) at?)

Jonathan Jeremy Sarah
TEALE TEALE CAMPBELL
b 3 Dec 1969, b 13 Feb 1973, b 9 Oct 1981,
Aldershot Aldershot Fleet

(13)
Very Rev = Annie Louisa
Richard William : SPARSHOLT
HERRICK : b 16 Apr 1915,
b 3 Dec 1913, : Peterborough,
Retford, Notts : Cambs
(m Ashton-on-Mersey, Cheshire)

Air Cdre
John Newall
TOMES
b 7 Feb 1913
[PAGE (G13) 1]

Col Leslie ('Dick') Thurstan = Jane Birnie
TOMES OBE | COOKE
b 14 Feb 1915, Exmouth, Devon. | b 11 Feb 1925,
Served Royal Warwickshire Regiment; | Crawley,
Commissioned 1935; pre-war in India; | West Sussex.
prisoner of war (Dunkirk) 1940-45 (dur- | Codist for
ing which made several escape attempts); | M.I. 6 before
post-war in Belgrade, Trieste, Egypt, | mar
Cyprus, USA & India, OBE 1959. Retired
1962 & ran bookshop in Axminster, Devon.
Live in Hawkchurch near Axminster
(m 25 Oct 1952, St Pauls, Knightsbridge, London)

Michael John Thurstan TOMES BA + Jill STEWART
b 19 Apr 1956, (um) STEWART
Lyme Regis, Dorset
Principal at North London homeless hostels

(14)
Julia Birnie = Martin John
TOMES HERRICK
b 28 Feb 1954, b 27 Feb 1946,
Lyme Regis, Dorset Portsmouth
A nurse; spent 2 years nursing Doctor (anaesthetist)
in Sierra Leone before mar in Cambridge
Live in Fulbourn, nr Cambridge
(m 25 Sep 1982, Hawkchurch, Dorset)

(15)
Philippa Helen Eirnie | Nicholas Richard Mark | Alice Stewart | Rose Ella
HERRICK | HERRICK | TOMES | STEWART-TOMES
b 23 Apr 1985, | b 29 Jan 1987, | b Dec 1994 | b 27 Feb 2000
Cambridge | Cambridge

(G12) 1

13TH GENERATION

Generation

(12)

[PAGE (G12) 1]

[ANNEX A. MAXWELL]
[ANNEX B. ABERDEEN]
[ANNEX C. Linking of MAXWELL & ABERDEEN]

Francis = ? : ? = ?
RULE (1) [English] (2) [Spanish
: Descent]

Emigrated to Mexico, from Camborne, Cornwall

Carlos = Consuelo
RULE [Mexican] : NARVAEZ [Mexican]
b 28 Feb 1903 : b 1 Sep 1919
d 9 Feb 1965 :

(13)

Air Commodore John Newall = Joan ('Jeanne')
TOMES CBE MAXWELL
b 7 Feb 1913, Shorncliffe, Kent. b 28 Sep 1913,
Served Royal Air Force, 1935-63; including Egypt pre-war, Woodon, Northants.
Bomber Command (Squadron Commander, 57 Sqn), Secretary, before mar,
Mention in Despatches and American DFC, World War 2, with Imperial Airways
post-war in Canada, England & Air Attache, West Germany. in Egypt, where met
After retirement, worked for Bristol Siddeley in Paris & then husband
Rolls Royce in Brussels; then became writer of guide books (m 1952)
of European countries. Inherited King's Lodge in 1972 and
which was then sold in Nov 1975.
(m 22 Jun 1936, Merrow, nr Guildford, Surrey)
After retirement, lived Paris, Brussels & then Chelsea up to 1987.
Now live in Bath

John Newall TOMES &
Joan MAXWELL (m 1938)

Major Colin L.B. = Susan A.
GILLESPIE : CURSHAM
b 10 May 1925, : b 9 May 1930.
Chatham, Kent : Bunny, Notts
Served Royal Engineers : Trained as a caterer,
1943-71 : London Hospital
After his retirement, ran a vineyard at North
Wootton, Nr Wells Somerset. Moved to Wells
in mid 1999

Simon Rollo = Maria Christina
b 26 May 1955, : RULE [Mexican]
Aldershot, Hants : b 20 Dec 1952,
Picture restorer : Mexico
specialising in 18th
Century Dutch oils :
(m 19 Nov 1976, Mexico)
Live in London

(14)

Major Ian Maxwell Lt Patrick Thurston
TOMES b 7 Aug 1941.
b 8 Jan 1940 Amersham Dist
Served Royal
Warwickshire Regiment.
Killed in military traffic
accident, near Hameln,
West Germany,
19 Mar 1963

[PAGE (G14) 1]

Simon Christopher = Nicola Janet ('Jan')
b 15 Feb 1944, GILLESPIE
Ruislip, Middx b 24 Jan 1953,
Was executive with International Loughborough, Leics.
Business Machines (IBM) Secretary at House of
in Australia, Paris & England Commons before mar
Now Company Secretary
for a management consultants
firm 'Organisation Resources'
(m 29 Apr 1978, Wells Cathedral, Somerset)
Now live in Mudgley, near Wedmore, Somerset

Oliver Rollo Alexander
GILLESPIE
b 21 Jan 1979,
London

Alexander Dominic Petrock
b 31 Mar 1982,
London

Harry Benedict Athel
b 8 Aug 1984,
London

(15)

Katherine Sarah ('Katie')
TOMES
b 31 Oct 1980,
London,
br Westminster Dist

Camilla Frances
b 26 Jul 1983,
Bristol

Peter Mark St. John
b 6 Apr 1988,
Weston-Super-Mare,

(G13) 1

LONGM (As at 6 Sep 2001)

Verena Meyer (1968)

Kieran Malcolm Tomes (1986)

Generation

<u>14TH GENERATION</u>

(13)

(14)

[PAGE (G13)1]

[ANNEXES A, B & C]

Major Ian Maxwell = Verena
TOMES MBE MC MEYER *[Swiss]*
b 8 Jan 1940, Edinburgh, SCT. b 5 Sep 1941, Winterthur, Switzerland.
RMA Sandhurst 1958-60: Commissioned Jul 1960 into A nurse (Swiss Red Cross & RGN UK qualified)
Royal Warwickshire Regiment (later absorbed into the Served in remote bush Mission Hospital in Tanzania
Royal Regiment of Fusiliers); served in Hong Kong, & then (where met husband) in Nairobi, Kenya
(the then West) Germany, Kenya, West Berlin, Northern before mar.
Ireland (MC 1973), Nigeria, Ghana (MBE 1990),
Zimbabwe & England. Retired Jan 1995 & then South
West Regional Welfare Officer for the Ex-Services
Mental Welfare Society until Jan 2000
(m 16 Aug 1968, Ober-Winterthur, Switzerland)
Now living Upper Weare, nr Axbridge, Somerset

Kieran Malcolm
b 30 Jan 1973,
Ascot, Berks
Ed Manchester Metropolitan University
Fashion stylist in London

Major Sacha Christopher
TOMES
b 10 Oct 1969

[PAGE (G15)1]

(G14) 1

Ian Tomes (1989)

(15)

Sacha Christopher Tomes (1982)

15ᵀᴴ AND 16ᵀᴴ GENERATIONS

Generation

(14)

[PAGE (G14)1]

James Geoffrey Lennox = Hon Petrina Francis Anne
PUGH ; MITCHELL-THOMPSON
b 14 Oct 1942; : b 7 Apr 1945,
Marylebone Hospital, London : Nursing Home, 5 Collingham Gdns, London
Captain in Grenadier Guards :
(m 5 May 1967, Guards Chapel, Birdcage Walk, London)
Run an exclusive 'B & B' at their home in Gloucestershire

Emma

(15)

Major Sacha Christopher = Countess Louisa Isabelle Zofia   = Emma Louise
TOMES (1ˢᵗ) RICHTER von MORGENSTERN   (2ⁿᵈ) PUGH
b 10 Oct 1969, British Military Hospital, West Berlin   b 22 Dec 1969, Roehampton, London   b 27 May 1969, Queen Charlotte's
Ed London (BA) & Cranfield, Wiltshire, Universities (MA)   Song Writer   Hospital, Hamersmith London
Major in Household Cavalry, 'Blues & Royals;'   Catering Manager
Has served in England (including London mounted
duties), Northern Ireland, Bosnia & Iraq;   (m, 2ⁿᵈ, 5 Jun 2004, Holy Innocent's)
currently Army Training Adviser in Kenya (2007)   Highnam, Gloucestershire
(m,,ıst, 16 Dec 1995, Church of the Immaculate Conception (RC),
Mayfair, London) (Divorced 27 Feb 2002)

(16)

Harvey Maximilian Roman   Jasper Peter Newall   Milo Archie William
TOMES   TOMES   b 29 Aug 2007,
b 8 Jan 1997,   b 12 Oct 2005,   Nairobi, Kenya
Hillingdon, West London   Chelsea, London

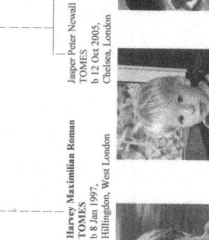

Sacha

Harvey (2005)

Jasper (Aug 2007)

(G15) 1

Milo (29 Aug 2007)

Without Ian's skill and willing help we would simply not have the genealogical information necessary for this book.

MAJOR IAN TOMES FINDS THE NEEDLE IN THE HAYSTACK! THE AMERICAN COUSINS.

Back To The Search - Eureka!

Now, picking up again where we left off with the search. Major Ian Tomes returned to England from Africa in 1993, retired from the army and resumed his interest in genealogy. In February, 1994 he astounded me by sending a detailed genealogy of Francis Tomes's ancestry!

By an extraordinary stroke of luck, through Ian's genealogical research, he discovered that my great-great grandfather Francis Tomes probably knew and was collaterally related to Ian's great-great-great uncle, Robert Fisher Tomes, a Cotswold bachelor farmer, and the English Tomes family's 19th century genealogist! Our ancestors had compared genealogies in the 1850's and Robert Fisher Tomes had kept all the records in a large " tin box" that ultimately was passed down through the generations to Ian.

Francis Tomes – At Last

By this serendipitous chain of events we found the "needle-in-the-haystack" information, which reunited our two branches of the Tomes clan. And we finally had the information about the identity and ancestry of Francis Tomes. What we didn't know then was just how much more was yet in store for us to discover.

Lord Edward Baldwin

The next stroke of serendipitous luck came about while I was rummaging through my late father's own "tin box" of family records. My father had died in 1975 in California and although I had been with him during the last few months of his life I had to leave the gathering up of his few things to a friend. The friend packed up his things in two suitcases and sent them to me and I stored them in our basement next to the furnace to keep

Top: Lord Arthur Windham Baldwin and Joan Elspeth Tomes on their wedding day in London, 1936.

Middle: Lady Elspeth Baldwin with her son Edward Baldwin and her husband Lord Baldwin.

Bottom: Edward and his father Lord Baldwin

them dry, but didn't open the suitcases until 1994 after Ian had found the contents of his "tin box". One of the items I found was a scrap of a newspaper item sent to my father by his sister in 1936, announcing the marriage of one of their New York City cousins, Joan Elspeth Tomes (1901-1980), to Arthur Windham Baldwin (1904-1976), the son of Lord Stanley Baldwin (1867-1947) who was three times prime minister of England in the 1920's and 1930's. I had never even heard of this bit of family history, but I sent it on to Ian. Elspeth was the youngest daughter of Charles Alexander Tomes (1854-1933) who I learned later had witnessed my grandfather's will.

Ian, characteristically, researched the descendants of Stanley Baldwin and found the present Lord Baldwin (born 1938), who turned out to be a graduate of Trinity College in Cambridge, and in 1994 a friendly teacher in Oxford, England. This Lord Edward Baldwin apologized for not being able to help us because of his wife's illness, but referred us to his "American cousin" Alexander Hadden Tomes, then living in Boston and New York.

Lord Baldwin, "Edward" to the family, has "made the cut" during the recent reductions in the House of Lords, and is currently still serving as a member of its Select Committee on Health. He has sadly however suffered the loss of his lovely wife, Lady

Ian Tomes with his wife Verena and Josie Tomes

Sarah "Sally" whom we met in 1997. Edward continues to live in Oxford with his three sons. Josie and I have had the pleasure of seeing Edward in London for dinner and for a few luncheons as Edward's guests at the House of Lords, most recently in January, 2006. Edward is a charming, modest, accomplished man whose friendship we cherish.

Ian's "Pedigrees"

By November, 1994 Ian had produced a detailed "pedigree" of our branch of the Tomes family, focusing on great-great-grandfather Francis Tomes who was born in Chipping Campden, England in 1780. His father, Richard, was baptized in March, 1745 in Bidford-on-Avon and his grandfather, Benjamin (1711-1786) "the saddler of Bidford", was baptized, married and buried at St. Laurence Church in Bidford, and his great-grandfather, also Benjamin (born 1680) was married in 1702 at St. James's Church in Chipping Campden and moved to Broadway, where they baptized two of their children at the beautiful ancient 12th century church, St. Edburgha, which still sits in an isolated rural setting, and then moved to Bidford. We have no records further back about their ancestors, but since people didn't move about very far in those days it is probable that they lived in Campden, Broadway and Bidford for many prior generations. They had to have been a hardy lot, suffering through the plagues and the English Civil Wars in the 1600's and worse, in the centuries before. (For the Tomes USA pedigree see appendix)

So, starting with our grandson, Alexander Steel Tomes, our Tomes ancestry goes back ten generations to the 1600's. Our collateral Tomes ancestors, via Ian's family, trace back to the 1500's. I was now beginning to take a very personal interest in English history. We had visited Chipping Campden, Broadway and Bidford on previous trips to England, without having any idea they were actually the homes and churches of my ancestors.

Now we had a pedigree documented by our own family's genealogist. Ian Tomes always says he is just an amateur, but he certainly does professional work. Ian and his wife Verena have since retired to a beautiful small farm overlooking the hills above Cheddar in Somerset. Without Ian's skill and willing help we would simply not have the genealogical information necessary for this book.

The American Cousins – Alexander Hadden Tomes, Jr.
In 1994, following up on Edward Baldwin's lead I telephoned Alexander Hadden Tomes, Jr. who turned out to be a genealogy buff whose permanent home was in Tuxedo Park, New York. We arranged to meet at the Racquet Club in New York City where he turned out to be quite friendly and generous, but a very eccentric and tragic figure. He was about 6' 6" tall, wore disheveled clothes and a baseball cap, had extremely thick glasses, and carried a #7 iron golf club as a cane. He was almost an apparition! He was born in 1931 as the son of a very successful Wall Street investment banker who later experienced a financial disaster during the Great Depression in the 1930's, and then, through more bad luck caused Hadden to have a debilitating medical treatment. As a young man Hadden had been an outstanding athlete, winning championships in golf, tennis, billiards and squash while at St. Paul's prep school, and at Harvard University, following his father's and grandfather's footsteps. He also graduated from Harvard Law School, but by then had developed a severe glaucoma. The treatment selected for curing the glaucoma

Alexander Hadden Tomes. Jr next to one his many trophies distinguishing his athletic achievements

failed and left him legally blind, forced to wear very thick magnifying glasses, which isolated him from his athletic interests and the practice of law. When I met him in 1994 he was living alone in a small cottage in Tuxedo Park, NY, down the hill from his family's former mansion, surrounded by family memorabilia and his memories of better days. We became good friends quickly because he was quite happy to meet a new cousin with an interest in genealogy. He gave me the original 270 page handwritten manuscript of Francis Tomes's 1837-1839 travel journals and a perfect copy of a bound printed book, "Our Great Grandfather", an 1875 book of over 300 letters written by Francis to his daughter Mary Elizabeth, "Polly", Tomes Burckhardt. He also gave me an original 1855 oil painting portrait of Francis Tomes painted by J.C. Horseley, R.A. It was in bad shape, but I have had it restored.

Hadden also gave me the names and addresses of all my other American cousins and therefore provided me the link to my extended American family. He tragically died in 1997, just a few years after we had met in 1994. After he died I learned from one of his friends that he had asked that I give his eulogy at Christ Church, in Greenwich, Connecticut where his family had worshiped and had been buried for generations. I was of course honored, and did so where I met many of his life-long friends. (See appendix for eulogy)

Beginning in 1994, I introduced myself to the other newfound cousins through letters and some personal visits and they welcomed me into the greater Tomes family. They have all generously given me pictures, letters and other memorabilia from my side of the family that had been handed down through their ancestors. When they learned that I was then in the publishing business they also began to give me the originals of some of our ancestor's journals, memoirs, books and letters, which I then undertook to transcribe and publish for them. It was an extraordinary experience to discover a complete, and very friendly, but previously unknown extended family.

The only problem created by Ian's and Hadden's gold mine of information, was that we now had almost too much information. Certainly too much for a one-hour talk. There were eight new-found cousins: "Hadden" Tomes, Arthur Tomes Lewry, Arthur C. Tomes, Mary Tomes Prinz, Francis Philip Tomes, Gordon Fairburn, Jim Pott and Lord Edward Baldwin. And they each had their own sets of collateral ancestors and siblings and children and grandchildren.

Alexander Hadden Tomes Jr. (1931-1997)

Now, back to "Hadden" Tomes of Tuxedo Park, New York. When I first visited him in New York City in June of 1995 I realized that he was a truly unique and eccentric person. He requested we meet at the Racquet Club on Fifth Avenue, where I was told at the front desk to find Mr. Tomes in the upstairs lounge.

I explained that I had rented a car, which we could pick up at Second Avenue and 50th, and could stop by the Trinity Cemetery at 155th Street on our way to Tuxedo Park. He agreed, but first he wanted to show me some things in the Racquet Club, then stop by St. Thomas' Episcopal Church on Fifth Avenue on the way to our car. Hadden then showed me what must have been thirty plaques on the walls of the Racquet Club attesting to the tennis, racquetball, squash, and billiards championships won by him, and also by his father, Alexander Hadden Tomes Sr.

At St. Thomas' Church Hadden showed me the baptismal font donated by his great-great grandfather, David Hadden, one of the founders of the church in lower Manhattan in the early nineteenth century. I was certainly getting a graphic genealogical tour.

When I mentioned again that we would stop by the Trinity Church Cemetery at 155th Street, Hadden said he had never known about it. But when I told him the records indicated a Hadden family plot immediately next to the Tomes plot he was of course very interested. I was able to show him both of these plots, which are also adjacent to the Astor plot. The Haddens and Astors were neighbors for a time in lower Manhattan when they lived on Lafayette Street.

As we drove out to Tuxedo Park Hadden began telling me about his family's fall from economic grace. Tuxedo Park was originally developed by the Lorillard family as a fancy New York City retreat for the wealthy in the 19th century. As we drove past the mansions, still grand, Hadden pointed to one that he said was his birthplace. We drove on until we came to a small cottage perched on the side of the road overlooking a pond. This was the house to which Hadden's parents

Hadden Tomes next to St. Thomas' baptismal font, in his right hand is his baseball cap and his golf club cane

Francis Tomes's store at 6 Maiden Lane New York City. Pre Civil War. He sold Fine cutlery, shears, soaps, toiletres, cologne, brushes and sundries. Figures may be Charles, Francis, Jr and Ben.

Charles Alexander Tomes with his wife Nettie Hancock Tomes.

had moved during the great economic depression of the 1930's, and where Hadden now lived.

Hadden then began telling me the story of his family's generational odyssey. This was to be genealogy by story telling, the old fashioned way.

Francis Tomes, Jr. (1813-1898)
Hadden was the great-grandson of Francis Tomes Jr., the eldest son of our mutual great-great-grandfather, Francis Tomes Sr. from England. In the 1850's Francis Jr. became responsible for running the family's import-export business, which had been started by Francis Sr. in 1815. The business had thrived, and Francis Sr. retired back to England where he lived as a country gentleman in the

1850's. The business continued thriving through the Civil War until 1871. At that point something went awry and bankruptcy occurred during the economic crash of the 1870's. Fortunately, Francis Sr. died before the crash in 1869 at age 89, and did not live to see his business fail.

Charles Alexander Tomes (1854-1933)
Francis Tomes Jr.'s eldest son, Charles Alexander Tomes, graduated from Harvard in 1871, but with no future in a bankrupt business he struck out on his own with a few hundred borrowed dollars and a letter of recommendation from John Forbes, sailed to Shanghai, and then Hong Kong, where he ultimately became the "Taipan" of a large trading company, "Shewan, Tomes".

"Gough Hill", Tomes' home on the peak in Hong Kong.

One hundred years later, in 1970, when I was doing business frequently in Hong Kong, I was asked by the British Taipan of Hutcheson's, Sir Douglas Clegg; if I was related to the Charles Tomes whose Shewan, Tomes Company was the founding company of Hutcheson's. Since I had no knowledge then of my ancestry, I could only plead ignorance. As a sign of the times since then, Hutcheson's has subsequently been acquired by Chinese interests and is now the largest trading company in Hong Kong, under the name of Hutcheson's Whampoa.

Sitting with Hadden in his Tuxedo Park cottage, he handed me pictures of Charles Alexander Tomes' 19th century Hong Kong. Charles was obviously successful, with a large mansion, "Gough Hill," on "The Peak", and married to a handsome Scottish girl named Hariot Hancock. Some of their treasures can be seen at the Peabody Museum in Salem, Massachusetts. They had five children, the eldest of whom was Hadden's father, Alexander Hadden Tomes Sr., born in Hong Kong in 1891. Hadden's father was an exceptionally handsome, athletic young man who graduated from Harvard and married a beautiful and wealthy Boston girl. They had two children, Elizabeth in 1926 and Hadden Jr. in 1931.

And, further to this story, in 2006 my son Robert Tomes and his wife Cynthia Zeltwanger visited Hong

Robert Tomes with the Tomes Cup at the Royal Hong Kong Yacht Club in 2004.

Over the years, the Royal Hong Kong Yacht Club has acquired a considerable collection of trophies as prizes for its yachting and rowing events.

The most impressive silverware in this collection is on display at Kellett Island. Each trophy tells its own story and by reading the inscriptions engraved on each cup, it is possible to learn something of the history of the Club.

In 1945 at the end of the Occupation, all existing trophies, along with everything else in the Club, were looted. Many of them ended up in the "antique" shops of Cat Street, but they were saved by Noel Croucher who scoured the shops and bought them back.

"He bought all the silver cups that were available and put them back in the showcases in the bar," explained Gordon Dewar who joined the Yacht Club soon after the War. However, not all the trophies that he found were Yacht Club ones so the names of their former owners were "sweated off" and a Yacht Club inscription added. "For years afterwards, members of other clubs visiting the Yacht Club would look at certain trophies and say 'we used to have a cup like that'," added Gordon.

The Club's oldest surviving trophy is the Tomes Cup. It was presented in 1880 by Mr A.H. Tomes in memory of his godmother, Dora Delano Forbes, who was the wife of William H. Forbes of Russell & Company. The first winner of the cup on 1st April, 1880 was the yacht *Naomi*. It was later given for a staggered all Classes pursuit race.

Top: Mrs. Alexander Hadden Tomes and Bridal
Attendants. The former Miss Elizabeth Whiting,
of 326 Beacon Street, Boston, was married in the
autumn to the son of Mr. and Mrs. Charles
Alexander Tomes, of London. From left to right the
group shows: Misses Mary Burr, Anita Sturgis,
Leila Fiske, of Boston; the bride; Misses Elspeth
Tomes, of London; Katherine Knapp, of New York;
Faith Stanwood, of Boston, and Marie Audibert, of
New York. 1912

Right: Alexander Hadden Tomes, Sr. circa 1910.

Kong and found the "Tomes Cup", a sailboat-racing cup given to the Royal Hong Kong Yacht Club by Charles Alexander Tomes. The cup is still awarded every year along with the Lipton Cup as part of the annual yacht club regatta. (see photos)

Alexander Hadden Tomes, Sr.
Hadden's father also became a champion athlete at Harvard, in baseball, golf, tennis and billiards. He went from Harvard to serve as an American Army officer during World War I in France and came home to become a partner in a Wall Street investment firm. So far, so good, but things began to unravel over time.

Unfortunately, Hadden's father bought a seat on the New York Stock Exchange during the summer of 1929, just a few months before the stock market crash. According to Hadden his father lost heavily, eventually having to sell the big house in Tuxedo Park and move his family into rooms in the Country Club, before he could buy the small cottage. Nevertheless, he remained in business on Wall Street and ultimately paid off all his creditors. He was also able to enroll his son at St Paul's prep school and Harvard University (class of 1950), where Hadden, just as his father, and grandfather, was a champion athlete, and later graduated from Harvard Law School (class of 1953).

Elizabeth "Betty" Tomes

Elizabeth Tomes
In 1944, after Hadden's sister, Elizabeth, had been introduced to society as a beautiful young debutante, the family's fortunes began to take a more serious turn for the worse. She apparently suffered what was then called "a nervous breakdown", not an unusual event for a beautiful young girl in east coast society. But her parents, on the advice of well qualified medical doctors, the same ones who advised many other families who were struggling with their children's mental illness, authorized a lobotomy. It seems incredible now, but it was then looked to as a cure

of choice. Well, we know now that it was a disastrous mistake, not just for Elizabeth Tomes, but for many thousands of other lobotomy patients. For poor Elizabeth, it left her so mentally damaged, she was institutionalized for the rest of her life, which ended finally in 1990. Personal tragedy number one for Hadden's family.

Then, as a young adult after finishing law school, Hadden developed glaucoma. Once again, the best medical advice available counseled surgery, which, tragically, was bungled. It left Hadden functionally blind for the rest of his life. He lived alone, could not work, and was increasingly isolated by his blindness and resulting frustration. Personal tragedy number two. In spite of all these difficulties Hadden had an indomitable spirit and was keen to share with me all that he knew about our family.

While he was telling me this long story of his family's history he was gathering things to show me in his cottage. Literally the first thing he handed to me were the original notebook journals (1837-1839) handwritten by our mutual great-great grandfather, Francis Tomes Sr. They were in quite a dilapidated condition so I offered to restore, transcribe and publish them for the family, to which Hadden quickly agreed.

He also gave me a copy of a beautifully printed and bound book of over 300 letters written by Francis Sr. to his daughter "Polly" from 1840 to 1864, and other memorabilia. The book also contains photographs of all the family members. "Polly" was Mary Elizabeth Tomes Burckhardt, was one of Francis Sr.'s two daughters, sisters to my great-grandfather, Robert Tomes.

A copy of this book, published by Polly in 1875, had serendipitously arrived in the mail on the very day that Hadden and I were meeting in his house in Tuxedo Park. It had been sent from the estate of Hadden's recently deceased aunt, Lelia Tomes. Hadden opened the package and, showing me the book, said; "You have a copy of this, don't you?" When I said no, he immediately handed it to me with spontaneous generosity saying I should keep it. I have since had the book rebound and keep it in a protective box in my library.

Over the course of the following two years Hadden also sent me other things, including an original 1855 oil portrait of Francis Tomes, Sr. by his friend, J.C. Horseley, (R.A.), which I had restored and which hangs in our home. I have learned since that Horseley was a well-known Victorian painter and member of the Royal Academy, and also a friend of Charles Dickens and Sir Henry Cole who commissioned him to paint the first commercial Christmas card in 1843.

Sadly, Hadden died in 1997, shortly after taking me to visit his family's church, Christ Church, and family cemetery in Greenwich, Connecticut. Hadden was a remarkable person who had a very tragic later life, and was the last of his line of Tomeses. Hadden and I became instant friends when we met in 1995, carried on a lively correspondence by mail and telephone, and met occasionally in New York City and Connecticut. But his general health was poor and he didn't survive for long after we met. Hadden is buried in the Tomes family plot at Christ Church. I am privileged, to have known him.

The Tomes – Higgins House
During Hadden's and my visit to Christ Church Hadden also showed me the "Tomes-Higgins" house, a grand Victorian mansion on five acres adjacent to the church on Putnam Ave. near downtown Greenwich. The house was built in 1861 by Francis Tomes Jr. The architect of the house was Calvert Vaux and the landscape design was by Frederick Law Olmsted. The house is featured in Vaux's classic 1865 work on American architectural design, Villas and Cottages. Vaux later designed the original Metropolitan Museum of Art and the American Museum of Natural History in New York City. Vaux collaborated with Frederick Law Olmsted to become most famous for designing Central Park in New York City and Prospect Park in Brooklyn.

The Tomes-Higgins house was later sold to a New York financier, A. Foster Higgins in 1877, whose family retained it until 1963 when they sold it to Christ Church. It has been recently restored to its former glory as a National Historic Monument for use by the church and for public functions in Greenwich. It is well worth a visit.

Joanna Bailie Gunderson

I was referred to Joanna by Hadden Tomes who had just recently in 1995 met her by chance (serendipity again) at a cocktail party of a mutual friend in her New York City apartment building. When he was introduced as Hadden Tomes Joanna said she was related to the Tomes family and Hadden then sent her some family information and introduced her to me by letter. I promptly followed up with a phone call and sent her copies of the transcribed Tomes manuscripts. She wrote back and graciously invited me to visit when next in New York. So, in August of 1996 my son Robert and I were guests at a very nice dinner hosted by Joanna at her apartment on Fifth Avenue in New York.

Joanna Bailie Gunderson is a descendent of Margaret Ann Tomes Iselin, one of great-grandfather Robert Tomes's two sisters. Margaret and her husband, John Iselin were the couple with whom Charles Tomes had left his children after his wife Isabella died in 1842 and he went to North Carolina to study for the ministry. The Iselin's and the Tomeses were close friends. Charles Tomes gave the Iselin name to one of his sons of his second marriage to Henrietta Otey, Francis Iselin Tomes (1848-1866) and his daughter Susan married John Iselin, a son of Margaret and John Iselin.

During our dinner with Joanna she showed us silverware bearing the name and initials of Francis Tomes and letters and a diary written by her great-grandmother Margaret Tomes Iselin. The diary recorded travels in Europe and meetings with her brother Robert Tomes and his family in Wiesbaden and her sister Mary Elizabeth Tomes Burckhardt and her family in Paris. The Tomeses enjoyed European travel and society in the 1860s and 1870s. I returned to New York in November 1996 and made photocopies of the diaries, which have yet to be transcribed.

When we met in 1996 Joanna was the founder and owner of small press publisher of poetry named Red Dust. Her husband, Warren Gunderson, was the executive director of the New York Japan Society. Joanna and Warren have two children, Lucy, born 1971, and Thomas, born 1976, both college students in 1996.

Reverend Harold Bend Sedgwick

In 1995 I also learned from Hadden Tomes about the Rev. Harold Bend Sedgwick (1908-2004) and contacted him by letter at his place of retirement in Lexington, MA. Rev. Sedgwick was a graduate of Harvard in 1930 and was an Episcopal minister, serving from 1938 to 1947 as Rector of All Saints Parish on Beacon Street in Boston, MA and then as rector of St.

John's in Williamstown, MA until his retirement. He was an admirer of his great grandfather Rev. Charles Tomes and contributed to the restoration of his memorial.

Josie and I met him at his retirement home in Lexington, MA in 1997 and had a wonderful visit during which he told us some interesting stories about the Sedgwick family burial plot in Stockbridge, MA. It is called "The Sedgwick Pie" because it is a large circular plot in the Stockbridge town cemetery. The patriarch of the family, Theodore Sedgwick (1747-1813) was one of the members of the American Constitutional Convention and was the lawyer who represented "Mumbet" a mistreated slave of one of his friends, a Col. Ashley. "Mumbet" had been injured by Mrs. Ashley and had come to Sedgwick seeking help. She also asserted that she had heard Sedgwick say that the Massachusetts Constitution provided that "all people are created free and equal" and wondered if that law included her. Sedgwick was intrigued and took her case and won it at the Court of Common Pleas in Great Barrington, MA in 1781. It was one of the earliest cases asserting that slavery was illegal in the state of Massachusetts. Mumbet also came to live and work for the Sedgwick's in Stockbridge. The court case compensated her for her time as a slave for the Ashley's and she was employed by the Sedgwick's as a free person. She became such a beloved member of the Sedgwicks that when she died in 1829 she was buried in the "Sedgwick Pie" alongside the Sedgwicks.

Rev. Sedgwick's grandmother, Mary Aspinwall Bend, the wife of Theodore Sedgwick, and daughter of Isabella Tomes Bend and General William Bend, is also buried in the Sedgwick Pie. We kept in touch with Rev. Sedgwick until a couple of years ago and now it appears that he has passed away. I found on the Internet an entry showing that a contribution has been made by "The estate of Harold Bend Sedgwick", and only learned recently from a cousin of his in Lexington that he died in 2004. He never married and left no direct descendents.

Cousin's reunion at the summer home of Art and Lolly Lewry. Left to right, Josie and Jim Tomes, Verena Tomes, Goleta "Lolly" Lewry, Beverly "Bev" and Arthur "Art" Charles Tomes, and Arthur "Art" Tomes Lewry.

OUR OTHER AMERICAN COUSINS

**Arthur Tomes Lewry
(born 1935) and Lolly Lewry**
The next cousin to meet was Arthur Tomes Lewry, (born 1935), a retired Ford Motor Company design engineer, and his wife Goleta, "Lolly", then living in Bloomfield Hills, Michigan. (they have since moved to Rochester, Michigan) Arthur Lewry is my second cousin, as a great-grandson of Dr. Robert Tomes. His grandfather, Arthur L. Tomes, and mine, Dr. William A. Tomes, were brothers. Art and Lolly have three grown sons, Matthew, Mark and Thomas who are each married with children.

Art and Lolly organized and were the generous hosts for a unique three-day "Tomes Family Reunion" at their year-round "summer home" near Saugatuck, Michigan in 2003. Attending were Ian and Verena Tomes from England, Art and Beverly Tomes from Minnesota, and Josie and I from Illinois. Walter Keith Tomes of Tennessee was unable to attend because of a family member's illness.

The reunion was of course well organized and full of interesting family stories. It was certainly happy testimony to the meaning and joy of kinship.

It is Art and his wife Lolly who had possession of great-grandfather Robert's memoirs, which they generously gave to me to restore and transcribe. Art has shared the cost of most of this work with me and has donated the original memoirs to The Newberry Library in Chicago. We have also donated a complete set of Robert's books and copies of all the transcribed memoirs and journals to the Newberry's Special Collections Library. Art has also been a very important help in converting my type-written transcriptions into computer language for editing and printing.

Eugenia Lewry Stilwell
Art referred me to his sister-in-law, Eugenia Lewry Stilwell who lived in Taunton, Massachusetts as another person who could be helpful in searching my genealogy. He was so

Art Tomes, Lolly Lewry, Bev Tomes and Art Lewry.

right. I happened to be traveling to Providence, Rhode Island soon on business (more serendipity!) so I made an appointment to visit Eugenia.

We had a wonderful visit during which she showed me many family pictures and gave me some of my grandfather William's memorabilia, such as his Yale University fraternity pin, and some of his letters and photographs. Then, a few years later Eugenia sent me a large package containing my great grandfather's own copy of a 1775, Fourth Edition, Johnson's Dictionary of the English Language. It has Robert Tomes's name inscribed by him on the flyleaf and includes a note, also in Robert's penciled handwriting, describing the provenance of the book on the sub-

scription page. It is a rare treasure, which I have had rebound in leather.

Thanks to Eugenia's kindness and generosity we have now added this rare book to the collection of Robert's books.

Arthur Charles Tomes (born 1920)
The next new-found cousin, Arthur C. Tomes, of Burnsville, Minnesota, a retired commercial pilot, and highly decorated World War II B-29 pilot, (two Distinguished Flying Crosses and two Air Medals), has also been most helpful to me in sharing documents and stories. Art and his wife Beverly divide their time between places in Winter Haven, Florida, Burnsville, Minnesota and their fishing retreat at Lake Vermillion,

Lolly and Josie in front of the Lewry's summer home.

Art Tomes, with cousins Ian Tomes and Art Lewry

Ian and Art enjoying the Michigan beaches.

Verena and JosieTomes

Ian and Verena Tomes traveled from England to reunite with their American Cousin's.

Minnesota. We are frequent correspondents keeping up to date with news of their four children and grandchildren.

Shortly after we met at my office in Washington, DC in 1994, Art was invited to Japan by a World War II Japanese Air Force combat pilot veteran, Shigeo Imamura, to celebrate fifty years of peace since the end of the war. Shigeo Imamura had the unusual life experience of being born in the U. S., then taken to Japan by his Japanese national parents before WW II, then surviving as a pilot in the Japanese Air Force during the war. After the war he was able to return to the United States where he ultimately became a Professor of English at Michigan State University. Then, after he retired from Michigan State, he returned to his Japanese hometown, Himeji, which he discovered through his research had been bombed by Arthur Tomes's B-29 Squadron in 1945!

Arthur referred the invitation to Ambassador Walter Mondale, a fellow Minnesotan and then Ambassador to Japan, for advice. Mondale encouraged Art to accept the invitation, which he did, and made the trip with some of his surviving squadron mates in July of 1995. Art, who is a typically taciturn Minnesotan, gave a very moving talk in Himeji, pulling no punches, but appreciating the spirit of reconciliation shown by the invitation and warm welcome by the towns-

people of Himeji. (A copy of Art's talk in Himeji is in the appendix)

One symbol of that reconciliation that now shows up on the Tomes Pedigree is that one of Art and Beverly's daughters, Mary, is married to a third generation Japanese-American, Gary Yanagita, and they have two children, Brian Tomes-Yanagita and David Tomes-Yanagita.

Reverend Charles A. Tomes (1814 - 1857) His Memorial
Art also told me on the phone about his great-grandfather, the Reverend Charles Tomes, my great- grandfather Robert's next oldest brother. When Art told me about Rev. Charles he casually mentioned that he was buried in Olivet Cemetery in Nashville, Tennessee. More serendipity! By another odd coincidence I was then scheduled to travel to Nashville on business, for the first time in my life, the following week.

When I told Art about my upcoming trip he gave me the particulars about visiting the cemetery, as well as Rev. Charles's home, "Glenoak", in Nashville near what is now Vanderbilt University. Art also told me about the three churches in Nashville that Rev. Tomes had served. I visited all these places and also subsequently met with the historian of Christ Church in Nashville, Mrs. "Fletch" Coke, who was most helpful to us in restoring and reconsecrating the Rev. Charles Tomes cemetery memorial.

We discovered that the memorial, which had been built in 1857 by the City of Nashville and Christ Church, had fallen into disrepair. It had been built to honor Rev. Charles's heroic efforts on behalf of his parishioners, the poor, the sick during two cholera epidemics, and the prisoners in jail. He had also organized the building of another Episcopal Church in downtown Nashville, Holy Trinity, and been called to serve a new "free pew" Advent Church, when he was untimely felled by pneumonia in 1857.

We financed the restoration of the memorial, and, together with Mary Tomes Prinz and her husband Jules from New Orleans, Fletch Coke and her husband, Arthur and Lolly Lewry, Arthur and Beverly Tomes, and the Episcopal priests and congregants from each of Rev. Charles Tomes's three Nashville churches held a rededication ceremony. Rev. Charles Tomes's life is not forgotten.

The tragic irony of Charles's life was played out further during the American Civil War, which occurred after Charles had died. Charles's first marriage was in New York City to Isabella Hadden with whom he had two children, Isabella and Charles Jr.

Arthur Lewry, Goleta Lewry, Mary Tomes Prinz, Beverly Tomes and Arthur Tomes at the Rededication of restored Memorial for Rev. Charles A. Tomes Olivet Cemetery, Nashville, Tennessee.

Portrait of Reverend Charles Tomes.

After Charles's wife Isabella died in Charles Jr's birth, Charles was so distraught that he left his two children with his sister Margaret Tomes Iselin, in New York City, and started studying for the ministry. He studied first in North Carolina, then in St. Louis under the tutelage of a cousin, Rev. Stephen Cicero Hawks, Bishop of Missouri. He then transferred to Nashville, Tennessee, living with Bishop James Otey, Bishop of Tennessee. They became close friends and Charles soon married Bishop Otey's daughter, Henrietta. Charles and Henrietta had many children, among them two daughters, Margaret Otey Tomes, Sarah Iselin Tomes and a son, Francis Iselin Tomes.

Charles Tomes, Jr. and his half brother, Francis Iselin Tomes

Thus, when Charles died at age 42 in 1857, he left two families of children, two in New York City and at least three in Nashville. Then, during the Civil War, Charles's oldest son Charles Jr., served first as an enlisted man and later as an officer in the Union Army. His other, younger son, Francis Iselin Tomes, (Charles Jr's half brother) was a cadet at Virginia Military Institute in Lynchburg, Virginia as a Confederate officer candidate. By 1864 Francis was a 17-year-old cadet at VMI when the Confederate Army called upon the VMI Commandant to supply some cadets to help defend against the advancing Union Army coming down the Shenandoah Valley. Many cadets volunteered, including Francis, and they served during the now famous Battle of New Market, which resulted in a Confederate victory. "Little Frank", as he was called by his classmates, was ordered to stand guard at VMI during the battle. After the battle Francis was assigned to the defense of Richmond, Virginia where he became ill in December of 1864. VMI's archives show that he was then given a medical leave, but there is no further record of his military service.

But we do know that Francis Iselin Tomes was buried in the Tomes plot of the Trinity Church Cemetery Annex in 1866. The only explanation possible is that Francis, still ill from the effects of the war in the spring of 1865, somehow transported himself to New York

Rev. Charles Tomes House in Nashville "Glenoak" built by Charles in 1854.

City to find his half-brother Charles Jr. and the other members of the Tomes family. He was however fatally ill and died in 1866. It is a grim historical fact that over one-half of the 600,000 total confederate and Union soldier's deaths in the Civil War were from illness.

And Charles Jr. didn't live much longer. He died a few years later in 1870 at age 29 of a "self inflicted gunshot wound". Charles Jr. is also buried in the Tomes cemetery plot. An all too personal reminder of the terrible costs of war. Francis and his half-brother Charles, soldiers on opposite sides of the truly fratricidal American Civil War, lie buried together in the Tomes family's cemetery plot.

Much of the information we discovered about Francis and Charles was obtained through the Internet Civil War websites and the VMI website.

Mary Tomes Prinz
Beginning in 1995 I also corresponded with other newfound cousins who were most helpful in telling me family history. First was Mary Tomes Prinz of New Orleans. She is descended from Charles Jr., who had four children between 1865 and his death in 1870. His first born, Charles Francis Tomes

(born in 1865 in New York), married Emma Lafitte of New Orleans, lived the rest of his life there and died there in 1938. They in turn had two children, the eldest of whom was Jacques Lafitte Tomes, Mary's father. Mary married Julius F. Prinz III and they have five children. and live in New Orleans. Julius is a retired airline pilot so he and Mary are now constantly on the go. Mary is an enthusiastic, energetic and well-informed family genealogist who has been very helpful to me as a careful editor of this book.

Hilary Clarke

In 1995 Mary gave me information about Francis Tomes Sr.'s burial place in Great Longstone, England and the name of Mrs. H.A. (Hilary) Clarke, the Secretary of the Longstone History Group. When my wife, Josie, and I visited Great Longstone in the spring of 1995 we were given the grand tour of the local area by Hilary. She met us at the Longstone Church, where a church has stood on the same ground since the ancient year of 1262. She showed us Francis Tomes Sr.'s grave, which we duly honored, then also showed us the house of Francis's close friend, William Longston, at Little Longsdon nearby. We had a delightful dinner with Hilary and her husband Harry and have corresponded with them since.

Francis Philip Tomes

In 1995 I was also in touch with the present Francis P. Tomes, now 94 years old, (born 1914) who lives with his wife, Dorrit in Colorado. Francis is descended from Rev. Charles Tomes marriage with Henrietta Otey, so he has known another branch of the Tomes family better than ours. Among that branch of the family was a prize-winning children's book illustrator, Margot Ladd Tomes, who was born in 1917 had died in 1991. I had known of her existence by reading some of her books to our growing children, but I didn't know of our family relationship then and was unable to contact her through her publisher.

Thomas Tomes actually survived a scalping, fighting on the American side at the Revolutionary War Battle of King's Mountain in 1780

SOME EARLY AMERICAN TOMESES

Francis P. Tomes was also most helpful to me by sending copies of correspondence great-great grandfather
Francis Tomes Sr. had with his cousin
the Rev. Francis Hawks, about whom
we will say more later. Included in
this material was a note from Hawks
referring to the Quaker Francis Tomes
who had come to America in the
1600s. I researched this further and
found that The Quaker Francis Tomes
had first come to Virginia as an inden-
tured servant, then migrated to North
Carolina where he became a Quaker,
a leader in the Quaker church and
the North Carolina government, and
the patriarch of the Tomes family that
subsequently propagated itself west-
ward to Kentucky Tennessee and
Ohio. I have come to refer to these
Tomeses as the "Southern Tomeses".
Another early American Tomes,
whom Ian includes in what he

describes as the "Tomes of Kentucky
family" was Thomas Toms who
actually survived a scalping, fighting
on the American side at the Revolutionary War Battle of King's
Mountain in 1780. We know this
because the event is recorded in his
Revolutionary War soldier pension
record. His descendants spell their
name "Tomes".

Francis Philip Tomes also sent me
a copy of a book, *The Mountain of
Names*, by Alex Shoumatoff, which
I highly recommend as reading for
anyone interested in genealogy. It
is a classic.

Reverend Francis Lister Hawks 1798 – 1866.

THE HAWKS AND POTT FAMILIES

The Hawks Family

Reverend Francis Hawks was the grandson of John Hawks, the brother of Sarah Hawks, Francis Tomes Sr's mother, from Shipston-on-Stour, England. Shipston is a village in the Cotswolds, about ten miles east of Chipping Campden, where Francis Tomes's father, Richard Tomes (1745-1785) lived.

Ian Tomes recently gave me a charming hand-colored 18th-century e t c h-ing, entitled "A View of "Shipston-on-Stour", showing a landscape view with a man in the foreground walking on the old road towards the village (See page 97). It is easy to imagine that man as Richard Tomes, in the fall of 1773, making his way from Chipping Campden to court his lady-love, Sarah Hawks. Sarah and Richard were married in the church at Shipston-on-Stour in February, 1774.

John Hawks, Tryon Palace

Sarah's brother, John Hawks (1731-1790), was also Rev. Francis Hawks' grandfather, and was said to be the architect of Tryon Palace in New Bern, North Carolina. I had never heard of Tryon Palace until 1996, but since Josie and I had previously planned a driving trip with a law school classmate and friend, Gabe Burton, to visit Charleston, South Carolina and Savannah, Georgia later that year, we added New Bern to our itinerary.

We stayed in New Bern at an excellent bed and breakfast then had an entire day to visit the palace and the town, all beautifully restored. We learned that the palace had, in fact, been designed, and built, by John Hawks for the Royal Governor William Tryon who was appointed Governor of North Carolina in 1764 by King Charles III.

John Hawks went to London as a young man, was apprenticed to Stiff Leadbetter of Eton, who was the Surveyor of St. Paul's Cathedral in 1756. John may have then helped design the palace at Kew Gardens, and was ultimately chosen by the Governor to be the architect and builder of "Tryon Palace". Hawks traveled to North Carolina with the Governor in 1764. The cornerstone was laid in 1767 and the palace was completed in 1770. New Bern was the first colonial capitol of North Carolina and John Hawks was the first American Architect - Builder. Gov. Tryon remained only a few years in New Bern and then became the Royal Governor of New York, just a few years before the American Revolution. He left New York at the outset of the revolution and returned to England.

John Hawks joined the-American revolutionary cause in New Bern. After the Revolution he was Tax Commissioner of New Bern, a Trustee of Dobbs Academy and a North Carolina State Council member. The Capitol of North Carolina moved to Raleigh in 1774, and the Palace was not well maintained thereafter. It subsequently fell into ruin during the war and burned to the ground in 1798. We learned during our visit that the house John Hawks built for himself and his family still stands in New Bern where it is a National Historic Monument.

In the 1930s Mrs. James Edward Latham, a wealthy tobacco heiress and native of New Bern, decided that she wanted to rebuild Tryon Palace on its original foundation and refurnish it as it had been under Governor Tryon. She achieved this ambitious goal during the 1940s and 1950s, and the

Tyron Palace Source: http://commons.wikimedia.org/wiki/File:Tryon_Palace.JPG

Palace stands today as a magnificent tribute to her vision and dedication to restoring a significant piece of American history.

Necessary for this successful restoration was the discovery of the original palace plans. They were found in the custody of the New-York Historical Society where they had been placed by John Hawks' grandson, Reverend Francis Lister Hawks. He had inherited them and was once involved in the management of the Historical Society.

Tryon Palace is an extraordinary example of Georgian architecture, rebuilt exactly as it was planned. It has also been refurnished as it was originally, based on an insurance inventory of Gov. Tryon's furnishings. It is therefore a remarkably accurate restoration.

Now, back to our story of the serendipitous search for family history. While touring the palace, our friend, the late Gabe Burton (1926-2003), mentioned to a docent that John Hawks was one of my ancestors. This put us quickly in touch with the Curator of Tryon Palace with whom we had an informative discussion. We also discovered a problem - that John Hawks' English birthplace was described in their official biography as "the north of England in Lincolnshire." 'Since this was contrary to our family information I told the Curator I would send her what information I had, which I did after we returned home. But our pedigree information was only about John Hawk's supposed sister, Sarah Hawks.

Jim and Lois Pott

We heard nothing further until 1998 when I received a telephone call from Jim Pott, a retired engineer living in California. He related that he had recently visited Tryon Palace and was a direct descendent of John Hawks, so was interested in identifying his origins. Jim Pott is also an amateur genealogist and wanted to know more about the Shipston-on-Stour home of Sarah Hawks. I told him that we had visited the Shipston church, but could not obtain any historical baptismal or birth records, nor had Ian Tomes been able to discover any information about any Hawks in Lincolnshire.

A few more months passed when I received a letter from Jim Pott telling me of his surprising success in finding that the Mormon Church's Family History project had microfilmed the Shipston church's records a few years ago and these showed that Sarah Hawks's brother, John, was in fact born there in 1731. Jim forwarded to me copies of the records that were microfilmed by the Mormons. So, the serendipity of my Pedigree being sent to Tryon Palace, found there by Jim Pott, who then researched the Shipston-on-Stour church records via the Mormon Church's Family History microfilm program, solved another mystery! Jim Pott also advised Tryon Palace of John Hawk's corrected birthplace. Jim and his wife Lois visited England the following year where they met Ian and his wife Verena Tomes. I visited Jim and Lois at their beautiful home in Long Beach, California in 2003. The family connections kept growing.

Reverend Francis Lister Hawks (1798-1866)

Francis Lister Hawks, son of Francis Hawks and grandson of John Hawks, was a protean, but capriciously flawed character who had many links to the Tomes family during the 1800s, beginning with my great-great grandfather

Rev. Francis L. Hawks, September of 1850.

Francis Tomes, who visited the Hawks in New Bern shortly after he arrived in America in 1815. Francis Hawks and his brothers, Bishop Cicero Stephen Hawks, and John Hawks, visited the Tomes's house in New York City during the years before the Civil War. Francis Hawks enlisted Robert Tomes's help in a number of his literary projects. He also sailed to England with Robert and his father enroute to Edinburgh when Robert started medical school in 1836.

Francis Lister Hawk's father, also named Francis, was born in 1769, and was also active in government as the Customs Collector of the Port of New Bern.

Francis Lister Hawks' first choice of occupations was law, graduating with first honors at the University of North Carolina in 1815. He then studied law under William Gaston and later went to then famous law school of Reeve and Gould at Litchfield, Connecticut. He succeeded quickly at the bar and in 1820 was made reporter of the Supreme Court of North Carolina. In 1826 he gave up the practice of law to enter the Episcopal ministry, and was ordained a deacon and priest in 1827. He then served as an assistant at Trinity Church in New Haven, Connecticut, St. James's in Philadelphia, Pennsylvania, and then as rector of St. Stephen's and St. Thomas's in New York City until 1843. Rev. Hawks was renowned as a spellbinding preacher and he wrote prolifically on church history and other subjects while serving as a minister. He was appointed Bishop of Rhode Island and missionary Bishop of the Southwest, but he declined both.

Then, unfortunately for him, in 1839 he established a church school, St. Thomas's Hall, at Flushing, Long Island, N.Y. The school was built and run on a grand scale, but in a few years became bankrupt, leaving Rev. Hawks and the founders of the school in serious debt. The school's failure caused him to resign as Rector of St. Thomas Church and move to Mississippi where he was soon elected Bishop, which he also declined. In 1844 he became Rector of Christ Church in New Orleans and was also elected the first president of the University of Louisiana, now Tulane, which began operations under his guidance, and which he led as president until 1848.

Rev. Hawks then returned to New York as Rector of the Church of the Mediator and Calvary Church. In 1862, because of his Southern sympathies, he resigned and went to Christ Church in Baltimore. Returning to New York in 1865 he formed the parishes of Our Savior and Iglesia de Santiago, where he preached and conducted services in Spanish His first wife was Emily Kirby of New Haven,

Connecticut, by whom he had two children. She died in 1827. He remarried Mrs. Olivia Trowbridge Hunt of Danbury, Connecticut, and they had six children. Rev. Francis Hawks died in 1866 and is buried in the cemetery of the Tomes's Christ Church in Greenwich, Connecticut.

My great-grandfather Robert Tomes spent considerable time working with Rev. Francis Hawks, and wrote that "he was a man so full of energy that he required a wide scope for its activities…The church was too limited a field….he sought beyond, in the wide domain of science and literature, occasions for the exercise of his superabundant vitality and force." (Robert Tomes' personal memoirs)

Hawks revitalized the New York Historical Society, and was one of the founders of the Ethnological Society and the Antiquarian & Geographical Society. He also edited an Ecclesiastical History, Perry's Expedition to Japan, the Church Journal and a Biographical Dictionary and Heroes of History, each of which he started, but soon abandoned in favor of his next project. In two of these projects, Robert Tomes was invited to help, and ended up doing all the writing; namely Perry's Expedition to Japan (1856) and Heroes of History (1858)

Robert Tomes enjoyed Hawk's friendship and company, but was frustrated by his inability to complete his projects. "Dr. Hawks, however, was changeful and capricious, and after he had made his design, constructed the machinery and once set it to work, generally left its conduct to others. It was so with all these societies, which after being so zealous in their revival or organization he soon abandoned forever. It was the same with all his literary undertakings. …" "He showed in his frequent changes from church to church, and by his varying interest in the establishments more or less connected with them, his Bible classes, and Sunday schools, his associations for this and that benevolent purpose, the same spirit of caprice." (Robert Tomes' personal memoirs)

Robert continued to describe his frustrating, but remarkable cousin by saying, "He was always an incautious, free-spoken man, and as a Southern man early imbued with extreme views of 'state's-rights', which he regarded as his own peculiar country. He was no supporter of slavery in the abstract, and never so perverted his holy office, like many clergymen, as to pretend that this institution with its manifest wrongs and horrors was authorized by the teachings of the founder of our faith, or could be reconciled with the spirit of Christianity. He would not from principle continue to be a slaveholder himself, having immediately emancipated those slaves which had fallen to his inheritance, as a portion of his father's estate…"

Rev. F.L.H. Pott

As a postscript to the life of Rev. Francis Hawks, one of his daughters, Josephine Hawks Pott, named one of her children after him, Francis Lister Hawks Pott (1864-1947). This man was the grandfather of the James Pott who called me about the John Hawks who built Tryon Palace. The Rev. F.L.H. Pott had immigrated to China, married a beautiful and educated Chinese woman, Huang Su-wu (Susan N. Wong, 1867-1918) in 1888, and became president of St. John's University in Shanghai. (see their wedding photo) Rev. Pott served as president until his death in 1947. His wife, children and grandchildren returned to the United States where one of his grandsons, Jim Pott (born 1927), lives in California today. Jim's eldest brother, William Lister Pott (1920-1944) was killed serving as an American Air Force pilot in Burma. St John's University was taken over by the Communist regime in 1949 and closed as an Episcopal institution in 1951. Jim Pott has researched and published an extensive genealogy of his family. (see photos)

Wedding Photo of Reverend Francis L. H. Pott to Susan Wong, in Shanghai China, 1888.

1 Francis Hawks b: Abt. 1711 in Warwick, England
.... +Elizabeth Sabin b: 1710 in England d: March 12, 1772 in Shipston-upon-Stour, Warwick, England m: April 9, 1732
.. 2 Francis Hawkes b: July 1, 1733 in Shipston-upon-Stour, Warwick, England
.... +Ann French b: Abt. 1736 in Warwick, England m: October 15, 1750
...... 3 Elizabeth Hawkes b: October 22, 1751 in Shipston-upon-Stour, Warwick, England
...... 3 Ann Hawkes b: June 22, 1753 in Shipston-upon-Stour, Warwick, England
...... 3 Sarah Hawkes b: December 30, 1754 in Shipston-upon-Stour, Warwick, England
...... 3 Francis Hawkes b: October 12, 1763 in Shipston-upon-Stour, Warwick, England
.... +Mary Wigginton b: Abt. 1765 in Warwick, England m: November 3, 1788
.... 4 Francis Hawks b: May 30, 1789 in Shipston-upon-Stour, Warwick, England d: Abt. 1796 in Shipston-upon-Stour, Warwick, England
.... 4 Ann Hawks b: December 20, 1791 in Shipston-upon-Stour, Warwick, England
.... 4 William Wigginton Hawks b: July 23, 1794 in Shipston-upon-Stour, Warwick, England
.... 4 Mary Hawks b: September 12, 1799 in Shipston-upon-Stour, Warwick, England
.... 4 Elizabeth Hawks b: January 5, 1802 in Shipston-upon-Stour, Warwick, England
.... 4 John Hawks b: August 25, 1805 in Shipston-upon-Stour, Warwick, England
.... 4 James Wigginton Hawks b: November 28, 1808 in Shipston-upon-Stour, Warwick, England
.... 4 Francis Hawkes b: January 27, 1797 in of London, London, England
...... 3 John Hawkes b: November 4, 1765 in Shipston-upon-Stour, Warwick, England
...... 3 William Hawkes b: September 22, 1768 in Shipston-upon-Stour, Warwick, England
.. 2 John Hawks b: January 15, 1734/35 in Shipston-upon-Stour, Warwick, England d: October 31, 1790 in New Bern, N.C. Occupation: Architect & Builder Tryon's Palace
.... +Sarah Ann Rice b: August 1, 1743 Occupation: Grndtr of Gov Nathaniel Rice m: 1768
...... 3 Francis Cicero Hawks b: December 10, 1769 in New Bern, NC d: December 20, 1831 in New Bern, NC Occupation: Customs Collector, New Bern
.... +Julia Airay Stephens b: December 1, 1773 d: April 3, 1813 in New Bern, NC Occupation: Mother - 9 children m: March 7, 1793 Event 1: Died during childbirth
.... 4 Mary Lister Hawks b: August 8, 1794 d: October 11, 1794 Event 1: October 10, 1794 Baptized by Rev. Solomon Halling. Died next day.
.... 4 John Stephens Hawks b: March 21, 1796 in New Bern, NC d: October 16, 1865 in Washington, NC Occupation: Lawyer Event 1: May 18, 1796 Baptized by Rev Solomon Halling
.... +Mary Holliday b: Abt. 1799 m: 1820
.... 4 Francis Lister Hawks b: June 10, 1798 in New Bern, N.C. d: September 27, 1866 in New York City Occupation: Clergy, author, Pres Tulane Univ Event 1: October 4, 1798 Baptized by Rev Thomas Pitt Irving
.... +Emily Kirby b: November 19, 1803 in New Haven, CT d: July 12, 1827 Occupation: Mother - 2 children m: November 11, 1823
.... 5 Julia Ann (Susannah) Hawks b: October 16, 1825 in New Haven, CT
.... +Eaton Pugh Guion b: Abt. 1823 m: March 4, 1845
.... 5 William Walter Hawks b: 1827 in New Haven, CT
.... *2nd Wife of Francis Lister Hawks:
.... +Olivia Trowbridge b: August 11, 1798 in Danbury, CT Occupation: Mother - 6 children m: Abt. 1830
.... 5 Emily Hawks b: Abt. 1831
.... +Richard Oakley b: Abt. 1827
.... 5 Olivia Hawks b: Abt. 1833
.... +Edward Bogart b: Abt. 1829
.... 5 Francis Tomes Hawks b: June 9, 1832 in New York City Event 1: October 7, 1832 Baptism by Dr. Milnor
.... +Hannah Manly b: Abt. 1839 Occupation: dtr of Judge Wm Gaston & Hannah McClure
.... 5 Josephine Hawks b: Abt. 1837 in New York? d: Abt. 1902 in New York?
.... +James Pott b: 1827 in New York City d: February 8, 1905 in New York Occupation: Publisher, James Pott & Co.
.... 6 James Pott b: Abt. 1861 Occupation: Publisher
.... +Katherine Maud Mason
.... 7 Eleanor Pott b: 1886
.... 7 Josephine Pott b: 1889
.... 7 Helen Mason Pott b: May 26, 1892 in Greenwich, CT d: January 1972 in Roxbury, CT
.... 6 Kate Pott b: Abt. 1862
.... 6 Francis Lister Hawks Pott b: February 22, 1864 in New York, NY d: March 7, 1947 in Country Hospital, Shanghai, China Occupation: Clergyman, President St. John's Univ
.... +Susan N. Wong b: Abt. 1867 in China d: May 11, 1918 in Shanghai, China Occupation: Headmistress, St. Mary's School m: August 23, 1888

For complete Hawks genealogy please see appendix.

Home of John Hawks, New Bern North Carolina.

Family of Jim, upper right and Lois Pott, upper center.

They were, in their genteel, well-educated, literate way, latter-day "jet-setters". All in all, the Burckhardts and their kin, were an exceptionally talented family.

THE FAIRBURNS, AND BURCKHARDTS AND JOHN SINGER SARGENT

Gordon Fairburn (1941 - 2000)
and Phoebe Fairburn
Gordon Fairburn was next in the line of serendipitous connections. Sadly, I was privileged to know Gordon for just the few short years between 1996 and 2000 when he died of a recurring cancer. He was a wonderfully intelligent, witty and well informed person who welcomed me and joined in our mutual search for ancestral information. My wife and I are fortunate indeed to have also met and continue our friendship with Gordon's charming wife, Phoebe.

As the pedigree shows, Gordon was a descendent of Mary Elizabeth (Tomes) Burckhardt (1828-18??), my great-grandfather Robert's youngest sister. Mary Elizabeth, "Polly" to her friends, married Edward Burckhardt a Swiss businessman from Basel, who was a friend of John Iselin, also from Basel, who had married Polly's older sister

Margaret. Both the Tomes sisters were born in New York, but were raised and schooled mainly in England and the Continent under the care of their mother, Maria Roberts Tomes, Francis Sr's wife. Polly is the person who published the letters her father wrote to her from 1849 to 1869 in the family book, Our Great Grandfather (circa 1875).

Polly and Edward Burckhardt had three daughters, two of whom died tragically young. May died first, in 1875, age 19, of typhus while she was in boarding school in Switzerland. The next eldest, Charlotte Louise, died at age 29 of tuberculosis. Both diseases can now be easily cured, but were then quickly fatal.

The surviving daughter, Valerie (1859-1932), had six children with her husband, Harold Hadden. Two of Valerie's uncles, Charles Tomes and Francis Tomes Jr., had married Hadden women (Isabel and Eleanor, respectively), Harold Hadden was a nephew of these Hadden women. So, the close connection between the Tomes and Hadden families continued to another generation.

After I met Alexander Hadden Tomes he sent a copy of the pedigree to Gordon's older brother, who was not keen on genealogy, but passed it on to Gordon. Gordon was quite interested so he contacted me and our friendship started in 1996. Gordon was the editor of "Art World", a fine arts magazine, in his early adult life, but had subsequently become a practicing psychologist, living and working in New Canaan, Connecticut. His interest in the family genealogy caused me to send him copies of the Tomes memoirs and journals we had transcribed and published, and we began correspondence.

Gordon was then particularly interested in correcting a well-known art critic's erroneous interpretation of the history of the painter John Singer Sargent's relationship with the Burckhardt family. To make another long story short, Gordon and I collaborated on setting the art critic straight, and my wife Josie and I became very good friends with Gordon and his wife Phoebe in the process.

"Lady with the Rose",
John Singer Sargent, Henry James
From this experience I learned that John Singer Sargent had in fact been a close friend of the Burckhardts and for a time had courted Charlotte Louise who was a beautiful young girl of 19 when they met in Paris. Sargent offered to paint her portrait as a gesture of friendship while his and Charlotte's families were living in Paris during the 1870-80's. The painting, "Lady With The Rose", is one of Sargent's masterpieces, which Henry James considered significant in Sargent's artistic growth. (See Henry James's 1887 Harpers Monthly article on this subject.)

Ultimately the painting was given by Charlotte's sister Valerie to The Metropolitan Museum of Art in New York City, where it still hangs next to another of Sargent's famous works, the portrait of "Madame X." Sargent also painted portraits of Charlotte Louise and her, mother, Mr. Edward Burckhardt, Valerie Burckhardt, and even one of their pet dog, "Pointy." Sargent never did marry, but the record of his courtship of Charlotte is noted in the diary of one of his close friends and fellow art student, James Beckwith. (see John Singer Sargent, His Portrait by Stanley Olson (St. Martins' 1986.)

Left: Mrs. Burckhardt and Daughter *79 1/4" x 55 1/2" Oil on canvas. 1885*
Center: Portrait of Valerie Burckhardt *16" x 29" Oil on canvas. 1878*
Right: Portrait of Edward Burckhardt *22" x 18" Oil on canvas. 1880*

*All paintings by John S. Sargent. Mrs. Burckhardt was Mary Elizabeth Tomes,
Robert Tomes youngest sister.*

The Burckhardt Family

Before Gordon Fairburn died, he told us that he and Phoebe had just visited Basel, Switzerland to look up his Burckhardt family history and found it most interesting. My wife and I were visiting in Alsace, France in October, 2002, so we also visited Basel on Gordon's recommendation. It is located on the Rhine just across the French border, has beautiful museums and lovely ancient architecture. We also found the Burckhardt family mansion, now a museum, in the center of Basel. Portraits of eighteenth and nineteenth-century Burckhardts, some of their furniture and other household effects, as well as many other items of Basel history are on display.

The Burckhardt family goes far back in Basel's history. Many in this family were very successful textile manufacturers, merchant bankers, Protestant ministers and senior government officials. The Burckhardts were also serious art collectors and academics. One, in particular, Jacob C. Burckhardt (1818-1897) was the author of two famous works in the mid nineteenth century, *The Civilization of the Renaissance in Italy* and *The Age of Constantine the Great*, both of which are still in print. His lecture notes have also been recently transcribed and published. He is still recognized as one of the first modern historians who characterized the Italian Renaissance as the historical break from the Gothic past to the modern era of Humanism and individuality, and who was very prescient about the rise of nationalism and the future of Europe.

Another Burckhardt, Johann Ludwig (1784-1817), was a Swiss born, British-sponsored explorer of the Near East the African Continent, who anticipated the other great explorers of the 19th century. He was the first modern European to discover Petra.

Edward Burckhardt, Polly's husband, was a very successful textile manufacturer and merchant who also had professional artistic skill. I found, and had copies made, of his panoramic drawings of the city of New York which he drew as he observed the city from a Manhattan church tower in 1845. The originals are on display at the New York Historical Society.

Edward, Polly, and their three daughters spent many happy years, before May's untimely death. They traveled in Europe where they had homes in Paris and Basel, as well as a home in New York City. Edward's brief memoir, sent to me by Gordon Fairburn, tells of frequent visits to meet friends such as the Iselin's, and my great-grandfather Robert in Wiesbaden, Paris, Baden, etc. The Iselin's great-granddaughter, Joanna Gunderson of New York City, let me copy her great-grandmother Margaret (Tomes) Iselin's diary of those times. They were, in their genteel, well-educated, literate way, latter-day "jet-setters". All in all, the Burckhardts and their kin, were an exceptionally talented family.

My direct ancestor Francis Tomes from a painting by J. C. Horsley. R. A. Francis's manservant, John Nicol, in the doorway.

FRANCIS TOMES SENIOR AND HIS ENGLISH ROOTS

Francis Tomes (1780-1869)

Now, getting back to the beginning purpose of this search in 1959 - to discover the identity of my great-grandfather Robert Tomes's father, Francis Tomes. By transcribing the many original handwritten journals and memoirs of both Francis and Robert given to me by Hadden Tomes, Arthur Lewry, and Arthur Tomes, plus interpreting the genealogical information given me by Mary Tomes Prinz and Francis Phillip Tomes and Major Ian Tomes, and others, we have discovered the identity of both Francis and Robert in great detail.

The journals and memoirs of Francis and Robert are so personal and detailed that I feel as if I know them both better than I do many friends. Their writings have taught me that my own love of language, reading, writing and books is not original with me - it is clearly an inherited trait. As Francis wrote in his journal

on Monday, on June 18, 1838, while sailing in the mid-Atlantic bound for Liverpool, "How dreadfully monotonous must such a life be to one who has not taste for books."

We learned from transcribing the journals that Francis Tomes' was born in 1780 in Chipping Campden in the Cotswolds and, as the second son of a farmer/sackmaker, Richard Tomes, who died when Francis was a young boy, was apprenticed to a merchant in Birmingham. He ultimately emigrated to New York City in 1815, with his wife Maria and their two eldest children, and founded an export-import business. They had five more children in New York, including my great-grandfather, Robert who was born in 1817.

Francis maintained a family home in New York for all his life, but during the 1830s and 40s he began to live separately from his wife at another home he established in England. Maria also spent considerable time in England educating their two daughters in private schools there. Francis and Maria both died in 1869, Maria in New York at age 79, and Francis in England at age 89.

Francis's 297 page journal for the years 1837-1839 describes four sailing ship crossings of the Atlantic Ocean and a seven month overland trip from New York City to Chicago, then to New Orleans and back to New York, via stage coach, river and lake boat, wagon, and horse-back; staying in a variety of accommodations and meeting an even wider variety of frontier Americans in a very rough-and-ready new democracy. When Francis arrived in Chicago in 1837 it was a frontier town of 4,000 people celebrating the first year of its incorporation. Fifteen years earlier, in 1812, its inhabitants had been massacred by the Indians at Fort Dearborn and it was not until 1833 that the Federal Treaty of Chicago moved the Pottawatomie, Ohowa and Chippewa Indian Nations to west of the Mississippi.

Francis And Maria Roberts Tomes

In 1812 Francis, at age 32, married Maria Roberts, age 22. She was originally from Dolgelly, Wales and had been raised by an aristocratic cousin after her parents died while she was a young girl. Francis tried to start his own trading business shortly after they were married, but it failed and they lost both Maria's £1000 dowry and all of Francis's savings. Francis went back to work for Lewis and paid off all his debts. Lewis then staked Francis to start a new jointly

Sketch Chicago 1837

Francis Tomes, Robert Tomes Father

Maria Tomes, Francis' wife

owned trading business based in New York City in 1815. The British loss of the War of 1812 and the defeat of Napoleon at Waterloo in 1815 combined to put England into a very serious economic depression, but opened the possibility of trade with America.

Francis and Maria had two sons in Birmingham; Francis Jr. (born 1813) and Charles (born 1814), and then moved to New York City in 1815. Francis left England for New York by sailing ship and Maria followed him by herself with a maid and the two boys, nursing one, on an arduous storm-tossed, eighty day sailing voyage, via the Azores, in 1816. They established their home in New York City and had four more sons and

three daughters; Robert (born 1817), George and Maria (twins born 1819), Richard (born 1820), Margaret Ann (born 1821), Benjamin (born 1825) and, Mary Elizabeth (born 1827). For a more detailed history of the family's life in New York, please see The Private Memoirs of Dr. Robert Tomes, which I transcribed and printed in 1996.

Francis soon bought out Mr. Lewis's interest and continued his trading business at No. 98, then No. 6 Maiden Lane in New York City, first as "Tomes & Miller", then as "Francis Tomes & Sons". (The building and storefront was still there in 2003.) It was on Maiden Lane, just 25 years before Francis started his business there in

View of the back of the house in Moseley Grove.

1815, that Thomas Jefferson, in 1790, met in his rented house with Alexander Hamilton and James Madison. "In the course of the night, Jefferson recalled, they brokered one of the great political deals of American history. Under the terms of the arrangement, the national capital would be situated on the Potomac, and the federal government would agree to take on the enormous debts of the 13 states. Had that meal never taken place, New York might still be the nation's capital. But even more important, the primacy of the central government might never have been established, says Ron Chernow, the Hamilton biographer. The assumption of state debts was the most powerful bonding mechanism of the new Union. Without it, we would have had a far more decentralized federal system." (New York Times, July 2, 2006)

Francis Tomes' business succeeded, enabling Maria to return to England frequently with their daughters, and to send their sons to attend private schools in Manhattan. Francis maintained a house on Washington Place in "Greenwich Village", as well as a country house, Moseley Grove, near Birmingham in England. We estimate that Francis made over 30 round trip Atlantic crossings during the years between 1815 and 1850. Francis eventually retired in the 1850s to live at Moseley Grove and also at Little Longstone in the Peak District of Derbyshire, the home of his friend and business associate, William Longsdon.

Francis's mother was Sarah Hawks, born in Shipston-on Stour, about ten miles east of Chipping Campden. Sarah was one of the daughters of Francis and Elizabeth Hawks, and sister to John Hawks, who was to become the architect and builder of Tryon Palace in New Bern, North Carolina, described previously in this book. Richard Tomes and Sarah Hawks were married on February 28, 1774 in the Parish Church of Shipston-on-Stour. This church record is preserved in the database of the microfilm-records of the original Parish Register, which can be obtained via the Mormon Church's Family History Center. (I have a wonderful 18th century colored landscape etching, given to me by Ian Tomes, depicting Shipston-on-Stour nestled in the Cotswold Hills with young man walking on the road toward the village. It surely could be Richard Tomes walking to pay a courting call on his bride-to-be Sarah.)

Francis Tomes was a bright young lad who learned quickly in grammar school, where he was a good student of Greek and Latin, and was nominated to be a "King's Scholar". But his schooling ended at grade five because the early death of his father left the family without the means necessary to even support the King's scholarship. However, Francis, continued throughout his long life to be an avid reader and became a perceptive observer and good writer. His many references to the joys of reading good books, and his son Robert's comments on Francis's love of Shakespeare, attest to the importance of language and thought in his life. One of my other favorite quotes from Francis's journals is: "A state-room to myself - good books - good health - fine

An 18th century hand colored etching "A view of Shipston on Stour."

weather - fair wind - orderly company - and some of my best friends about me - what more on earth, or water, could man desire!" (June 10, 1838 on board the sailing ship George Washington, bound for Liverpool from New York City)

Francis's older brother, Charles (1774-1837), was able to continue his education and became a practicing lawyer in London. But Francis, as the second son without any financial means, had to go to work as a young man. He did so as a clerk to a Mr. Edward Lewis, a trading merchant in Birmingham, who ultimately brought him into his business. Francis's younger brother, Benjamin, was apprenticed as a clerk in a London banking house, but died of consumption at age 21. Francis also had two sisters, Ann and Sarah.

Francis did not like American democracy - he said so, "I could be a Republican. A Democrat I shall never be - I hate democracy", at page 95 of his journal. Democracy was for him too full of drunken, gambling, corrupt and uncouth people, particularly on the then western frontier along the Mississippi River. He was particularly dismayed by witnessing the Mississippi State legislature in session.

Francis was always a loyal British subject, but not an aristocrat. He was born during the reign of George III, and lived his life during the reigns

Pencil Sketch of Mr. Tomes. Drawn by a fellow passenger on board ship. March 1848.

of George IV, William IV and Queen Victoria (from 1837 until he died in 1869.) He enlisted in the British Militia Reserve in 1797 in response Napoleon's first threatened, but postponed invasion of England. Napoleons' threat didn't end until Nelson's victory at Trafalgar in 1805, and finally, the Duke of Wellington's victory at Waterloo in 1815, the year Francis came to America.

Francis's journals and letters show him to be a hardworking, honest, sober, frugal, self-disciplined man. He was not a fancy dresser - in fact his frugal repairing of his worn clothes was remarked upon by his son Robert. His expense accounts show this frugality in detail; "repair of trowzers (sic) 50 cents", "lodging, 50 cents", "cigars, 25 cents", etc.

When I was transcribing his journal I wondered why he hadn't traveled through Atlanta, Georgia. I learned subsequently by reading some history that the city now called Atlanta wasn't founded until 1845 and incorporated in 1847, almost ten years after the period 1837-1839 covered by Francis's journal. Before it was called Atlanta it was called "Marthasville" after Martha Atalanta Lumpkin, daughter of the former Governor of Georgia who was also a proponent of the Western and Atalantic Railroad planned to terminate at a place called "Terminus", which was really then just a small group of buildings developing around a depot. Economic hard times slowed the building of the railroad, but recovery occurred and by 1845 the W&ARR was joined by the Georgia Railroad, and the Macon & Western Railroad in 1847. The chief engineer of the Georgia RR, John Thomson, proposed Atlanta (an altered version of Martha's middle name "Atalanta"), and the name was changed. So, Atlanta came into existence as the place where three new railroads intersected in the newly developing south.

Filling in many of the details of the rest of Francis's life is a collection of letters he wrote between 1840 and 1868 to his daughter, Mary Elizabeth "Polly" Tomes Burckhardt, who published them for their grandchildren.

For other commentary on America in the 1830s and 1840s through the eyes of other Europeans, (see Charles Dickens' "American Notes" (1841), Frances Trollop's "Domestic Manners of the "Americans" (1832), and Alexis de Tocqueville's "Democracy in America" (1835)).

Francis was however quite conflicted on the subject of slavery which was legal until 1827 in New York City, second only to Charleston, South Carolina as a slave trading center. Francis never owned slaves himself, but he did considerable business with slave owners in the American south, selling imported British goods and buying cotton to ship back to his English partner, John Longsdon, in Great Longstone, Derbyshire, England. Cotton Was America's largest export business and it was based upon the continued availability of slave labor.

Francis wrote about slavery and said he knew it was immoral, but he also wrote that he was "not an abolitionist" and that, compared to the poor in London's slums, he saw some "happy slaves" in America. These assertions both surprised and disappointed me since he appears by his other comments to be a mostly skeptical man. But Francis was not alone in this self-contradiction. Most of the men who wrote and signed the Declaration of Independence and the

Bill of Rights owned slaves, all the while they said it was wrong. Also surprising and disappointing, with the benefit of 21st century hindsight.

One of the compliments Francis paid American culture was that he thought the "society" in Nashville, Tennessee was very congenial, "combining the industry of the North with the civility of the South". Except for his conflicted comments on slavery, reading Francis's journals made me think I would have enjoyed traveling with him.

Francis's observations on politics, commerce, slavery and "society" identify him clearly as a man of his time.

Coincidentally, in 1838, during the years covered by Francis Tomes's journal (1837-1839) Frederick Douglass successfully escaped his cruel slave master's plantation near St. Michael's on the eastern shore of Maryland and made his way north to the protection of abolitionists in Boston. In his first autobiography, "Narrative of the Life of Frederick Douglass", he states flatly "There are no happy slaves". As is well-known, Douglass (1818-1895) eventually bought his freedom from his master and became a world famous abolitionist and confidant of Abraham Lincoln whose Emancipation Proclamation was inspired by Douglass.

Francis enjoyed the rest of his life reading, writing letters, visiting his

English friends, such as William Paxton, the great gardener and manager of Chatsworth, the estate of the Duke of Devonshire. Francis had taken his 13-year-old son Robert to visit Chatsworth in 1830 where they met and talked with Paxton. Paxton was also the architect of the renowned Crystal Palace, which housed the Great Exhibition in Hyde Park in London in 1851.

Francis was also a good friend of J.C. Horseley, a member of the Royal Academy, who painted at least two portraits of Francis. One portrait shows him in Scotland, with his manservant John Nicol in the background, was sent to his daughter in 1855, and another one of him seated

Francis Tomes in his later days.

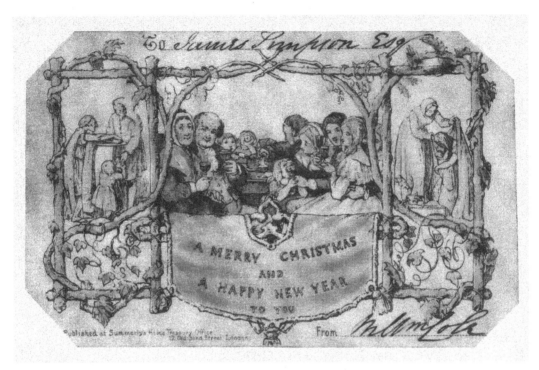

The world's first Chistmas card. Designed by John Calcott Horsley and commissioned by Sir Henry Cole under his "Felix Summerly" pseudonym. Published in 1843 by Joseph Cundall as a hand-colored lithograph.

in an armchair was given to me by Hadden Tomes in 1995. It was badly deteriorated, but I had it restored and it now hangs in a place of honor in our home. (see photos) Horsely was also the artist who made the first Christmas card commissioned by Sir Henry Cole in 1843. Some of Francis's many affectionate letters to his daughter Polly show he was happiest when he was fishing at the Dalmally Inn, as he said, "killing salmon", in Dalmally, Argylshire, Scotland.

Francis and Maria became separated sometime during the 1840's, but remained married throughout their lives, communicating with each other through their children. Robert recorded his views of the reasons for the separation in his Memoirs where he blames Maria's aristocratic aunt for her "class consciousness". It must also be said that Francis might not have been an easy husband, with his constant travel and absorption in his business, and his three cigars per day. Francis's daughter Polly also refers to her mother's "strong will and uncontrolled impetuous temper", but also refers to her "generous heart" in the preface to her book of Francis's letters. But Francis also expressed frequent love and concern for Maria's welfare and needs and provided generously in his will for Maria as his "beloved wife."

Francis and Maria both died in 1869. Maria died at age 79 in New York City and is buried in the family plot in the Trinity Church Cemetery Annex at 153rd Street overlooking the Hudson River Drive. The family had been members of Trinity Church in Manhattan for many years, then later joined St. Paul's nearby. In 1845 Trinity's downtown cemetery had reached capacity and the ornithologist, James Audubon also a member of Trinity, donated 26 acres of his farm on the Hudson River for use as an additional cemetery. Audubon himself is buried there. Francis bought a family plot there in 1851, next to the plot of David Hadden, two of whose daughters married Francis Jr. and Charles Tomes. The Hadden plot is also next to the Astors, their neighbors on Lafayette Street in Manhattan.

Francis died in 1869 at age 89, in Little Longstone and is buried in St. Giles Church cemetery at Great Longstone, Derbyshire, England, next to the family plot of his good friend and business associate, William Longsdon.

Francis Tomes's Coat Of Arms

Francis was very much a self-made man. But even though he overcame financial adversity and had little formal education, created a very success ful business in America, and had a large thriving family, and was mostly a very modest and frugal man, he apparently wanted some greater

recognition. As a life-long Englishman he would have seen a Coat-of-Arms as such a mark of recognition. The only problem was that he was never officially granted a Coat-of-Arms by an English sovereign, as required by English custom.

But that technicality didn't stop him from creating his own Coat-of-Arms, which it appears he did with the probable help, or at least acquiescence, of another member of the "Tomes Clan".

"Burke's Armory", the principal record of Coats-of-Arms, shows that there were thirteen different Coats of arms identified with various people named Tomes, Toms, Thomes, and Tommes. One of these Coats shows four Cornish "choughs" (a European crow-like bird) arrayed on a shield around a sheaf of grain, identified with a certain John Tomes (1760-1844), a member of Parliament from Warwick Borough in the 1820s. Although we have no evidence that there was communication between Francis and John, they lived near each other so it was possible. This John Tomes was directly related to the Tomes family of Long Marston, but no record of an official grant of a Coat-of-Arms to him has been found. We do know, however, that Francis was somehow in contact with Robert Fisher Tomes of Long Marston, who compiled Francis's genealogy in the 1860s. Robert Fisher Tomes's notes also show the John Tomes Coat-of-Arms, so it was clearly known at the time of the notes.

Whatever the actual circumstances, it is the John Tomes Coat-of-Arms that was used by Francis Tomes for the rest of his life, with a motto and Crest added (The Crest is a large Chough and the motto is "Non Dominus Frustra" - "Without God all is in vain"). All I can surmise from this limited evidence - or lack of evidence - is that Francis admired John's Coat-of-Arms and either asked permission, or simply "appropriated" it for his own use.

I have related this story about Francis's Coat-of-Arms simply to set the facts as straight as we can because the Coat-of-Arms with Crest and motto have been reproduced and printed in various commercially offered "Tomes Family Histories" in America. Most of these so-called histories are reprints of Social Security records without any genealogical information. Anyone using such information should know that Francis's Coat-of-Arms was not officially granted, but it probably gave Francis some pleasure and certainly did no harm.

To complete these comments on Tomes Coats-of-Arms it should also be noted that an official Coat-of-Arms was in fact granted to Sir John Tomes (1815-1895), a Fellow of the

Royal College of Surgeons, by Queen Victoria in 1888. It was actually granted retroactively to Sir John's grandfather, John Tomes of Long Marston, and it descends to all his male descendants. The original embossed and sealed "Citation" is now possessed by Major Ian Tomes (retired) at his home in Somerset.

The Sir John Tomes Coat-of-Arms is shown at the English Tomes's pedigree.

Francis Tomes's father was Richard Tomes (1745-1785) described as a farmer and sackmaker from Bidford-on-Avon. This area, from Bidford-on-Avon to Chipping Campden, including Broadway, Long Marston and many other "Warwickshire" towns south of Stratford-on-Avon, was for many centuries the site of the "Tomes Clan" from which many branches of families bearing the name Tomes, Thommes, Thombs, Tombs, Toms, etc. have come.

Josie and I have visited Broadway, Bidford-on-Avon and Chipping Campden many times. We have enjoyed many holidays at Buckland Manor, a charming and well-managed manor house inn located in the village of Buckland, which is very near Broadway. Both Bidford-on-Avon and Chipping Campden are also nearby. And Shipston-on-Stour, where Francis Tomes's mother was from and where she married Richard Tomes, is just a few miles down the road from Chipping Campden. So the churches where our Tomes ancestors were baptized, married and buried are all nearby as well. Please see the pictures of each of these churches in this book.

A Brief Diversionary History Of Buckland

The very small village of Buckland, because of its ancient origins, is worth a short detour to give the reader a sense of the history of this part of England. The "Manor of Bokeland" was granted to St. Peter's Abbey in Gloucester by Kynred, the King of Mercia and "Rex Gentis Anglorum" (chief king of the seven kingdoms of the English nation) in 709 A.D. The name "Boc" or "Bokeland" (now Buckland) indicates the ownership was granted by book or charter.

In a guide written in 1939, the author singled out Buckland as "one of the most out-of-the-way and one of the best built hamlets in the whole of the County. The secret of Buckland is in its isolated position, for the road to it ends at the dwellings, which are almost hidden, in the great elms and poplars of a small "combe" Among the great elms of southern England. Otherwise, the village appears much the same today, a mellow string of buildings along a lane beneath a wooded hill crowned by prehistoric earthworks."

"At Doomsday (the "Doomsday Book" was King Williams's mandated record of all the properties in England in 1086 A.D.), "the ten hides of the demesne, consisting of 15 plough tillage's and ten acres of meadows, were worked by 22 villains, 6 borders and 12 slave. Villains were customary tenants who worked for the lord unpaid for a certain number of days each year; borders were cottage tenants who worked whenever required but at a fixed wage, and twelve were slaves. None was free and two centuries later, according the 1266 subsidy roll, there were still no freed men on the manor Buckland. Among a villain's many duties and services to his lord was the undertaking not to alienate a son from the manor nor to marry away a daughter without paying redemption." (Buckland Manor History, 2000)

"A Church existed in the hamlet in the time of Pope Clement III, that is around 1190, and the present building was begun at about the time of the 1266 roll. Since the place is set on the side of an escarpment, like many others in the Cotswolds the Church was dedicated to the Archangel Michael, patron of high places." At Christmas of 2005 Josie and I attended a very moving midnight Christmas service in St. Michaels, presided over by the Anglican priest who serves the combined "livings" of Buckland with Laeverton, and Stanton-cum-Snowshill.

Photos of St Michael's, Buckland Manor on Christmas eve, 2005.

St. Michael's and Buckland Manor.

St. Michael's and Buckland Manor survived the Dissolution when the Manor was acquired by a Sir Richard Gresham (1485-1549) who had also bought Fountains Abbey and some other monastic plums from King Henry VIII. Buckland also survived the bubonic plagues, which ravaged the population in the 1600s, and various successive ownerships changed by inheritance and sale to the Grafton and Granville families.

In the 1720s John Wesley, one of the three founders of the Methodist Church, preached at St. Michaels and stayed with friends, the Kirkhams, who lived in Stanton, the neighboring parish. Like the Granvilles, the Wesley brothers were friendly with Rev. Kirkham, Rector of Stanton. Kirkham's son Robert was a fellow undergraduate at Christ Church, Oxford with Charles Wesley and was one of the three original Oxford "Methodists". Betty Kirkham was also friendly with John Wesley and corresponded with him, but they never met again after 1730.

One of the more fascinating entries from John Wesley's Journal, dated June 11, 1731 is: "We have made another discovery too, which may be of some service that it is easy to read as we walk ten or twelve miles; and that it neither makes us faint, nor gives us any symptom of weariness, more than the mere walking without reading at all." What a man - walking and reading at the same time! I also remember seeing, during a visit to

Bristol with a Methodist Church group guided by Rev. Phil Blackwell, a drawing of John Wesley writing a sermon on a small table mounted on his saddle while he rode to his next preaching destination. Walking and reading, riding and writing; what if he had a cell-phone?

The neighboring village of Stanway also has an ancient, and recent, history of interest. It is the site of the 16th, 17th and 18th century "Stanway House" with a very striking gate-house. The house, which is now inhabited by its owner, has a Great Hall, visible from the outside, and stands by an ancient church and a beautiful 14th century Tithe Barn. More recently; during the late 19th and early 20th century, the house was owned by Lord Hugo and Lady Mary Elcho who entertained many of the Edwardian intellectuals, politicians, scientists and artists. Lord Balfour, prime minister from 1902 to 1905, H.G. Wells, James Barrie, Harry Cust and the Duchess of Rutland were frequent guests who became dubbed "the Souls", because of their discussions or the arts and religion. In 1908, Edith Wharton, the well-known American writer was introduced to "the Souls" and became a frequent visitor and life-long friend of Lady Elcho. (See "Edith Wharton, A Biography", by R.W.B. Lewis, Harper & Row, 1975). The names of two

young men, Charles and Herbert Thombs, of Stanway are inscribed on the bronze sculptured World War I memorial on the road to Stanway. Maj. Ian Tomes has also compiled a pedigree of many Tomes, Toms, Thomes, and Tommes from the towns of Stanway, Blockley and Broad Campden.

In 1802 Buckland Manor was sold to Thomas Phillips (1742-1818) who also bought the Middle Hill estate, just across the Broadway-Snowshill road from St. Eadburgha. Thomas Phillips died and left Buckland and Middle Hill to his illegitimate son, also Thomas Phillips (1793-1872) who became an extraordinary biblio-phile and antiquary. His manuscript collection alone numbered some 60,000 items, and his books, drawings, printings, coins and prints were auc-tioned of by Sotheby's from 1886 through 1981. Buckland ultimately, in 1970, became the property of a Peter Ansdell, who retained the Lordship of the Manor, and who developed it into a very civilized small Country House hotel where we have stayed for many years. In 2004 it was sold to new owner.

Broadway, St. Eadburgha
The 12th century church at Broadway, St. Eadburgha, escaped both the Dissolution in the 1540s and the Victorian "restorations", because it was superceded by a Victorian church closer to the town. The result is that

St. Eadburgha

St. Eadburgha is pristine in its simplicity and very rural setting, isolated from the village on the narrow road from Broadway to the neighboring village of Snowshill. (Snowshill has a National Trust manor house, which was once the private home of Catherine Parr, the last and surviving wife of King Henry VIII.) The old church is dedicated to St. Eadburgha, Alfred the Great's granddaughter, one of the patron saints of Pershore, the now ruined mother Abbey a few miles to the north. Services are held in this still active church in the summer months. My ancestors worshiped in this church during the 18th century when they lived in Broadway. Broadway is a beautiful old English town and which was visited frequently in the earlier 20th century by the painter John Singer Sargent and his friend the writer Henry James.

Bidford-On-Avon, St. Laurance – Shakespeare's Sojourns
Bidford-on-Avon's ancient church of St. Laurance is one that was certainly seen by William Shakespeare (1564-1616) when he wrote his well-known bit of doggerel about his occasional sojourns just four miles up the Avon

Bidford-on-Avon's St. Laurence church.

from Stratford with his drinking contest buddies:

"Piping Pebworth, dancing Marston, Haunted Hillsborough, Hungry Grafton, Dodging Exhall, papist Wexford, Beggarly Broom and drunken Bidford."

"Bidford is not drunken now; it is only sleepy; a long steep street, with, at the top, the church and beautiful old house, now cottages, once the Falcon Inn, where Shakespeare used to drink...And at the foot the Swan Inn and old bridge" "The Slow Coach", by E.V.Lucas.

My great-great-great grandfather, Richard Tomes (1745-1785) was baptized in St. Laurance church in March, 1745 in Bidford, as were his three brothers and two sisters. Richard married Sarah Hawks (1748) in

August 1748 at the Church of St. Edmund in Shipston-on-Stour. Richard became a sackmaker in Chipping Campden where he died in 1785 and is buried in St. James church cemetery.

My great-great-great-great grandfather, Benjamin Tomes (1711-1786) "the saddler of Bidford" and his wife Elizabeth Tomes, were both baptized married, and buried at St. Laurance. Benjamin's father, also Benjamin, born circa 1680, married Elizabeth Maids on February 3, 1702 at St. James's in Chipping Campden and moved to Bidford. We have no records further back about their ancestors, but since people didn't move about very far or frequently it is probable that they lived in Campden and Bidford for many prior generations. They had to have been a hardy lot, suffering through the bubonic plague and the English Civil Wars in the 1600s, and worse, in the centuries before.

Chipping Campden, St. James

Parts of St. James, the parish church of Chipping Campden, date from the 1100s, but most of the present structure was built by wealthy wool merchants in the 14th and 15th centuries. The nave was rebuilt over the Norman foundations with raised walls to hold a row of clerestory windows and a large window over the chancel arch. The church's 15th century altar hangings are the only complete set of English medieval altar hangings known to survive in England. The great Perpendicular tower houses bell and ringing chambers with a

clock room between. The entrance walk to the church is bordered by avenues of ancient and now large lime trees planted in 1770, ten years before my great-great grandfather, Francis Tomes (1780-1869) was baptized in the church, as were his three brothers and two sisters. His father Richard Tomes (1745-1785) was buried there when Francis was just five years old.

This beautiful, large, spacious church stands on a rise overlooking Chipping Campden so it is a landmark to be seen for miles around, and to be heard with its "peal of eight bells". Descending into the town is a row of ancient almshouses, which have been modernized and are still inhabited by tenants. At the side and back

Church of St. Edmund, Shipton on Stour

of the church is a ruined manor house that was destroyed in the English Civil War, but whose open farmlands provide a vast open view of the church and the surrounding countryside. The church and its setting are altogether lovely to see.

The town of Chipping Campden is one of the most beautiful in the Cotswolds. The high street is bounded on both sides by houses and shops of amber colored Cotswold stone, with an extraordinary stone wool market building dominating the street. "Campden", as it is locally known, was the main center of the English wool market in its hey-day in the 15th through 17th centuries. It is now one of the premier tourist destinations in the Cotswolds, but it has kept its traditional character intact.

"Very Brief History of England" From The Beginning Of "England" Until The Present

Thus, our Tomes ancestors lived during interesting, albeit difficult times during the 17th, 18th and 19th centuries in the Cotswolds of England.

The more ancient history of people in England goes all the way back to the end of the first Ice Age (circa 10,000 B.C.E.) when there was a land bridge to the European continent. The earliest settlers would have been Celtic people from Europe, or, as recently discovered by DNA researchers, descendants of migrants who came up along the Atlantic coast from Spain. The "English Channel" was formed by the rising of the seas after the Ice Age "melt", about 6500 B.C.E. From then on new people inhabiting England

St. James's church at Long Marston.

CHIPPING CAMPDEN PARISH CHURCH

A popular tourist destination in Coltswolds.

were immigrants or invaders from Europe, the Mediterranean, and Scandinavia. These people, in turn, were all the descendants of those who had come before them as Homo sapiens from Africa to Europe and the Middle East, some fifty to one hundred thousand years before. When I checked my own personal DNA a few years ago I learned that one of my genetic "markers" showed that I am partly descended from a central European people. It had to be - we all have to come from somewhere else in the distant past. We Americans are all, in this remote sense, "African Americans". At this point in time we are all the product of rich amalgam of an incredibly complex gene pool. With ancestors from England and Scotland I must have a goodly share of Celtic, Spanish, Roman, Scandinavian; French, German and middle European genes.

For perspective on how many generations it takes to get from the remote past to the present, consider the following: At 15 years per prehistoric generation there would be 800 generations from 10,000 B.C.E. to the present; and 567 generations from 6500 B.C.E. to the present; and 133 generations from the time of the Roman conquest of Britain to the present; and 87 generations from the time of Alfred the Great, the Danes and the Vikings in England, to the present; and 35 gener-

ations from the time of Henry VIII. Modern generations tend to be longer than 15 years - my own is 30 years from the 1600s to the present - about 300 years for 10 generations.

The Ordinance Survey Maps of England are incredibly detailed. The OS Landranger series covers the whole of England in 204 maps on a scale of 1:50,000, about one and one-quarter inches per mile. A brief reading of any of these maps will give you another sense of the long and complicated history of England. The maps show not only the towns and roads, but all archeological and historical information, such as battlefields (with dates), visible earthworks, Roman Villas, non-Roman castles, stone monuments, hill forts, tumuli, stone circles, moats, long barrows, motts, farms, tithe barns, granges, churches, Roman roads, footpaths, courts and woods. The maps also show railways and dismantled railways, brooks, creeks, rivers, ponds and lakes. The OS the maps show at a glance how completely covered England is with evidence of the distant and recent past. To be in England is to be immersed in history.

One of the best histories of Britain is Simon Schama's three volume "A History of Britain" (Hyperion, 2000) also accompanied by a recent television documentary with the same title.

Opposite page: A map of the Coltswold region in England.

Dr. Robert Tomes, Crrca 1840.

DR. ROBERT TOMES, THE MEDICAL DOCTOR WHO BECAME A WRITER

Dr. Robert Tomes (1817 - 1882)
The memoirs of my great-grandfather, Dr. Robert Tomes, describe his life, beginning with growing up as a boy in Manhattan when Greenwich Village was still a village.

Robert was born in 1817 in a house at Washington and Liberty Streets in what is now downtown Manhattan. The house was located at the exact site of what were the World Trade Towers.

For years, whenever I visited New York I always looked at the Towers to mark Robert's birthplace. By an awful coincidence I was in Manhattan very near the Trade Towers on the morning of September 11, 2001, and witnessed the terrorist attack and the collapse of the Towers. I just happened to be walking to a meeting on lower Fifth Avenue that morning when I looked up at the Towers and saw the tragedy happen, stood mesmerized while it unfolded before our unbelieving eyes, and realized that the world had changed, once again

for the worse. Fortunately I was safe and only inconvenienced for a few days until I could rent a car to drive back to my home in Chicago.

Robert attended various grade schools in Manhattan until 1830 when he was enrolled in the Columbia College Grammar School on Murray Street with his life-long friend Evert Duyckinck, who later became a literary patron of many well known nineteenth century authors, including their fellow classmate and mutual friend, Herman Melville. Robert remembered, for instance, meeting Daniel Webster on a few occasions, and also being carried on his father's shoulders as a seven year old to see the parade of General Lafayette's triumphal return to America in 1824.

Robert's schooling continued, at age 14, at Washington College (now Trinity College) in Hartford, Connecticut, then medical school from 1836 to 1840 in Edinburgh, Scotland and graduate medical studies for eighteen months in Paris, France. His descriptions of life and studies as a young medical student in both Edinburgh and Paris are interesting and colorful. He describes the French system of medical education in detail and comments on the excitement of being a young student in the Paris of 1841 under the reign of King Louis-Phillipe.

It was still the "old Paris", before Napoleon III and the Haussman boulevards, with gas-lit street lamps and horse-drawn carriages. Robert rode to Paris from Boulogne in a "Diligence" stagecoach drawn by six huge white horses whipped on by "Postillons". It was the Paris of Honore de Balzac. Robert's memoirs describe his sixth floor student's walk-up flat on the Rue de Buci and the medical, school on the Rue des Ecole d'Medicin, all of which are still there. He also enjoyed the Louvre museum, the theater and opera, and dining out, even in the elegant Trois Freres and Grand Vefour, which Josie and I have also enjoyed, sitting at "Balzac's table".

Robert returned to New York in 1842, began his medical practice in the Alms House (now Bellevue Hospital) and the prison hospital on Blackwell's Island – (now Welfare Island). His descriptions of the corrupt Sixth Ward, and the Five Corners gang warfare are well documented in many recent

books and films. He also started writing as an avocation, with articles for The Democratic Review, The Literary World, and The New York Post. He engaged briefly in the private practice of medicine, but in 1846 he became a ship's surgeon crossing the Atlantic, and in 1848 he became ship's surgeon on The Panama, a steam/sail ship sailing from New York around the Horn of Tierra Del Fuego to San Francisco, one of the first ships to bring prospectors to the Gold Rush. These memoirs, of transporting prospectors from Panama to San Francisco, and then gold from San Francisco to Panama on the return trips, during 1849, are full of extraordinary images, observations and characters.

Robert Tomes also mentions finding the balustrade at which George Washington was inaugurated America's first President, relegated by 1842 to the Alms House in New York City. It has been recently (2006) reported that this same balustrade was somehow rescued from the Alms House and is now on display at the New York City Historical Society.

Robert returned again to New York in 1849 and soon began writing full time as the author of biographies, travel books, and articles for Harper's Monthly. He also wrote an interesting book about traveling as the reporter of record on the inaugural run of the Panama Railroad, across the Isthmus,

"Panama in 1855." David McCullough cites Robert's book in his best-selling The Path Between the Seas (1977).

During the American Civil War Robert wrote a history, "Battles of America," and a serialized Civil War history, "The War With the South," while also serving as a medical officer for the Sanitary Commission, the forerunner of the American Red Cross. Robert wrote a fascinating letter to his friend Evert Duyckinck in 1861 telling of his attempt to get medical aid to the Bull Run (First Manassas) battlefield. He was turned back by the mass of fleeing, panic-stricken Union troops who had been routed by the Confederates under General Beauregard.

After the Civil War Robert became U.S. Consul at Reims, France from 1866 to 1867, and wrote an interesting book about the experience, and the making of champagne, "The Champagne Country." He knew the famous "Widow Cliquot" ("Veuve Cliquot"). He then spent most of the rest of his life living and writing for Harper's Monthly in Wiesbaden, Germany with his wife, Catherine,

Dr. Robert Tomes circa 1879

Dr. Robert Tomes wife Catherine circa 1879

Wiesbaden, 1870s

Catherine M. Tomes

Arthur L. Tomes

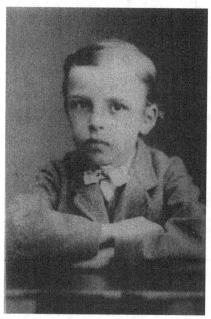

William A. Tomes

Tomes family residence in Wiesbaden

and their three children, Catherine, Arthur and William. The two boys attended the Wiesbaden Gymnasium where they received what Robert thought was the best possible education. And Catherine was sent to a convent at Chateau Thierry where she could learn French. When she came home to Wiesbaden Robert personally taught her history and literature by reading Shakespeare to her aloud.

I have obtained copies of all the Harper's Monthly articles Robert wrote from Wiesbaden, including one, which describes the city and also shows an etching of the Tomes's spacious apartment building. Robert enjoyed living and traveling in Europe and also appreciated the economic benefits of living and educating his children there.

In 1879 he began writing his personal memoirs, which were never published until 1996 when Arthur Tomes Lewry and his wife, Lolly, loaned them to me to transcribe and publish privately for the family. The first part of his memoirs had been published as "My College Days," in 1880, describing his education from grammar school through medical school at the University of Edinburgh, but the bulk of Robert's personal and family history had not. I published them in 1996 as "The Private Memoirs of Robert Tomes."

Art and Lolly also found another, memoir, "My Later Days," covering the years from 1840 through 1849 when Robert attended graduate medical school in Paris, returned to New York to practice medicine and began writing. We also transcribed and published My Later Days privately.

And there are yet other manuscripts of unpublished articles written for Harper's. In one of those articles he decries the unequal educational opportunities afforded young girls compared to young boys. His own reading Shakespeare to his daughter shows how deeply he felt about the importance of providing his daughter with an education. We have bound and deposited all of these original handwritten memoirs in the special collections of the Newberry Library.

By another bit of serendipity we have also found copies of 130 letters Robert wrote to his friend Evert Duyckinck from 1831 at age 14 to 1878, when Duyckinck died. Professor Donald Yannella, who was for a few years a scholar at Barat College in Lake Forest, Illinois, and also a member of The Caxton Club, gave a Caxton Friday Lunch talk in 1999 about Duyckinck and told me about the existence of the letters, then very kindly gave me a full set of copies. The letters had been kept by Duyckinck and left with his other papers to the Lenox Library, which was merged, into the New York Public Library. All of Robert's original letters are available for inspection in the manuscript library of the New York Public Library. Interestingly, the letters from Robert are kept in a box at the NYPL along with other letters from Duyckinck's correspondents whose last names began with the letter "T", such as then New York Governor Samuel J. Tilden and Henry David Thoreau. (Coincidentally, it was Governor Tilden whose bequest in 1889 was left to establish the New York Public Library, which was formed by merging the Lenox, Astor and Tilden libraries. Also by coincidence, the merger was organized and managed by John Bigelow, a Washington (Trinity) College classmate and long time friend of Robert Tomes)

We know from Robert's extensive writings and his letters that he was, in marked contrast to his father Francis, an admirer of the blessings of democracy, proud of the American Republic, and he abhorred slavery. He wrote that the Confederate claim of "State's Rights" was merely a political attempt to justify slavery. Another of Robert's Harper's articles, "The Fortunes of War-Made and Spent" condemning war profiteering during the Civil War, was recently reprinted in a 150th Anniversary collection of Harper's

articles, "An American Album (2000)." (see appendix) Incidentally, all of Harper's and most other 19th century articles are available on the Cornell University website.

Robert brought his family back to Brooklyn, New York in 1880 to start his two sons in American colleges. Robert died in Brooklyn in 1882 at age 65. He is buried in the Trinity Church Cemetery Annex at 153rd street.

More complete biographies of Francis and Robert are available in the prefaces to the memoirs and journals, copies of which are in special collections at the Newberry Library. A list of all of Robert's books and articles are included in the Appendix of this book.

Other authors of the 1850's, 60's and 70's also republished in Harper's, "An American Album" were: Herman Melville, Nathaniel Hawthorne, Stephen Douglas, Horace Greeley, and Walt Whitman.

Residences purchased by Robert Tomes for himself, his wife and their children in 1880 at 500-502 Classon Avenue Brooklyn, N.Y.

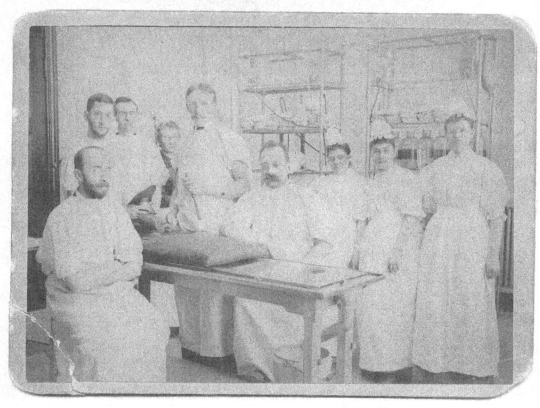

Dr. Tomes (standing) at German Hospital, New York City (Now Lenox Hospital).

MY GRANDFATHER
DR. WILLIAM A. TOMES

My Grandfather,
Dr. William Austin Tomes
Dr. William A. Tomes (1865-1920) was the third child of Dr. Robert Tomes (1817-1882) and Catherine Fasnet Tomes (1839-1923). William had an older brother, Arthur Lloyd Tomes (1863-1922) and a sister, Katherine (1861-1920). William and his brother Arthur attended school at the Gymnasium (high school) in Wiesbaden, Germany where the family lived while Dr. Robert Tomes continued his career as a writer, primarily of books for Harpers and articles for Harper's Monthly Magazine.

One of the reasons Dr. Robert Tomes gave for moving his family to Wiesbaden was to provide his sons with the excellent education available in a German Gymnasium. Katherine was sent to learn French at a convent in Chateau Thierry, France and Robert also tutored her in Wiesbaden by

reading her Shakespeare's history plays. Robert was seriously concerned about giving his children a good education. He also wrote an unpublished article, in a manuscript, which we have, criticizing the unfairness of discriminating against girls in the public and private educational systems.

When the family returned to America in 1880 they acquired two side-by-side brownstone houses at 500 and 502 Classon Avenue, then a fashionable part of the New York suburb called Brooklyn. (named by early Dutch-American settlers after the town of Brueklin in Holland). These houses were lived in for many years thereafter by the families of William at 500 and Arthur at 502.

Both William and Arthur attended Yale in America. Arthur subsequently graduated from Columbia Law School, and William from Columbia Medical School. Arthur practiced law in New

York City and William practiced medicine as an orthopedic surgeon in New York City and Brooklyn, at what was then the German Hospital (now the Lenox Hospital). The picture (see page 112) of William standing at an operating table holding a mallet and chisel was taken at the hospital in the 1890s. It was reprinted recently in a fund-raising calendar published by the Lenox Hospital, sent to us by one of Josie's college sorority sisters, Judy Magner Pasquale. Judy is the wife of Dr. Nicholas Pasquale, Lenox Hospital's chief cardiac surgeon.

Dr. William Tomes married Julia Hall (1870-1945) from Brattleboro, Vermont in 1887 and they had three children, Valerie (1890-19?), Yvonne (1896-19?), and my father, William A. Tomes, Jr. (1894-1975). My father's mother, Julia, and Dr. William were divorced in 1908; the two daughters went to Julia, and my father went to Dr. William who remarried in 1918, but had no other children, and died in 1920, leaving his estate to his second wife, Gertrude. Arthur died in 1922, leaving his widow Jennie E. Schauer, and a daughter, Margaret Iselin Tomes, who married Edward Thomas Lewry, the parents of my cousin, Arthur Lewry.

William A. Tomes

MY FATHER, WILLIAM A. TOMES, JR., HIS LIFE, WORLD WAR I, WILFRED OWEN

My father's parents divorce and the children's custody arrangement turned out be very unfortunate for my father since Dr. William allowed him to drop out of high school which ended his formal education.

Dad was a very bright, naturally articulate, athletic young man who was willing to work hard, but was continually stymied by not having an education. He had a privileged life as a boy but a difficult life thereafter, beset by unfulfilled promise. The separation of his parents when he was 14 years old left him badly scarred emotionally, and probably made him vulnerable to the alcohlism, which plagued him, and our family, all his life. My father's married life was however blessed with his first wife, my mother, Betty Steel (1897-1957), and then Helen Foote (1897-1972) who was also a lovely person.

So my father was very much on his own after he came home from World War I service, without financial or educational resources. By dint of hard work he did make his way in the world until he died in 1975 at age 80.

We know a great deal about my father's life through another serendipitous event that resulted in my getting the letters he wrote to his mother, starting from his age four, through World War I and a few years after. The letters were kept in a shoebox that was sent to me along with his few other possessions after he died in 1975. I was with him when he died, in California from injuries he sustained in a car-railroad train accident, but I had to rely on a close friend of his to collect and send his things to me. When they arrived in three suitcases at our home in Wilmette, Illinois, I inspected them in a cursory way and stored them in a dry place in the basement. Fifteen years later, in 1990, I was cleaning out the basement and I opened the suitcases and inspected the contents more carefully. Among the things was the shoebox marked

William Tomes as boy (left) and as a young man.

in my mother's hand "Bill's letters to his mother".

It was a treasure-trove. They told of his boyhood, his service in World War I, and some of the events of his later life. There is even one letter of thanks from a young man whose life Dad saved from drowning. I will tell here the story of the essential elements of his life. I have also written his detailed biography, "Dear Mother" (2001), and published it for the family, with many photographs.

After leaving school at Erasmus High School in Brooklyn in 1912, "Bill" Tomes held a variety of beginner's jobs in New York City. One of them was literally as a "runner" on the old "Curb" Exchange, a stock

exchange where the investors stood at the curb in the street shouting their orders to the brokers in the windows. The runners carried the written order confirmations. Dad was still living with his father who was a successful medical doctor, so he lived a rather fast life, driving his father's newfangled cars, drinking and dancing at the, Knickerbockers Hotel, etc.

Seeking independence and adventure Dad joined the elite Brooklyn "Troop C" of the First Cavalry of the National, Guard in 1916 at age 22. The Guard was activated in 1916 and sent to the Mexican border, chasing Pancho Villa, the Mexican revolutionary. They were under the command of General John J. Pershing, who later was the supreme

Bill Tomes (center) "Troop C" N.Y. National Gaurd, Texas Border, 1916.

Bill Tomes (left) on Horseback with rifle and saber, 1916.

commander of American Forces in France in World War I. They served as cavalry soldiers on the Mexican border, at McAllen, Texas and elsewhere. We have wonderful photographs of Dad sitting astride his horse among his buddies all in their campaign hat uniforms. It still amazes me that my father was actually a cavalry solider! Dad's military service was certainly symbolic of the transition from the 19th century "cavalry wars" to the 20th century "machine gun wars".

Pancho Villa successfully eluded the American Army and Pershing brought Troop C and the other American Army cavalry soldier's home to a kind of victory parade on March 15, 1917. Two months later, in May, 1917, shortly after America declared war on Germany, the New York National Guard was remobilized as the 27th Division and sent to Spartanburg, South Carolina, for retraining as an infantry division. No more cavalry. Dad's particular unit was transformed into a machine-gun battalion. They were issued British Vickers machine-guns and trained to use them while sailing on their troop ship to St. Nazaire, France.

The 27th (New York) Division and the 30th (Tennessee) Division were the only two American Divisions assigned to serve under the command of British Forces. One other, the 93rd Division, mostly American Negro soldiers,

was assigned to the French, under whose command they served with valor, equipped with French weapons and uniforms. All the other American Divisions were consolidated under the command of General Pershing who jealously guarded the independence of the American Army. The 27th and the 30th served their combat in World War I under British Command. For this reason American histories of WWI don't say much about them, and, since they were American and not British, British histories don't say much either. Because their history is so little known I recite it here. The records show that they fought valiantly and successfully in three major battles and many other engagements.

For perspective, by 1917 World War I had a history of catastrophic attempts by the Germans, British and French to make huge assaults across otherwise static trench lines that formed in 1914, after the first assault by the Germans.

Each assault was designed "to end the war", but each attempt failed and the front line remained virtually static all during the war. The carnage in dead and wounded was horrific. World War I saw the first use of the machine-gun and poison gas. By the end of the war the Germans had lost 1,900,000 killed, the French 1,700,000, and the British 950,000. America, coming late to the war, lost 110,000. Each country lost ten times as many wounded as killed.

The Battle Of Mount Kemmel

The 27th division's first combat was at Dickebusch and Mount Kemmel, near Ypres, Belgium in July, 1918. Ypres had been the scene of constant trench and artillery war for the entire four years of WWI. The area around Ypres is still covered with over 200 military cemeteries where the presence of WWI is palpable. The town of Ypres was leveled by artillery fire during WWI, but when it was rebuilt the eastern gate of the medieval town wall; the "Menin Gate", was inscribed as a memorial to the soldiers who were still missing at the end of the war. There are 55,000 names on that gate! And there are another 35,000 names of the missing listed at Tyne Cot, a British military cemetery at Paschendale, five miles east of Ypres. 90,000 names of the missing within five miles! To say nothing about the equal number of missing German dead. It has been estimated that almost one-half of the dead in WWI were never found. Literally, blown to bits. The total casualties of both sides, dead, wounded and missing, for 1914-1918, in the Ypres salient alone, was approximately 1,000,000 men!

To this day, 90 years after the end of WWI, the town of Ypres stops the traffic driving through the Menin Gate at 8:00 PM every night, and a small group of uniformed honor guards stands in the road under the gate and play British "Last Post", the equivalent of the American "Taps". I have attended this very moving ceremony three times with various members of our family.

The 27th Division fought near Ypres at Dickebusch Lake, Vierstraat Ridge, Wytschaete and Mount Kemmel. There are monuments recording their combat at each place. Mount Kemmel is a small, 250-foot high hill, southwest of Ypres. But it commanded the surrounding flat plain so it was a valuable height for military purposes. It was held for a long time during WWI by the Germans, then captured by the British, then recaptured by the Germans during their spring, 1918 offensive. The Americans were positioned in front of Mt. Kemmel under British command to prepare to retake it in August, 1918.

My father used to describe Mt. Kemmel as "Hell". His Erasmus High School friend, William Clarke, who served in the same machine-gun company with Dad and wrote a detailed book, "Over There," in 1966, about their daily experiences. We therefore have eyewitness testimony of someone who was in the same unit as my father's, telling what they went through day by day.

As machine-gunners they were ordered to set up their guns each night "in front of the front" in "No Man's Land," between the opposing front lines. Their written standing orders were to "hold their position until relieved, alive or dead." Should their gun be put out of action, they were ordered to use rifles, revolvers or grenades. Surrender was prohibited.

The German offensive in March of 1918 had pushed the British back many miles, causing the British Commander, General Haig, to issue his famous "Backs To The Wall" order: It read: "With our backs to the wall, and believing in the justice of our cause, each one of us must fight on to the end... Every position must be held to "the last man." (The same order given to Dick Tomes in 1940!)

The landscape in No Man's Land in front of Mount Kemmel was the result of constant artillery shelling, mortar, rifle and machine gun fire, and frequent gas attacks for the entire four years from 1914 to 1918. The ground was pulverized into hillocks of shell holes, full of putrid water, lingering pockets of gas, unexploded shells, discarded and broken weapons and equipment, human waste, and the broken remains of countless numbers bf dead soldiers of both sides, and thousands of rats.

The machine-gunners were ordered to set up their guns at night in shell holes in No Man's Land, in front of the front line, prepared to defend their positions if attacked, then return back to the front line when relieved 24 hours later. They were constantly under artillery and gas shelling, mortar, machine gun and sniper fire. The 27th Division, during their-two

months on the "East Poperinghe" line in front of Mount Kemmel, lost 167 killed, 50 died of wounds, 819 wounded, 279 gassed, 13 captured and 10 missing in action.

Clarke's telling of the fear and terror experienced by soldiers cowering in shell holes during a sustained artillery barrages rivals the same telling by Eric Maria Remarcque in "All Quiet on the Western Front" (1929), written by a German soldier about the very same Ypres sector of the war.

The 27th Division was assigned the task of retaking Mount Kemmel after first retaking Dickebusch Lake and the Vierstraat Ridge before it. The 27th Division was successful in repelling a counterattack from Mount Kemmel and retook it after the Germans retreated.

Mount Kemmel still exists, now peacefully, about a fifteen-minute drive southeast of Ypres. Its steep sloping sides are now covered by a forest of large trees, but they have grown out of the hundreds of shell holes that remain to this day as a reminder of the hellish fighting that took place there. There is also now a pleasant inn and restaurant located at the top of Mount Kemmel, overlooking a French "Ossuaries", memorializing the French dead at Kemmel.

In 1983, sixty-five years after the 1918 battle of Mount Kemmel, I happened to have a business meeting in Ypres and, at the end of the meeting my French colleague mentioned to Monsieur Ribot, the elderly president of the Picanol Company with whom we were meeting, that my father had fought as an American at Mount Kemmel. M. Ribot immediately stood up and warmly shook my hand and told his colleagues about my father having been at Mt. Kemmel. They all, in turn, shook my hand and made comments of appreciation. I was embarrassed, but they insisted that all the citizens of Ypres will always appreciate the sacrifices of the Allied troops who liberated their land in World War I. In fact, they arranged for us all to have lunch at the restaurant on top of Mt. Kemmel and after lunch they took me into Ypres where we met the mayor. The sense of World War I is so palpable in Ypres, with its over 200 military cemeteries and other monuments everywhere in the town and the surrounding countryside, that you can't escape its presence.

The Battle Of The Hindeburg Line, At The St. Quentin Canal Tunnel
After Mount Kemmel, the 27th and 30th divisions were moved south and east to the St. Quentin area in France. An assault was prepared, coordinated with Australian and British troops, on the Hindenburg Line, the "impregnable" last line of defense of the German Army.

The resulting battle of "The St. Quentin Tunnel", on September 28th, 29th and 30th of 1918, was a very costly, but important victory for the allied forces. Breaking the Hindenburg Line was "the straw that broke the camel's back". As John Toland, author of "1918, The Last Act" said:

"All day long the German troops had fought from the defenses of their famous line with much of the same skill and ardor which had distinguished them in the past - their defeat was due mainly to the offensive spirit of the Americans and the Australians, and to the spirit of victory which animated the British and possibly to German luck, which had changed. For although no one realized it at the time, that afternoon Germany had lost the war. Under the accumulating strain, Ludendorff's nerve had cracked."

The Allied forces marshaled to attack the Hindeburg Line included American, Australian and British units. In command of these forces was a uniquely successful general officer, named General Sir John Monash (1865-1931), a reserve Australian officer who had been a successful engineer and businessman in Australia before the war. He was also the only Jewish general officer on the Allied side.

Monash was born in Melbourne, Australia in 1865 of Prussian-Jewish parents and as a young man showed exceptional aptitude as an engineering student and leader. He was called to active duty in 1914 and served in Egypt, then at Gallipolis in 1915, and then on the Western Front in France where he demonstrated his unusual talent for coordinating artillery, tanks, infantry and aircraft in offensive action. He was knighted in the field by King George V after leading a surprisingly quick victory over German forces at Hamel in the Somme in 1918.

Field Marshall Viscount Montgomery, a junior officer in World War I, later stated that, "I would name Sir John Monash as the best general on the Western Front in Europe." After the war Monash returned to Australia leading many public and private organizations. After his death in 1931 Monash University in Melbourne was organized and named after him. It now has a branch near Florence, Italy.

When Monash took command of the Australian, British and American troops on the Hindenburg Line in September, 1918 he planned and commanded the ultimately successful assault.

The 27th Division was assigned the job of "shock troops" attacking the center of the Hindenburg Line, over the top of the St. Quentin Canal Tunnel, which they did. In one of Dad's wartime letters he said, "it certainly was a shock". My mother's brother, Uncle Wilson Steel, was in that shock troop infantry assault with the 27th Division's 106th infantry, which took the most losses. The problem was that after the Americans had broken through, the Germans came up from the tunnel below and attacked the Americans from behind.

Dad, and his friend William Clarke, in Company A of the 104th Machine Gun Bn., were on the left flank of the action, on top of the "Knoll" overlooking the whole battlefield. In one of Dad's letters, and in Clarke's book, they both describe the breathtaking panorama of the battle. The 104th was then drawn into the battle moving down the hill to defend against a large German counterattack aimed at the Americans. The 104th fought head to head with the attacking German infantry and succeeded in stopping the counterattack.

Then, Clarke reported, "There is no cohesion along the line. The battle is no longer an organized military operation. The fighting is settling down to the bayonet, the bullet, the hand grenade, and Bowie knife between small groups. The German infantry and machine gunners have emerged from their hidden tunnels both in front of and in the rear of our troops. Each group is fighting its own little war. To these men, civilization has disappeared, replaced by primeval instinct. Three of the strong points are taken and then lost. Our men are now isolated in shell holes and small trenches as the hidden trenches disgorge fresh Boche to their rear and front."

Clarke's book reports "the losses were staggering" and, "when the falling shadows of night descend upon those on the battlefield, we do not know from our vantage point whether we have won. We cannot have lost because only a few injured are returning or are being carried from the field. No one retreats, no one gripes about long marches and lousy billets. To the men out there, all these gripes are crowded out by the pain of wounds, hunger and thirst. There have been on this day 1,480 American casualties."

"Two hundred seventy Germans have been captured, but there is no count of their casualties. One can still hear sporadic machine gun fire, a rifle shot, or the explosion of a hand grenade. What about the officers who led these troops into this inferno? Of the three battalions engaged that day, all were killed in the 1st, except one was wounded; in the 2nd, every officer was killed or wounded; and in the 3rd, every officer but one was killed or wounded. In the supporting battalion of the 105th infantry, both officers of Company M were killed. Who can give more than that? Who asked for more?"

On another note of serendipity, I learned recently from Dr. Fred Kittle, a good Caxton Club friend and a premier collector of the works of Dr. Arthur Conan Doyle, that Doyle actually visited the St. Quentin Canal Tunnel battlefield on the last day of the battle. Doyle wrote a great many

books besides the famous Sherlock Holmes mysteries, and one of them is a six volume History of World War I, generously given to me by Fred. Doyle's description of the battle and its aftermath is in Vol. 6. It is virtually the same as Clarke's.

There is now a large, well cared for American military cemetery at the site of this battlefield, near the small French village of Bony. There are over 1,800 graves there, mostly crosses, but many Stars of David. Three of the gravestones are marked with the Congressional Medal of Honor for the extraordinary bravery that stood out in a day where the bravery of everyone was simply ordinary.

There is also a large marble monument to the victory of the 27th and 30th Divisions, built in 1930 overlooking the battlefield at Bellicourt. The monument has a bas-relief diagram showing the locations and movements of the troops during the battle, but it also has a unique asterix cut in the marble at its upper right hand border. This asterix refers to a footnote, also carved in the marble at the base of the diagram. The footnote recites the fact that the notation on the diagram is wrong where it marks "the furthest advance of the American troops". The footnote, surely demanded by one of the veterans of the battle who visited the monument in the 1930s, states that: "Many Americans went beyond this line, joining up with small units of

Australians and carried the fight further north." The American veterans were not to be denied this evidence of their total victory.

There is also a large World War I German cemetery nearby, marked mostly with crosses, but also some Stars of David.

After the battle of the St. Quentin Tunnel the 27th Division was given a few days rest to reorganize and then returned to battle, chasing the German Army further north, through small French towns until they got to St. Souplet, "where they meet strong resistance. William Clarke describes the action he and Dad, of Co "A" of the 104th, saw:

"The 108th Infantry will lead the attack and was already formed up in front of the 107th whom we could vaguely see. Our limbers had come up from Busigny and had lined the field just back of the 107th. As the leaden skies begin to show signs of daylight, we are loaded up and ready to go."

"The barrage begins with its usual crescendo. Behind each limber is the gun team to which it belongs. The 107th moves off, a thin line of men, followed by us. We move off across the muddy fields as the German counter fire begins to fall upon us. It is high explosive, gas, and smoke, as well as machine gun fire. There is no wind, not even a little breeze.

Bill Tomes (top center with mustache) Corbie, France, December 1918.

The air is heavy and wet. The gas and smoke hug the ground. We cannot see where we are going. We maintain our steady pace regardless of the firing and the gas. I cannot see with my gas mask on and I can't breathe. I am choking and coughing so hard I feel that my stomach must come up with the next heave. I had ripped off my mask and reached for the tailboard of our limber. I hang on as I retch and vomit, the limber pulling me along, one foot after the other being sucked from the mud."

"Under cover of smoke, the 102nd Engineers had gotten a prefabricated bridge over the Selle. The air had cleared considerably after daylight, or about the time we reached the bridge. But the enemy counter fire was terrific. It hardly seemed possible for anyone to survive it. With the machine guns and whiz-bangs firing at us at point-blank range from the railroad embankment, we start "on the double" racing through the streets to our objective, the top of that railroad embankment. The streets of St. Souplet were running with the blood of our dead and maimed. Bodies were strewn all over the place, some without heads, some without legs or arms, or both. These are the horrors we see as we race for the railroad."

They get to the top the embankment, immediately after the infantry, and:

"Almost under our feet are two rows of German machine gunners, silenced, their crews all dead, lying about in a most grotesque fashion. We quickly drive through them and over them, across the track and set up our guns, ready to operate should a counter attack develop. This was our mission in this battle."

The Sambre Canal

After St. Souplet, the 27th continued on through some other small French towns and fortified farms, reducing the German defenses as they occurred. Finally, on October 21st, the 27th Division, having reached the top of the ridge overlooking the Sambre Canal, was relieved by the British 6th Division. The 27th was scheduled to return to the front on November 13th, but the war would soon end on November 11th.

The Commanding General of the 27th, John F. O'Ryan, commended Company "A" of the 104th, as veterans of the former "Troop C" of the First New York Cavalry, for their service after the battle of the Hindenburg Line, as follows:,

"I write to express to the officers and men of the 104th Machine Gun Battalion my admiration and respect for their valor, initiative and endurance during the great battle for the breaking of the Hindenburg Line and for the operations subsequent thereto."

Bill Tomes (Lower right without mustache) Corbie, France, December 1918.

"Almost continuously since that battle the Division has been fighting and marching, lying in shell holes at night, attacking at dawn, fighting throughout the day against the most determined machine gun resistance, and repeating this after only temporary relief which meant only lying in other shell holes or pits in positions of close support. The skill, endurance and determination of the machine gunners contributed largely to the success of the operations which resulted in our forcing the crossing of the LeSelle river, capturing St. Souplet, Bandival and the town of Abre Gueron, taking the farms of Jonc-de-Mer, and Le Roux, and reaching the Canal De La Sambre."

"Whether in attack or resisting counterattacks the conduct of the machine-gun units has been characterized at all times by the courage and skill of the officers and the valor of the men. The machine-gun units have won the respect and admiration of the entire division."

The 27th Division retired to Corbie near Amiens. Dad was on a two-day furlough in Amiens on November 11th when the Armistice was declared.

He wrote his mother on November 12th:

"Dear Mother, La Guerre finis! The armistice was signed and hostilities ceased yesterday morning at 11 o'clock..." I was on a pass in Amiens yesterday and that town went crazy. An American and an Australian band went all around the town followed by French civilians, American, Canadian, Australian, English, French and Italian soldiers all carrying French flags. Wine flowed like water. The only thing that ever beat it was New York on New Years Eve. French men and women with cries of "Vive L'Amerique" threw their arms around us and in some cases kissed our "blushing cheeks". I thought I was home...your loving son, Bill".

The Death Of Lt. Wilfred Owen WWI's Great Poet

In the meantime, the British forces that replaced the 27th at the Sambre Canal were ordered to press on with a suicidal attack across the canal, killing the great poet, Lt. Wilfred Owen, and 43 of his mates. The British Colonel in command had himself already been wounded ten times during the war, objected to executing the suicidal attack, but led it heroically and was posthumously awarded the Victoria Cross.

Lt. Wilfred Owen, who had been sent back to the front at his own request, after having suffered severe shell shock for prior combat and, just a few weeks before he was killed, was awarded the Military Cross for bravery in the fighting at Joncourt, near the St. Quentin Canal Tunnel.

The tragic story of Owen's life and death, and remarkable poetry, is told in Jon Stallworthy's biography of Owen. At the very end of the biography he also tells the doubly tragic story of Owen's last letter to his mother which she received in England on November 11th, the same day that the British War department notified her of Owen's death on November 4th, four days before the end of the war.

The insanity of both British and German general staff's ordering their men on suicidal missions just one week, or even one day before the end of the war, which they knew was imminent, could not be more dramatically shown.

Josie and I have visited all the St. Quentin Canal and St. Souplet battlefields, and also the site on the Sambre Canal where Owen was killed. We have also visited the French communal cemetery at Ors where Owen and his mates are buried in a British military cemetery plot. When we were there ten years ago there were a number of bouquets of flowers and messages of respect laid at Owen's gravestone.

Jon Stallworthy wrote in his biography of Owen:

"Wilfred Owen left perhaps the most famous literary manifesto of the twentieth century, not as a finished and final statement, but as a single rough draft of the preface to a book of his poems he intended to publish after the war:

"This book is not about heroes. English poetry is not yet fit to speak of them.

Nor is it about deeds, or lands, nor anything about glory, honor,

might, majesty, dominion, or power, except War.

Above all I am not concerned with Poetry.

My subject is War, and the pity of War.

The Poetry is in the pity.

Yet these elegies are to this generation in no sense consolatory. They may be to the next. All a poet can do today is warn. That is why the true poets must be truthful...."

See also the WWI poetry of Siegfried Sassoon, Edward Thomas, Robert Graves and Isaac Rosenberg, among others. See also Mark Twain's, "The War Prayer".

The Rest Of Dad's Life

The 27th Division returned to a homecoming parade on Fifth Avenue in New York City in March of 1919, and all the soldiers were mustered out to return to civilian life.

Although Dad was not physically wounded, he did fight on the front lines with the 27th Division in its three major battles and other "engagements" and "minor actions" and once had "a whiff of gas". As he said many times years later, "it was enough just to be there." We have his battle ribbons and bars for Ypres (Mount Kemmel) and the Somme (Hindenburg Line).

It is clear from the record of Dad's life, in his letters and in the documented history of the 104th Machine Gun Bn of the 27th Division, that he was a brave man who voluntarily did his duty, risking his life for others and for his country, and praising others but being modest about himself.

The rest of Dad's life was centered around his marriage to my mother Betty Steel in 1926, fathering me in 1927 and my brother Bill in 1929, and struggling to make a living during the endless Great Depression from 1929 through 1945. Dad and Mother moved in 1926 from Brooklyn to Milwaukee where my brother and I were born. We then moved to Cleveland, Ohio where my father owned a small shoe store and bought a house, both of which were lost during the Depression. We then moved to Chagrin Falls, Ohio while he managed another Hanan shoe store in Cleveland which ultimately also failed. We then moved to Chicago where he managed other shoe stores and sections of retail department stores. He never made much money, but was able to buy a small house in Northbrook, Illinois, a then small country town suburb of Chicago in 1940 with a $500 down payment borrowed from his mother. Dad and Mother became respected members of the Northbrook community. Mother was a member of the School Board and Dad, at one point in 1945 was simultaneously (!) The Commander of the local American Legion Post, the Chairman of the Zoning Board, and the Chairman of the Village Church Trustees.

During my high school days in Northbrook, from 1940 to 1944, Dad and I experienced considerable conflict, beyond the normal conflict between a teenage boy and his father. He was an alcoholic and his heavy drinking unleashed a very combative personality, which caused him to start physical fights in bars, which he would always lose. He was frequently driven home in a taxi after he had been badly beaten in some bar where he had been in a fight. It happened many times and it was always a very sad sight. The alcohol also caused him to be vocally very abusive to my Mother and me, which in turn caused me to try to restrain him physically, occasionally trying to take his bottle of booze away and smashing it on the floor. These times were of course very frightening for a teenage boy, as well as for my Mother and brother, Bill.

Bill Tomes from left to right 1958, 1953, 1925, 1921.

Bill and Betty Tomes, Northbrook, circa 1950s.

The only redeeming result of these experiences was that they taught me that I was actually on my own and could not rely on Dad for either guidance or financial help. We had virtually no money for any extras, just enough for modest meals and clothing. I always had an after school and summer job and contributed my small earnings to the family pot. Ironically, my father's weaknesses made me a stronger person.

Many years later, after I was married and had a family of my own, and had learned about the difficulties my father had in his life, we became reconciled. During the last ten years of his life we became quite close friends, for which I am grateful.

In spite of his lack of education, his parent's divorce and virtual abandonment by his father, his traumatic war experiences, and his serious alcoholism, he mostly overcame his difficulties and disappointments. He always worked hard, was a brave soldier and an honest and decent man of integrity who was loyal to his wife, family and friends. He was a real-life Willie Loman right out of Arthur Miller's "Death of a Salesman", a tragedy. He was a very bright, gregarious, sentimental man who could have had a much different and better life if he had only had more responsible parents and an education. He was, in spite of the limits imposed on him, an honorable man.

He derived his strength mostly from the love of his wife, Betty Steel. She was admired and loved by all who knew her. She organized and operated a pre-school day-care center and was a member of the Northbrook School Board for many years. She was a very quiet, thoughtful and religious person who held the family together through the difficulties of the Depression and my father's erratic personality. Her education after high school in Brooklyn was a two-year program in "Home Economics" at Pratt Institute in New York City. She died in a tragic automobile accident in 1957 and is buried in Memorial Park Cemetery in Evanston, Illinois.

In 1961 my father remarried another lovely woman, Helen Foote, a widow who had known both Dad and Mother many years before in Brooklyn. Dad and Helen moved to California in 1965 where she ultimately contracted ALS and, after Dad gave her loving care for many years, she died in 1972. Dad died in 1975, also as a result of a tragic automobile accident, and is buried in Memorial Park Cemetery in Evanston, Illinois next to Mother.

With dad, Wisconsin, 1929

With brother Bill, Northbrook 1942

My brother, William A. Tomes, Jr. with his grandchildren.

MY BROTHER'S LIFE - WILLIAM A. TOMES, JR.

My brother, William A. Tomes, Jr., was born in 1929, and now lives in Phoenix, Arizona. As a boy and young man Bill was a gifted athlete and musician, with an unquenchable sense of humor and mimicry. He spent a year in the Army and attended college at Northern Illinois State Teacher's College. He then married his high school sweetheart, a beautiful girl named Geraldine Slonaker, who has recently died in 2007. They had three beautiful daughters, Valerie (born 1953), Kimberly (born 1955), and Patricia (born 1957). They each have children so Bill is blessed with many grandchildren. Two of them have been married and one of them had a baby this year so Bill is now a great-grand-father! And I now have a "kid-brother" who is a great-grandfather!

Kimberly achieved much more than the so-called "allotted fifteen minutes of fame" when she became "Miss Texas", and "Miss USA" in 1978, and runner-up "Miss Universe" later that year. After her very successful beauty pageant career she returned to Texas A & M and finished her college work, married and had two children, both boys. Kim maintains her beauty; and her father's sense of humor, and is now a successful television commen-tator, sculptor and painter in Texas.

With my brother Bill, 1956.

Our Wedding day, June 26, 1954.

MY LIFE, JOSIE'S LIFE, AND OUR FAMILY AND SOME SPECIAL FRIENDS

A Personal Memoir

Each of our friends who read the first draft of this family history have urged me to write a more detailed history of Josie's and my lives and our family. Recalling the pleasure we have had reading the journals and memoirs of Francis and Robert Tomes we have decided to do so, hopefully giving our children and grandchildren the same pleasure. So, please forgive the length of these personal memoirs, but they have been written "by popular demand".

My own life has been a lucky and fruitful one. I was born in 1927 in Milwaukee, Wisconsin where my parents had moved after their marriage in Brooklyn, New York in 1926. We moved from Milwaukee to Cleveland and then to Evanston, Illinois by 1938. We then moved to Northbrook, Illinois in 1940 when it was still a very rural community of just a few hundred people - it even had a blacksmith who was still shoeing horses! I graduated from Northbrook High School in 1944

and enlisted in the Army that year at age 17. Northbrook High School was a small country school with 250 students from grade school through high school. Our graduating class had 30 students. We could each participate in student government and sports teams. So, I was class and student council president for a few terms and, even though I was not very athletic I ran track, and played on the tennis and football teams (second string guard).

Fortunately for us the school principal, Dr. Norman Watson, was a very capable educator and administrator. He assembled a unique faculty during the World War II years. We received an excellent basic education. I was the youngest boy in the class, graduating shortly after my 17th birthday. Many of our older classmates had enlisted in military service during the war, and in fact, two boys of our class of 1944, Jack Brown and Walter Koeberl, and two from the class of 1943, Donald Peukert and John Doty, had already been killed in action in 1944. World War II shaped our lives.

We have kept in touch with some of our classmates throughout our lives. Richard Dahlberg, Dale Bergstedt, John Boyer, Jim Serrin, Paul Lundell, Rudy Abel, Leonard Swensen, Betty (Schmidt) Hallen, and Lowell Peterson all survived the war and have lived long and productive lives. I just recently learned from Rudy Abel's son Timothy that Rudy died in 2001, but had a full life and left a thriving family.

I have also recently become reacquainted with Donald Hintz (now 90 years old), a 1939 graduate of Northbrook High School. I worked for Don after school at the Culligan Zeolite Company in 1943. When Don was drafted (at his request) in 1943 I drew a cartoon of him being fished

A happy 60th high schoolclass reunion in 2004 with friend Don Hintz (His 65th).

out of a pond. He kept the cartoon for forty years and reprinted it in the history of Culligan, "People of Culligan" that he wrote in 1986. Don Hintz and I agreed when we met at a Northbrook High School reunion in 2004 that;

"If you can remember the Great Depression, survived World War II, and like Jazz, you have got be an optimist."

As a young boy I was naturally adept at drawing, making small sculptures, model airplanes, and other craft and mechanical skills. I also took the high-school class in "manual training" ¬learning to use wood working tools - and automotive shop, learning how to repair cars. I actually rebuilt a "Model A" Ford roadster out of two junked cars, and made it run. I felt like I had invented the automobile! A part-time art teacher in high-school encouraged me to enroll in a drawing class at the

Cartoon drawn by Jim Tomes, a lab employee, when Don Hintz's third six-month deferment was about to expire, October, 1943.

Art Institute of Chicago, which I did for one session, but withdrew since all they taught was how to draw a Grecian Urn. Too static and dull for an active young boy who liked to draw action cartoon characters. Many years later, when I visited Florence, Italy with Josie and we toured the great Bargello Museum, I realized what a real art education might have been. There were Florentine art students, arrayed and sketching on the floor all around and among the magnificent sculptures of Michelangelo, Donatello, Cellini, Giambologna, Ghiberti, and Brunelleschi. And at the Uffizi there were endless galleries of all the Renaissance and other great painters. To have been born and lived and studied art in Florence would have meant a very different life. But, my early interest in the arts, and Josie's knowledge of art, has continued to enrich our lives, touring the world's art museums in Europe and America and appreciating their beautiful works.

Army Service

I served in the Army for two and one-half years, first as an ASTP (Army Specialized Training Program) civil engineering student at the University of Illinois, then after infantry basic training as a rifleman, two months as a code clerk in Washington, DC, and then paratroop training, as an infantry squad leader, then finally as a medic in the 508th Parachute Infantry Regiment of the 82nd Airborne Division in Germany.

Immediately after infantry basic training at Camp Robinson in Little Rock, Arkansas, I was sent to Washington, DC for a brief two months stint as a code clerk in the Chief of Staff Message Center in the Pentagon. I was depressed by the essentially clerical work, which was contrary to my youthful ideas of being an infantry soldier. I was able to prevail upon an airborne officer serving in the message center to get me reassigned overseas.

During my brief time at the Pentagon I did learn a couple of interesting lessons about military behavior. The first was that in the vast environs of the Pentagon there was no saluting. I saluted every officer I passed on my first day, until I was kindly admonished by a Master Sergeant who said, "Son, we don't salute here. There's more of them (officers) than us (enlisted men), so they did away with salutes!"

The second lesson was that, in the Top Secret Code room where I was assigned I learned that the higher a message's security classification, the slower it moved through the room. The merely "classified" messages whipped right through, the "Secret" ones were the next speedy, and the "Top Secret" ones moved the slowest. Even slower than "Top Secret" was "Eyes Only" intended to be read only by the named recipient. The reason for this apparently inverse urgency for message transmittal was simply that everyone in the code room wanted to read the more highly classified, and more interesting, messages before passing them on. Good old human nature. My short stay at the Pentagon proved unexpectedly beneficial a few months later in Germany.

After transferring out of the Pentagon, I went overseas as an infantry replacement soldier on a small Victory ship to Le Havre, France, and from there via "Forty-and- Eight" box cars to a "Repple Depple", Infantry Replacement Depot* at Marburg, Germany where I volunteered for paratroop training. The 82nd Airborne second lieutenant recruiting officer, sitting on a chair behind a card table on the company street, took one look at me, and seeing a skinny, pale-faced GI just off the boat from the U.S., said "Kid, you'll never make it". In true Horatio Alger style I saluted and replied, "Sir, I just want the chance." He shook his head and said, "O.K., its your neck" and signed me up. We few volunteers were then transported by truck to Heddernheim, a suburb of Frankfurt am/Main, where a jump school had been organized to train and replace the 82nd Airborne GI's who were returning to the U.S.

* For an unvarnished picture of the actual lives of infantry replacement soldiers during WWII see "The Boy's Crusade 1944-1945", by Paul Fussell (2005)

Paratroop jump school was a watershed experience in my life. I not only "made it", but I survived the rugged physical training better than the two-thirds of the other volunteers who didn't make it. We ran a mile before breakfast and seven miles before dinner, after calisthenics all day every day. I desperately wanted to prove myself, and I had been toughened up by infantry basic training, but the main force that pulled me through was a refusal to quit. There was a sign posted on the wall of the jump school barn that said it all "A Quitter Never Wins and a Winner Never Quits". That motto not only pulled me through the jump school and the five required qualifying parachute jumps as an eighteen year old soldier, but it served to strengthen my resolve in many other difficult situations later in life. It was a privilege to serve with the 82nd which had fought all through WW II in Europe, under General James Gavin, from Sicily, to D-Day in France, to Holland, to Belgium and finally Germany. My regiment, the 508 PIR, (Parachute Infantry Regiment) was kept in Europe after the war as the SHAEF honor guard in Frankfurt am/Main.

Military parachute jumping is designed to be a safe activity, provided you follow the rules. Each paratrooper carries two parachutes; the main one on his back, and a reserve one on his chest. The main parachute is automatically opened by the "static line", a fifteen

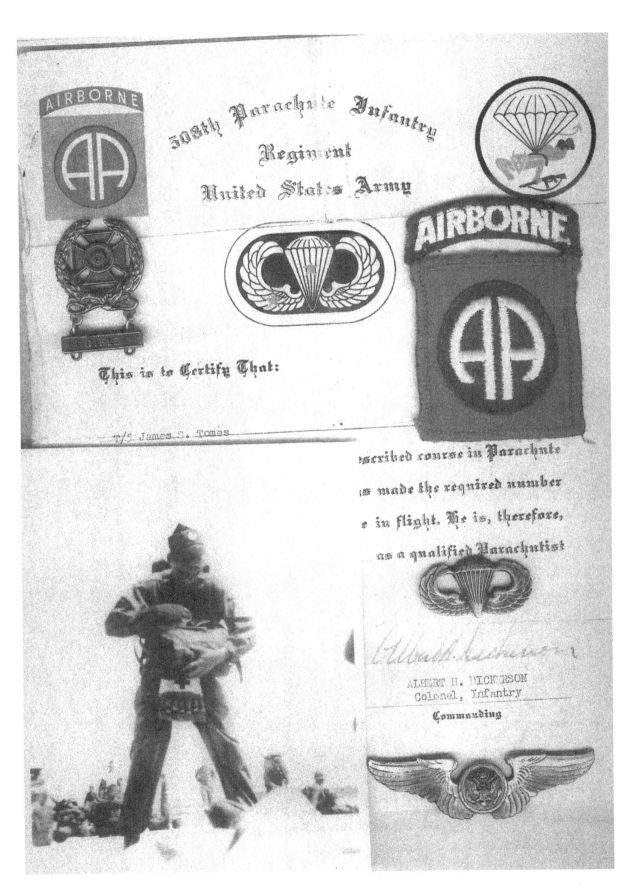

508th Parachute Infantry
Regiment
United States Army

This is to Certify That:

T/5 James S. Tomes

scribed course in Parachute

s made the required number

e in flight. He is, therefore,

as a qualified Parachutist

ALBERT H. DICKERSON
Colonel, Infantry

Commanding

foot long canvas strap folded across the back of the chute pack. It is connected at one end to a "pilot chute" on the top of each parachute canopy by a breakable cord which pulls it from the back pack, and on the other end to the woven wire "anchor cable" that runs the entire length of the interior cabin of the C-47 airplane at shoulder height. At the jumpmaster's command "Stand Up and Hook Up" each paratrooper hooks his static line on to the anchor cable before moving up toward the open door of the airplane preparatory to making the jump. At the command "Stand in the Door", the lead man stands in the door and when the command "Go" is given he and the men following him kick their right foot out the door with their arms folded over their chest and jump into the prop wash of the left engine of the C-47. Each man drops about 60 feet underneath the tail of the airplane before his parachute is blown open and he then swings under the parachute for the ride down to earth.

After a "stick", typically an infantry squad of twelve men, has jumped from the C-47 the used static lines are still hooked to the anchor cable and are flapping on the outside of the fuselage, aft of the open door. These used static lines must then be manually pulled back into the airplane and either thrown away, or returned to the parachute riggers to be re-packed with other parachutes.

So, the actual jumping out of the airplane is quite straightforward and safe. Problems can occur however after the parachutes are open and the paratroopers are descending to the ground. Combat jumps are usually made at a low altitude of a few hundred feet to get the men to the ground as quickly as possible. Training jumps are usually made at about 1,200 feet altitude to give more time to the trainees. If, during the descent of a number of paratroopers, one main parachute gets tangled with another, and starts to collapse, one or both paratroopers can pull their emergency ripcords to open their reserve parachutes. Or, as happened to me once, another paratrooper can accidentally descend above you and "walk" on the top of your canopy, risking the collapse of both his and your parachutes. The only way out of this predicament is to pull your risers, hard on one side as I did, and "slip" your chute out of the way. Accidents can also occur if a paratrooper fails to properly hook up his static line to the anchor cable. This actually happened to one of the men in my jump class - he luckily was able to open his reserve chute.

But the worst of these experiences for me was the result of my own carelessness by not wearing a parachute when I was helping a friend who was jumpmaster for a training jump one day in Germany. He wanted to jump with the jump school trainees, so he went out

the door with the two "sticks" of trainees and left me to retrieve the static lines and drop them on the drop-zone.(DZ). I did so by pulling them back into the airplane, unhooking them from the anchor cable and zipping them into a large canvas "kit-bag". I yelled to the pilot that I had the static lines in the kit bag and he made another lower altitude pass over the DZ so I could kick the bag out. I was the only one left in the back end of the C-47. The pilot and co-pilot were in the cockpit.

I stood in the open doorway gripping the anchor cable, watched for the DZ , kicked the bag out and yelled again to the pilot that the bag was out the door. The pilot then immediately, without any warning, put the C-47 into a steep left banking turn, so steep that I lost my grip on the anchor cable and was slammed down to the aluminum floor of the plane, sitting right in front of the open door, which was now below me because of the steep left bank. I found myself looking straight down through the open door hundreds of feet below and I had nothing to hold on to. Worse yet, I had carelessly not worn a parachute.

The aluminum floor was too slick to get any traction, and the sides of the open door were out of reach, so all I could do was look straight down in heart-stopping fear of falling out of the door for what seemed like an eternity. Fortunately for me, the centrifugal force of the turning airplane

pinned me to the floor, keeping me from falling through the open door, and, as the pilot leveled off, I was able to slowly make my way across the floor to grab the leg of the seat next to the open door. When I was safely in the seat I just thanked my lucky stars and realized how careless I had been.

I will never forget sitting on that slick aluminum floor looking straight down out of the open door at the earth far below. I still have occasional dreams about the experience. It was, however, another "maturing" experience. I learned in this very personal way that I might not live forever - that I was a mortal being. Most young soldiers have a natural feeling of invulnerability - of "immortality" - until they personally experience such a risk.

I arrived in Germany after the war ended so I was merely a witness to the chaotic and sometimes violent aftermath of war. Serving in Germany I saw towns and cities destroyed by war, civilian refugees streaming West, Wermacht POWs, and, en-route to Marburg, some recently released victims of concentration camps. Frankfurt am/Main had been bombed both night and day by American and British air forces. The streets were piles of rubble, the sickening smell of the buried dead was palpable, and Taunus Park at the center of the old medieval city was all bomb craters where the black market flourished at night. Zigaretten and Shokolade (cigarettes and chocolate) were the currency. Contraband and prostitutes were the products and services. It was a bizarre, surreal and otherworldly scene. Many years later I revisited Frankfurt am/Main on business and found the Taunus Park restored to its pristine, pre-war beauty, populated mostly by young mothers walking their babies.

Before leaving Marburg for Frankfurt I was shocked one afternoon while walking along the banks of the Lahn River, to come "face-to-face" with three young German hospital patients prisoners of war. They were in their marked POW hospital clothing and were obviously young soldiers, about my age. But they were each undergoing various stages of plastic surgery reconstructing their faces which had been shot-up or burned away. They each appeared like gargoyles, with noses, eyes and mouths out of place. After seeing them I quickly looked away and walked around them. A hideously dark side of war.

Seeing concentration camp victims in a town near Marburg was also appalling. They were still emaciated and wearing their striped uniforms, and they were trying to sell photographs of the charnel house conditions of their concentration camp. The only thing they owned was the photographic evidence of their horrendous tragedy. The awful toll of war was again made quite real and personal.

What I didn't know until years later was that there were hundreds of local slave labor concentration camps throughout Germany.

Having this brief, but very memorable contact with concentration camp victims became the basis for my subsequently acquiring a collection of 250 books and films about the Holocaust, which I ultimately gave to Northwestern University where it is being used as a resource in their Holocaust history course.

Many years later in 1985 I also wrote an essay expressing outrage at president Reagan' equating as "victims" the SS Nazis buried in a cemetery at Bitburg, Germany alongside the real victims of Naziism also buried there. The essay was titled "Where Are The Christians?" and was stimulated by the picture of Elie Wiesel pleading for Reagan not to attend the 40th Anniversary of the end of WWII at Bitburg. No prominent Christian clerics joined in his plea so I wrote my essay asking some Christian leaders to speak out. The essay (see appendix) was published in a Jewish weekly, "The Sentinel" and was responded to by a young Episcopal priest in Winnetka, Rev. Kirk Kubicek. I sponsored his traveling to Munich and Dachau where he was joined by a few other Christian clerics and some Jewish Rabbis. They held their own 40th Anniversary memorial at Dachau, reading my essay and others aloud, on the same day that Reagan and Chancellor Kohl held theirs at Bitburg. It was a small, but necessary protest. On his return, Kirk gave a series of powerful sermons about the Holocaust to his Winnetka congregation. This event also put Kirk in touch with Rev. Franklin Littell, a Methodist minister who had witnessed Naziism in Germany before WWII and had returned after the war to help in re-civilizing Germany. Rev. Littell had since become the leading Christian scholar of the Holocaust. In 1988 we invited Rev. Littell to speak at Trinity United Methodist Church in Wilmette, which he did, on the 50th Anniversary of Kristallnacht. His talk was "The Holocaust; Its Meaning For Christians", which I published on behalf of the church. Littel' s principal message was that Christianity must acknowledge its complicity in setting the stage for the Holocaust through its thousands of years of blatant anti-Semitism. Germany was, after all, a Christian country with a high level culture of learning, technology and the arts. As Littel said, "The Nazis were culturally sophisticated and technically competent barbarians. And most of them were raised as Christians." The talk was offered at the church to the public and we drew an overflow crowd, including many people from local Synagogues, a few of whom had been prisoners at Auschwitz and other concentration camps. It was a very moving experience.

We have also taken our children to visit the memorial camps at both Dachau, near Munich, and Matthausen, near Linz, Austria, to help pass on this historical knowledge to them. The only way the admonition "Never forget" can have real meaning is to keep retelling the story of the Holocaust. As memorials these camps are truly sacred places to keep the memory alive. World War II was an absolutely necessary response to the aggression and brutality of the Nazis and Japanese military governments. The Allies won the war unconditionally, but it was a dark time.

Occupation Duty In Germany
While I was a squad leader with the 82nd Airborne Division in Frankfurt my squad served mostly as armed guards, guarding prisoners of war and some of the hordes of displaced people (DP's) who had escaped from the marauding Russian army. We also guarded some Danish run de-Nazification teams while they arrested Nazis trying to escape, and some ex-Auschwitz SS and IG Farben officers and guards for their return to war crimes trials in Poland. The Danes told us they had been interned by the Nazis during the war and were therefore particularly zealous in tracking down the Nazi escapees. IG Farben was a large, Frankfurt based, chemical company which had actually built Auschwitz III to make synthetic fuel from coal, using thousands of Auschwitz prisoners as slave labor,

and had also owned a subsidiary that made "Zyklon B", the poison gas that murdered prisoners in the Auschwitz gas chambers. Many of the IG Farben officers had fled back to the company headquarters in Frankfurt at the end of the war. Years later, I learned that some of the Auschwitz SS Nazis and IG Farben officers were in fact arrested, returned to Poland, convicted of war crimes and executed or sent to prison.

After a few months as a squad leader I was surprisingly ordered one day by the First Sergeant to report to the Company Commander's office. When I arrived and saluted the Captain he told me to relax and sit down at a chair in front of his desk. All this informality was unusual so I was put on my guard. After asking how I was doing and what I wanted to do when I got out of the Army the Captain finally handed me a copy of an Army letter and asked me, "What the hell is this all about?" The letter was notification from Washington, DC that I now had a "Top Secret" security clearance. I explained that it must be from my short time at the Pentagon, but the Captain didn't seem very convinced. He told me to report back to the First Sergeant who also asked me what I wanted to do when I got out of the Army. I told him, as I had told the Captain, that I wanted eventually to study medicine. The next day the First Sergeant told me they were transferring me to the medics. He said it

would be easier than being an infantry squad leader and would be more in line with my civilian interests! This accommodating behavior was so unusual for the Army that I can only conclude they were worried that I was some kind of intelligence agent "plant" and they wanted me out of the way where they could keep their eyes on me more easily. And so, by dumb luck, I became an instant medical non-com in the 508th Parachute Infantry Regiment. The security clearance also explained why my Mother had written me asking if I was in any trouble because the FBI had been asking our neighbors about me back home in Northbrook.

I served the rest of my Army time as an infantry medic, in garrison, and tending GI's wounded or hurt during patrols and maneuvers along the East German border held by the Russians. I luckily had only a few "close calls", on live-fire maneuvers, some hairy parachute jumps, and a POW shot down directly in front of me by a reckless GI. (I put a tourniquet on his arm using my belt to stop the arterial bleeding from his wrist until we got an ambulance.) As members of an infantry regiment we were fully armed with rifles, carbines, pistols, BAR's hand grenades, machine guns, bazookas, mortars and even hand-carried 57 MM recoil-less anti-tank guns. Occupation duty, enforced by thousands of young GI's, armed with live ammunition, and plenty of liquor available, was not peaceful. The war was over, but the chaos and tragedy continued. It was the beginning of what the Germans called "Der Schrecklich Zeit", the five years of "Terrible Time" after the war.

In 1946 I delivered some CARE packages sent to me from home for delivery to my high-school classmate Rudy Abel's German relatives in Frankfurt am/Main. I found them, still living in the basement of their bombed out house, mostly sick and still dazed from the bombings, but of course very grateful. It made me realize again how lucky I was.

I also experienced the unusual coincidence of meeting a high school classmate, Leonard Swensen, on the tarmac of the Frankfurt am/Main airfield while putting on my parachute in preparation for making a jump. Leonard was in the Army Air Force operating the Ground Control Approach radar system at the airfield. The picture taken of me on the day we met is on a previous page. We met again in Frankfurt am/Main and had some good times together.

The 508th Parachute Infantry Regiment returned as a unit to Fort Bragg, North Carolina in November of 1946 and was demobilized, with most of us being transferred to the 504th PIR. I was discharged in February of 1947 and returned home to start college at Northwestern University under the GI Bill in the spring of 1947.

Northwestern University

After I was discharged in February 1947 the GI Bill helped me study science at Northwestern University, where I graduated in the class of 1952 with a Bachelor of Science in biology and chemistry.

Without the GI Bill I couldn't have afforded college, but by working at a variety of part-time jobs it was even possible to attend the relatively expensive Northwestern University. I washed dishes in a sorority house, waited tables at a hotel, ran another hotel's coffee shop, sold signs door-to-door, sold shoes (a most demeaning experience), sold toys at Christmas (I still cringe when I hear recorded Christmas carols), sold furniture and worked in a hardware store, painted interiors and hung wallpaper, and dropped out of school for six months to work as a common laborer on a brick laying and concrete crew (as a card-carrying member of the International Union of Common Laborers and Hod Carriers of America). All these experiences working at so-called "menial" jobs gave me a life-long appreciation for the difficult lives of most working people, as well as the real skill required for their jobs.

In spite of all the part-time work I was a good science student and was applying for admission to medical school when my studies were interrupted in December, 1950 and I was called up from the reserves to active duty in the Air Force during the Korean War. I was ordered to start pilot training, but I was soon "washed out" after a follow-up eye exam resulted in my being prescribed tri-focal glasses and disqualified from pilot training. So, I served for two and half more years as a flight engineer and crew chief on a B-25 bomber and a C-47, "Gooney Bird" cargo plane, flying all over the United States based at Vance Air Force Base in Enid, Oklahoma. With Reserve pilots we were at great risk because they weren't checked out properly on those old World War II airplanes, and they were careless. I had a few more "close-calls" and one real crash landing, but we all walked away from it so it qualified as a "good landing". One of my best friends from pilot training, Bob Hohtanz from Des Moines, Iowa, finished his pilot training and flew F-86 fighter planes in Korea. Sadly, the week before he was to come home his plane blew up in mid-air and he was killed. I attended his funeral in Des Moines and realized once again how lucky I was. I was discharged in March of 1953, returned to Chicago and started law school that fall. I had completed the requirements for my Bachelor of Science degree from Northwestern University while in the Air Force, and also taking night courses at Phillips University in Enid, and came home on leave for graduation with the class of 1952. My interests changed however during this second tour of military duty and I decided to switch from science to law.

While at Northwestern I had two professors in particular who were influential in causing me to change my academic course. One was Dr. Paul Winch, professor of sociology, and the other was Dr. Frank Haiman, professor of psychology, who later became a professor in the School of Speech. Frank ultimately wrote many books about freedom of speech, such as "Freedom of Speech - To Protect Those Rights", 1979; "Speech Acts and the First Amendment" 1993, and "Freedom, Democracy and Responsibility: The Selected Works of Franklin S. Haiman" 2000.

I met Frank for the first time when he was teaching a freshman psychology course in 1947. He not only taught the course content well, but he was such a welcoming, friendly man that he provided me with a classroom setting that enabled me to overcome a disabling stutter that had occurred when I was discharged from military service in 1947. Thus he truly gave me the actual "freedom to speak". He was an exceptional teacher. He also directed me to the University Library "stacks" where I could explore its incredible warehouse of knowledge free of any discipline. It was like discovering a gold mine. Many years later I became reacquainted with Frank when I was practicing law in Chicago in the 1960s and he was the Chairman of the Illinois Division of the American Civil Liberties Union, (ACLU) which he served well for many years.

Josie at Portland Oregon Rose Garden picture taken by her father in 1950.

Meeting Josie Raymaley via Bob and Helen Dentler

Josie and I met at Northwestern University in 1948, introduced by my roommate, Bob Dentler, via his fiancée, then Helen Hosmer. Helen, now Helen Dentler, had told Bob that "Josie is the best read girl at Northwestern", and that was enough to intrigue me. It turned out that she was also a very beautiful and charming young woman, making her even more intriguing.

Helen and Josie were sorority sisters in Delta Delta Delta and Bob and I were fraternity brothers in Sigma Nu. We were equally disillusioned by then with fraternity life. We roomed together off campus in an attic on Judson Avenue in Evanston. Bob was an English Masters candidate and I was a science undergraduate, so Bob became my introduction to the liberal arts. He loaned me copies of literary classics, some of which I just recently found I had never returned, and also introduced me to using the stacks at Northwestern Deering Library.

And Josie was my introduction to the arts. She was then a theater major and already had a good knowledge of music, art and literature. So my real cultural education began with Josie and the Dentlers at Northwestern in 1948. I was a member of the Dentler's wedding party in 1950 in Washington, DC. Josie and I happily shared in the celebration of their 50th wedding anniversary in 2000 and we are still in frequent touch through visits and correspondence. We have enjoyed wonderful life-long friendships with Bob and Helen Dentler. Sadly, both Bob and Helen died in 2008.

Bob ultimately earned his PhD in Sociology at the University of Chicago and had a long and productive career as an author, professor of sociology and consultant. Bob and Helen had four children and now many grandchildren, one of whom recently graduated from the University of Chicago. Another grandson, Lucas Segall is now attending Northwestern majoring in music.

Howes Memorial Chapel at Northwestern University on our wedding day.

Helen was an accomplished artist and is a leader in the First Unitarian Church of Lexington, Massachusetts, located on the Lexington Common, the site of the famous Revolutionary War "Minute Man" statue. And, pertinent to genealogy, Helen was directly descended from the Massachusetts Hosmers who fought in the Battle of Concord Bridge, which immediately followed "the shot heard round the world" at Lexington Common in 1775.

Josie and I were married on June 26, 1954 in Howes Memorial Chapel, located in front of the Methodist Garrett Theological Seminary on the campus of Northwestern University. Josie had graduated from Northwestern in 1951 and she was working in the Fashion Office of Marshall Field & Co, the women's fashion center of America west of New York City. Among her many college accomplishments Josie had won the national Mademoiselle Magazine writing contest when she

was a junior, whisked off to New York for lunch with Truman Capote etc., and her fashion career was launched. Josie was an excellent student and graduated with a Bachelor of Arts. A picture of her, taken by her father, Francis A. Raymaley, in 1950 at the Rose Garden in Portland, Oregon, on page 151. (Much more about Josie's genealogy later)

Josie continues through 2008 to work in the fashion business in Chicago, over 56 years since she began in 1951. And she is active in many Chicago cultural, theater, dance, and artistic organizations.

Josie is also the mother of our four children, whom she raised with loving care all the while she was pursuing her fashion career. Our four children are: Robert Steel Tomes (born 1960); Elizabeth Austin Tomes-Sandbo and John Wilson Tomes (born 1962 - twins!), and Julia Hall Tomes-Wells (born 1968).

Robert, our first born, married Cynthia Zeltwanger, a true "Pennsylvania Dutch" person in her own right, who is the president and chief executive of a thriving financial services business. Robert is a successful independent newsprint broker, and a consummate fly fisherman and author of articles and books on fishing.

Elizabeth married Scott Sandbo, who is now the chairman and CEO of a successful securities business, and

Josie and Jim's Family

Family at Dairymen's, 1994.

Some of our Family at Dairymen's, 2005.

Robert's Family

Right: Robert and Cynthia's wedding day with Josie and Jim Tomes.

Below: Robert and Cynthia.

Robert and Cynthia'shouse in Harbert, Michigan

Robert, Cynthia and Josie

Above: Scott and Betsy Sandbo with their children Elizabeth and John Sandbo on vacation. Above right: An evening together for the young couple.

Right: Elizabeth and John with Grandpa.

John Sandbo and Alex Tomes at Darymens.

Kate Tomes and Elizabeth Sandbo at Darymens.

John, Jennifer, Kate and Alex in Santa Fe with "Biscuit". Alex is in "pappas" shoes.

Jennifer and her mother Darby.

John with his buddy Biscuit.

Julia's Family

Our family at Julia and Art Well's wedding in Portland, Oregon, July 4, 1999.

Julia and Art with their children Flora and Erskine at our Chicago apartment, 2005.

they have two children, John Douglas Sandbo, age 11 and Elizabeth Austin Sandbo, age 13.

John is the founder and president of a successful equity investment business, and is married to Jennifer Harrington. They have two children, Alexander Steel Tomes, age 13 and Katherine Harrington Tomes, age 11.

Julia is a teacher and is married to Arthur Wells, a computer genius, and they have two children; Flora Raymaley Tomes, age 5, and Erskine Kersey Tomes, age 2.

Chicago-Kent Law School

I attended Chicago-Kent Law School (four nights a week for four years), graduating in 1957 with an LLB (Bachelor of Laws), later upgraded to a JD (Juris Doctor). I was a very good law student. During night law school I worked full-time, for two years as a management trainee at the Harris Trust & Savings Bank, and then for the final two years of law school as the law clerk for the firm of Berchem, Schwantes & Thuma, trial lawyers. On the recommendation of the Dean of Chicago-Kent I was hired by Doug Schwantes, the senior partner, who was then president of the Chicago Bar Association and also president of Chicago-Kent. I was in court every day, answering court calls, assisting the lawyers at trial, and sometimes arguing routine motions. I learned the reality of trial practice during the day while studying law at night - and over the weekends. I graduated and passed the Illinois Bar exam in 1957 and began the practice of law in Chicago with the firm of Petit, Olin, Overmyer & Fazio. "Bud" Petit, the senior partner, was a member of the Board of Trustees of Chicago-Kent.

The best law professor I had in law school was Warren Heindel who was tragically afflicted with a severe spastic palsy. His affection made it difficult for him to walk and he had to speak quite slowly. But his mind was as clear as a bell and his legal analytic skills were extraordinary. He was also a strict, but kindly teacher who would help a serious student think through and articulate a law case or problem and thereby truly teach the student. He was never demeaning or arrogant as some lesser professors were. His main subject was Administrative Law, which he practiced as a lawyer and which he also specialized in later as an Administrative Law judge in Chicago. He had an outstanding career as a lawyer, law professor and judge. He died in 2005. One of Professor Heindel's most memorable lines for me was his saying, after trying to get me to articulate a legal cause of action where the facts of the case didn't provide a valid basis; "Mr. Tomes, there are some wrongs for which there may be no remedy at law". It was particularly poignant coming from a man who so magnificently overcame his severe physical disability.

Bob and Nancy Gunn

In 1954 after I started night law school and was working during the day at the Harris Trust & Savings Bank in Chicago I met a co-worker, Robert Murray (Bob) Gunn, who had finished law school and was studying for his CPA. We quickly became friends and, after Josie met Bob's fiancée, Nancy Schweitzer, we became a friendly foursome. We were included in the Gunn's wedding party in Iowa in 1956, and were named Godparents to their first daughter, Phoebe, whom we dearly love. Bob has always provided me with good legal and tax counsel, and we cherish Bob and Nancy's friendship. We were also fortunate to have many opportunities to meet Bob's parents, retired Colonel Damon Gunn and his wife Helen, both of whom have since passed away. Colonel Gunn was a West Point graduate who later became a lawyer and served as General Omar Bradley's chief military government officer all through World War II, and after, during the Nuremberg and related trials of Nazi war criminals. Helen Gunn was also a remarkable lady who wrote a wonderful book, "The Colonel's Lady" and remained sharp as a tack and critical of world affairs until she died in her 90s. Both Colonel and Helen Gunn, and Bob's brother Alan, who was lost at sea while flying as a Navy pilot, are buried in Arlington Cemetery in Washington, DC.

Over the years during occasional discussions of genealogy, Bob and I learned that our families were probably related in the distant past. Bob's heritage is Scottish, "Gunn and Montgomery", and my Scottish side was Steel, Wilson and McEwan. Bob's ancestors emigrated from the north of Scotland to Canada in the late 19th century, then moved successively farther south through the Dakotas to Iowa where they settled on farmland which Bob still owns and manages. Bob's genealogy shows intermarriage with Wilson's, and my English side shows intermarriage with Gunns. So, we are probably distant cousins. And, Nancy is of Alsatian descent, her ancestors coming from the town of Ribeauville, which is very near Schaeffersheim, Josie's ancestral town in Alsace. "The acorns never fall very far from the tree."

Bob and Nancy Gunn.

Bob and Nancy have five children; Alan, Phoebe, Damon and Charles (twins) and Judy, each of whom is married and have children of their own. We were happy in 2006 to be included in Bob and Nancy's 50th wedding anniversary celebration with all of their family. It is truly incredible that the past 50 years have gone by so quickly and that we are each so fortunate to have large thriving families.

Bill and Caroline McKittrick
I first met Bill in the early 1960's when I was General Counsel for Bell & Howell Company and he was a partner with Vedder, Price, Kaufinan and Kammholz, our outside counsel for labor law. I arrived at the factory early one morning to find a line of union pickets from the Machinists Union seeking to organize our workers. We paid our workers over the market wage, had good communications and liberal benefits so it was a simple attempt to add our workers to their union membership. I called Bill and we met and he led us through a successful election, which resulted in our workers voting to keep the union out. During the course of the campaign I learned to respect Bill for his labor law knowledge and also his wisdom about human relations and communication. My respect for Bill as a lawyer has only grown over the ensuing years during which he also represented me and other companies where I was CEO on matters of labor and employment law.

Our personal friendship has also grown and includes Bill's wife, Caroline, who has become a very good friend to Josie. The McKittrick's interest, knowledge and generous philanthropy of the arts; the Chicago Symphony, the Lyric Opera, the Art Institute of Chicago, the Goodman Theater, and The Arts Club of Chicago has expanded our appreciation of the great cultural advantages of Chicago. We have also become acquainted with their children, Bruce (a well-known antiquarian book seller) and his wife Wendy, and their daughter Lynn, a successful businesswoman.

Bill is a graduate of DePauw University where he was a member of their truly unique football team of 1934, which still holds the distinction of being the only college team ever with the perfect record of no losses, and un-scored upon (!). Bill says he was only a second-string lineman, but he was on the team. He went on to Northwestern University Law School on a scholarship and, after passing the Illinois Bar, went to practice law for the American government in the Panama Canal. When World War II began Bill decided he didn't want to fight the war as a lawyer so he came back home and enlisted in the Navy as an able-bodied seaman, went to officer's candidate school and was commissioned as an armaments officer on a "Jeep" carrier. Jeep carriers were small aircraft carriers

Visiting with our good friends Caroline and Bill McKittrick.

made by the Kaiser shipbuilding company and called "Jeeps" because Kaiser also made the famous four-wheel drive Jeeps.

Bill's ship, the Kalinin Bay, was engaged in many combat operations in the Pacific theater of war, but the most remarkable and last operation was the Battle of Leyte Gulf on October 25, 1944. The Kalinin Bay was part of a small task force of a few destroyers, destroyer escorts, and Jeep carriers sailing in the Leyte Gulf in support of MacArthur's landing to retake the Philippines. On the morning of October 25th one of their carrier pilots spotted a large fleet of Japanese warships bearing down on them from the north. The task force commander, Captain Sprague, ordered all his carrier planes in the air and ordered his force to attack the Japanese, even though they were significantly out-gunned. They sank one of the Japanese cruisers, and some of their destroyers and damaged their battleship, but also lost a Jeep carrier, the Gambier Bay, one of their destroyer escorts and a destroyer. The Kalinin Bay was hit repeatedly by heavy point¬ blank fire from the Japanese and was struck by Kamikaze planes hitting their deck.

Incredibly, after a protracted, daylong battle, the Japanese fleet withdrew, probably because they mistakenly thought that such a ferocious fight put up by a small task force had to be backed up by the larger fleet of Admiral Halsey known to be in the area. So, Sprague's task force accomplished a great victory, but at great cost in lives and ships. Bill's ship limped to a nearby Navy repair base, was patched up and sailed back to Pearl Harbor with the rest of the task force where they were surprised with a hero's welcome home. Bill's ship was so badly damaged that it was scrapped at Pearl Harbor. Bill spent the remainder of the war instructing younger officers.

Bill and Caroline had been married during World War II, when Bill was a seaman and Caroline, who had enlisted in the Waves, was a commissioned officer. The rules in those days automatically discharged an officer bride from military service if she married an enlisted man, so Caroline spent the rest of the war following Bill around from port to port while he was at sea. After the war they returned to Chicago where Bill started to practice law and they had a family. It was Bill who introduced me to the Caxton Club and Caroline who introduced Josie to the Women's Board of the Goodman Theater. And Bill and Caroline have been most generous to our daughter Julia and her husband Art.

We have been fortunate to be long-standing friends with Bill and

Caroline and continue to have dinner once a month with them, exchanging stories of our lives and travels. Both Bill and Caroline are now in their 90's, and Bill is seriously disabled needing a cane and help to walk, but they are both bright and cheerful and actively engaged in the cultural life of Chicago. We have also become good friends with their son Bruce and his wife Wendy and see them often.

Other Long-Standing Friends

Josie's and my lives have been blessed by many other long-standing friendships. They are too many to even list their names, but they have each contributed to our happiness. We regret that we cannot identify them all here. Many have been listed in the body of this book.

Plus many other friends in the Caxton Club, the Chicago Literary Club, The Fortnightly Club of Chicago, the Cliffdwellers Club, The Arts Club of Chicago, The Fashion Group of Chicago, The Fashion Office of Marshall Field & Co, The Apparel Center, the Japan-America Society of Chicago, and the University of Chicago Library Society.

Marshall, Irene and Andrew Patner

During preparation for the 1951 Illinois State Bar examination I met Marshall Patner who had just graduated from the University of Chicago law school and was also preparing for the bar exam. We quickly became friends and after we passed the bar we also enrolled in a trial practice course. It was Marshall who introduced me to the Chicago Bar Association indigent prisoner defense program and also to the American Civil Liberties Union (ACLU). Josie and I then also met Marshall's wife, Irene, and during the ensuing few years became good friends and even shared a wonderful baby nurse, Earlene Brown, who helped us each raise our newborn infants in the early 1960s. The Patners had three sons; Andrew, Joshua and Seth. Our friendship with the Patners has grown and continued for all the years since, until Marshall sadly died of a heart attack in 2001. We are still close friends with Irene and their son Andrew who has become a well-known art, theater, dance and music critic in Chicago. Irene heads the

Education Committee for the Chicago Symphony and Andrew travels with the Chicago Symphony on their overseas tours and regularly hosts the WFMT radio classical music and arts interview shows. We are blessed with Irene and Andrew's continued friendship and their intellectual and artistic stimulation.

Marshall's life exemplified the best of the practice of law as advocacy of individual rights. He was for a while Counsel for the ACLU and always spoke truth to power, even though it cost him personally many times. We will always remember Marshall Patner as a man of extraordinary integrity. He was also a person of exceptional artistic sensitivity, an excellent cook, and a loving husband and good father. We will always miss Marshall Patner.

Julia Tomes, Irene Patner and Marshall Patner.

Private Practice and the American Civil Liberties Union

After law school graduation and passing the bar in 1957 I practiced law for three years at the firm of Petit, Olin, Overmyer & Fazio in Chicago. It was quite a varied general practice, including litigation, probate, contract negotiation and preparation, divorce, adoption, zoning, tax, corporate, banking and small business advice, etc. It was during this time that I became involved with the Chicago Bar Association's defense of indigent prisoner program and the ACLU.

I learned quickly that the ACLU is an extraordinary volunteer organization of lawyers and lay people dedicated to protecting the rights and liberties of American. It is in my judgment "America's most truly conservative organization", dedicated to conserving the rights guaranteed by the Bill of Rights and the American Constitution. I became a pro bono volunteer lawyer and speaker and board member of the Illinois ACLU, which we still support financially. The fundamental lesson guiding the ACLU is that "all power is abused", whether by government, corporate, military, or other institutions. Only by eternal vigilance and speaking out as citizens, and legal action where appropriate and necessary, can the individual liberties guaranteed by the Bill of Rights and the Constitution be secured so our lives can be free.

These rights uniquely provide Americans with a shield against government and other abuses of power. But, as Judge Learned Hand once wrote, "Once Liberty dies in the hearts of the people, no court can save it."

The American Civil Rights Movement

I also learned some new points of view about American history during my work with the ACLU. The essential lesson was that, as proud as we are and should be of our Bill of Rights, and of America's founding fathers, they were incredibly self-contradictory when it came to the enslavement of black people. They spoke loudly and clearly about individual liberty as in "All men are created equal", but continued to own slaves and even limited a slave's value for purposes of representation to "3/5th's of a person".

It took the American Civil War of 1860-1865, followed by Reconstruction, then a resumption of virtual slavery beginning in 1871 and lasting until after World War II during the "Jim Crow" and Ku Klux Klan years, and finally, the Civil Rights Movement of the 1960s until today, to begin to remedy the wrongs of slavery and racism. It literally took over 100 years after the Civil War to begin to implement the Constitutional Amendments passed in 1867 to grant freedom and enforceable civil liberties to black Americans. For the complete story of the failure and tragedy of reconstruction see "Reconstruction,

America's Unfinished Revolution"
by Eric Foner (1988 Harper & Row)

Men and women like Frederick
Douglass and W.E.B. DuBois in the
19th century, A. Philip Randolph, John
Hope Franklin, Rosa Parks, Thurgood
Marshall, and Martin Luther King in
the 20th century continued the fight
for liberty. The biographies of each of
these true American heroes should be
required reading for every American.
Please see my book "The Meanings
of Genealogy" for a more complete
description of this history. The best
history of this time is Taylor Branch's
three-volume work, "Pillar of Fire",
"Parting the Waters' and "At Canaan's
Edge". David Halberstam's "The
Children" is another great description
of this time.

One of the most effective, but also
most forgotten of these heroes was A.
Philip Randolph. He became the head
of the Pullman Sleeping Car Porter's
Union in the 1920s and after many
years of persistent advocacy finally
achieved recognition as a bargaining
agent with the Pullman Company.
Then, as World War II loomed, he
obtained equal employment rights
for blacks and other minorities in the
defense industries by threatening
President Roosevelt with a massive
march on Washington, DC. Following
World War II, in 1948, he obtained the
integration of the American Armed
Forces by threatening President
Truman with another massive march

and a black men's boycott of the draft.
And, in 1963, at age 74, he organized
the March on Washington for Jobs and
Freedom, where he passed the Civil
Rights Movement torch to Rev. Martin
Luther King, which resulted in the
Voting Rights Act of 1965.

Fulfilling the promise articulated by
our "Founding Fathers of equal rights
for all people is an "important part
of "Who We Are" as Americans.
Carrying on this cause to make and
keep America as a bastion of individual freedom is ongoing and will probably never end since "all power is
abused" and freedom will always be
under threat. As stated in the motto
of the ACLU, "Eternal vigilance is
the price of Liberty."

And now, back to the story of the per-
sonal memoir, to 1960 when I joined
Bell & Howell Company as Assistant
General Counsel.

Bell & Howell Company
In 1960 I left the Petit, Olin law firm
to become Assistant General Counsel
of Bell & Howell Company (B&H), a
photographic equipment manufacturer
in Chicago, in 1960. Unbeknownst to
me, Chuck Percy, the B&H CEO, had
attended night law school at Chicago-
Kent until he was made president
and CEO of B&H in 1950. Also, Ed
McDermott, a director of B&H and the
founder of the law firm of McDermott,
Will & Emery, B&H's outside legal
counsel knew of me because I had
been invited to consider a position as

an associate with his firm. I was made B&H General Counsel in 1961 for the purpose of forming a corporate and patent law department, which I did over the course of the next few years. I also provided direct legal services to the Board of Directors and to the international operations of the company. Bell & Howell diversified into an international conglomerate during that time, acquiring and organizing businesses in Europe, Japan and Asia. As a result of these business operations I was made a senior vice president and chief executive of the company's international operations, which I managed until 1972. (Incidentally, this new assignment afforded me the opportunity to pursue my genealogy in England.)

Chuck Percy resigned as the B&H CEO in 1962 and became a U.S. Senator for Illinois, and Peter Peterson, previously one of B&H's two executive vice-presidents, was named president and CEO. In 1972 Pete Peterson resigned to become part of Nixon's cabinet, and was later named U.S. Secretary of Commerce. Unfortunately for B&H, both Chuck and Pete Peterson put their personal ambitions ahead of their obligations to the company and its employees. Chuck had been a charismatic leader in his early days, and Pete was a very bright "deal maker', but a poor manager. When they left they compounded the problems caused by their excessive personal ambitions by naming a new B&H board member,

Donald Frey, previously of General Cable Company and Ford Motor Company as the new CEO. He also had excessive personal ambition, and was woefully unqualified as a CEO in management skills, temperament and integrity. Most of us longer term officers of the company resigned during the following two years because of conflict with Frey.

It was personally difficult to leave Bell & Howell because it had given me great opportunities, but it had become a great disappointment. Under Frey's subsequent control the company descended down the slope of poor management and it was finally acquired by outside interests who fired Frey and broke up the surviving parts of the original business. They even sold off the B&H trademark, which can still be seen occasionally, now applied to lamps and contract purchased cameras.

Bell & Howell had a great beginning based on the inventive genius of Albert S. Howell, the business savvy of Joseph McNabb, the charisma of Chuck Percy, the management skills of Bill Roberts, and the deal making of Pete Peterson. But it ultimately failed because of excess personal ambition, and then poor corporate management under Donald Frey. A sad demise.

By a strange quirk of fate Frey later became a professor at Northwestern Kellogg School of Management! Kurt Vonnegut's often repeated ironic phrase applies, "So it goes."

Lunch with special long-time friends Jackie and Dick Higgins.

Chuck Percy served three terms as a U.S. Senator, but was never able to achieve his main ambition of becoming President. He was beaten for his fourth term by the now late Paul Simon, an exceptionally good Senator. Pete Peterson became Chairman of Lehman Brothers, investment bankers, where he became involved in a destructive internal power struggle with its president, David Glucksman. Pete "lost" the battle, which is accurately portrayed in a great book, "Greed and Glory on Wall Street", by Ken Alueta. But, being Pete, he continued his fight and arranged for the acquisition of Lehman Brothers by another investment banking firm, making him and Glucksman even richer they already were. Pete then went on to become Chairman of The Blackstone Group, a huge "equity investment fund" that makes tons of money buying and selling distressed businesses. Josie and I visited Pete briefly a few years ago when we were staying at a business associate's place nearby his in the Hamptons. We found him to be the same old Pete, still very bright, very rich and still on the make.

During my fifteen years with Bell & Howell I worked with many good people. The best were Dick Higgins, Bill Montgomery, the late Fred Jahnke, the late Tom Rappel, David Craigmile, John Rosenheim, Bill Becker, Gordon Newman, Jack Hudson, Dick John, Everett Wagner, Gerald Perutz, Paul Beck, Hal Dotts, George Krtous, Arnie Zentz, Larry Howe, Milt Lauenstein, Dick Tobita, Frank Jones, and Nagakazu ("Nabe") Shimizu, president of Bell & Howell Japan.

They were each very skilled, hard-working managers and people of the highest integrity.

I must also make special mention of Mrs. Geraldine O'Connor who was my secretary for many years. Gerry is now 99 years old and still bright and cheerful. She was an excellent secretary and is a wise and thoughtful person. We visit her a few times each year and stay in touch by letter and telephone calls.

Dick Higgins is my longest standing and best friend from business life. We met at Bell & Howell in 1960 and we have continued as close friends ever since. Dick was a Navy fighter pilot during World War II. He was an excellent pilot so he served mostly as an instructor, but did serve on a "Jeep" aircraft carrier in the Pacific at the end of the war.

Dick was an invaluable friend in business because he was completely trustworthy and, while always very diplomatic, had a way of telling me what I didn't want to hear that made me listen. During the many years that I was responsible for B&H's international businesses Dick and I traveled interminable miles together around the world. We still frequently recount those experiences. Dick's second wife, Jackie, is a wonderful companion for him, and is also a professional editor who has provided me excellent services in producing this book.

Bill Montgomery is probably the brightest businessman I know. He came to work for me at Bell & Howell fresh out of the Harvard Business School. Unlike other "B school" graduates I have known, Bill was willing to do the difficult "grunt work" and

John Tomes, Josie Tomes, Ann Montgomery and Bill Montgomery

careful analysis that must be done to successfully manage any business.

After I left B&H in 1974 to join U. S. Industries, Bill followed me there and then, after I left there in 1978 to run Filtertek, Bill stayed and followed Russ Luigs, the president of U. S. Industries when he became president of Global Marine, an oil rig manufacturing company headquartered in Dallas, Texas. Bill has continued to live in Dallas, becoming a very successful business consultant and happy husband, father and grandfather. Bill's wife Ann is also a good friend. And, interestingly, Bill and I have recently discovered that we share a mutual interest in religion, in particular the writings of John Dominic Crossan.

After resigning from B & H in 1974 I became the chief executive of various other businesses, namely; the Consumer Group of US Industries, Filtertek, Inc., Bijur Machine Tool Co., and ultimately in 1984, becoming the president and CEO of Federal Publications, a law publisher headquartered in Washington, D.C. owned by Pearson, a British conglomerate.

For many years I had been a director of Development Systems Company (DSC), which had been founded by a long-time friend, Bob Kyle, who sold DSC to Pearson. Pearson had then kept me on as one of the directors of its American subsidiary through

which we acquired Federal Publications on behalf of Pearson. After the Federal Publications founder retired I became its president and CEO.

Federal Publications

The last fifteen years of my business career were spent as president and CEO of Federal Publications. They were the best years of my business experience. We made the business very successful by first improving its operating effectiveness and creating new publications, and then by finding and negotiating the acquisition of 13 additional small publishers over the course of the next 12 years. Surprisingly, even to us, each of these acquisitions was also successful and also improved its performance with us. We built the businesses on what I liked to call a system of "Risking Trust", by selecting the businesses mainly on our assessment of the integrity and skill of the managers. It worked. On the very few occasions

Gerry Swope's and my mutual retirement from Federal Publications, 1997. David Levendusky shown on the left.

From left to right, Josie Tomes, Dori Mebane, Mary Swope, Gerry Swope and Bill Mebane at the Woods Hole Marine Biological Laboratory Marine Resources Center.

where our trust was not reciprocated, we took corrective action quickly, but where the trust was reciprocated we could and did build very successfully.

We also developed a staff of people who were highly skilled, very productive, and very congenial. The best of them were Bill Brown, Helen Hoart, Rick Gibbons, David Levendusky, Mike Cavanaugh, Maury Roberts, Juan Osuna, Donald Reddit and Christine Hanson. My principal "partner" and chief financial officer, was Gerard L. ("Gerry") Swope, the best business partner I ever had. Josie and I also became good friends with Gerry's wife, Mary, who is a remarkable woman in her own right, as a poet and the founding producer of the "Washington Revels" for many years. We continue to see and cherish our friendship with Gerry and Mary Swope.

It must also be remembered that Federal Publications would never have existed if it hadn't been for its founder, Henry Kaiser, a brilliant and creative, but very eccentric and sometimes most difficult man, who sadly died a few years after he sold us the company.

Federal Publications had been acquired by Pearson PLC, a British publishing conglomerate, in 1984. After a year as a member of the board of directors of its American subsidiary I was asked to be the CEO of Federal Publications when Henry retired. The two best managers at Pearson were Tim Rix, Chairman of Longmans, and Michael Wymer, his deputy and the principal representative of Pearson in America. They gave me full support at Fed Pub and have remained good friends whom we continue to see whenever we visit England.

The Caxton Club

After I retired from Federal Publications in 1997, at age 70, I returned to living full-time in Chicago where I became involved in the affairs of The Caxton Club. The club was founded in Chicago in 1895 "To promote the arts pertaining to books, and to foster their appreciation." The club provides for lectures and exhibitions, and scholarships for book-arts students the occasional publishing of books designed to illustrate and support the objectives of the club. It was named after William Caxton (1422-1491), a soldier, diplomat, author, and the first printer in England. It has about 350 members and meets once a month for dinner and luncheon programs. It is a most congenial group of people who love books. I was elected program chairman in 1999 and president for the years 2001-2003 at the invitation of Dr. Fred Kittle, the previous president. Fred and his wife Ann have become good friends over the years, and the club has been the source of many other wonderful new friendships.

END OF PERSONAL MEMOIR
The Endless Search –
The Tomes Surname

Thus, the search for the Tomes genealogy has now its run course for the time being. The records of our family's direct Tomes line begins in the 1600's with Benjamin Tomes at Bidford on-Avon in England. Our Tomes surname has proceeded from then through ten generations to Alexander Steel Tomes, born 1995 and Katherine Harrington Tomes, born 1996. The heritage of course also lives on through their cousins, Elizabeth and John Sandbo, and Flora and Erskine Wells, who are also in the tenth generation.

But, as we have learned, the heritage is truly endless. We have, for instance, just recently learned of the existence of two people who are probably part of our line of the Tomes family, but about whom we need more information. They are Amanda LaFitte Tomes and Gloria and George Chapman Singer.

In the companion book, "The Meanings of Genealogy", we will explore just how endless the human generations are. We hope that tracing and recording our ancestry will interest some of our children or grandchildren to continue searching and making a more complete record.

Some of Our Special Friends

Top: Chick and Stan Kennedy with Chick's daughter Holly.

Middle: Mary Swope and Josie Tomes.

Bottom left: Ann Kittle and Fred Kittle.

Bottom right: Virginia Steele Wood, Josie Tomes and Jim Tomes.

Top: Giles Rigler, Lucy Rigler and Linda Newman Riglar

Middle left: Josie Tomes and Gabe Burton.

Middle right: Ray and Ann Mack.

Bottom: Gordon and Phoebe Fairburn and Alexander "Hadden" Tomes, Jr.

Top: Helen Dentler and Josie Tomes.

Middle: From left to right, John Straub, Cathy Wytmar, Jim Tomes and Rick Wytmar.

Bottom Left: Robin and Myron Goldsmith.

Bottom right: From left to right, Tom Scott, Simone Scott and Bob Dentler

Top: From left to right, Patrick O'Connor, Erin O'Connor Driscoll, Gerry O'Connor and Jim Driscoll.

Middle: From left to right, Bill Englehaupt, Francine McCrea, Bill McCrea, and Dorothy Fuller Englehaupt.

Bottom: Lou and Frank Stowell (1927-1995).

Top: Francine McCrea and Susan Glick

Middle: From left to right, Marcello Francini, Cass Racine, Bill Racine and "Liz" Armstrong.

Bottom: Gillian and Tim Rix with Josie at Buckland Manor.

James Steel with Sarah Mary Wilson Married July 23, 1895 in Paisley Scotland

MY SCOTTISH ANCESTORS

James Steel (1870-1947)

The earliest sense I had of having ancestors was at about age five when I recall meeting my Scottish grandfather, James Steel (1870-1947), after whom I was named, in Brooklyn, New York.

The most vivid memories I have of him were formed during visits to Brooklyn, "home" to both my mother and father. My brother and I would either take the New York Central train with my mother, or my father would drive us all in a two-door Chevrolet from Milwaukee (later from Cleveland), on the old two-lane roads. Such a trip in the early 1930s, before freeways, took two or three days, and we stopped enroute at "cabins", before there were modern motels. If we went by train my brother and I shared an upper Pullman berth, with my mother in the berth below. It was so exciting that we didn't sleep a wink, watching out the small window at each railroad crossing and listening to the crossing warning bell coming and going as we passed through the towns. We ate our meals in the dining car and were cared for by the cheerful Negro porters, all demeaningly called "George", after George Pullman. But in my memory they were all wonderful. Those annual trips to Brooklyn were my brother's and my first real adventures.

My grandfather and grandmother, Sarah Wilson Steel (1872 - 1951) lived in a row house in Bay Ridge, Brooklyn, just a few blocks from Riverside Drive, which overlooked the Narrows across from Staten Island and near Fort Hamilton. The Verrazano Bridge is now just north of Fort Hamilton. The row house had a small back yard where my grandfather had a neat garden. The house was also small which meant that while I was still a young boy I slept on the horsehair divan in the dining room.

Potrait of James Steel

cream, and "porridge" (oatmeal). All arranged on a white table cloth with china plates and tea-pots and sparkling glassware. My grandfather usually greeted me in the morning with a hearty, Scotch-brogue accented, "Get up lad and eat your porridge. It'll stick to your ribs". I tried to do as I was told, but my childhood memories of porridge are that it always stuck in my throat and almost made me gag. (I have since learned to love oatmeal - and Grandpa was right - It, and everything else I have eaten since, has "stuck to my ribs", and never gone away.)

This was for me a special privilege because I got to see my grandfather every morning as he had breakfast at the dining room table. When I woke up he would be seated there, already dressed for his job as a bank auditor, in his vest, starched white collar and tie, and also had white hair and a white mustache - the perfect picture of a grandfather. I certainly loved and revered my grandfather, particularly since I was named after him.

The dining room table was always laden with a full complement of Scottish jams, orange marmalade, and jellies, "Fin and Haddy" (steamed haddock), toast, scones, clotted

I also remember vividly that Grandpa once took me to a movie, "The Barrets of Wimpole Street," at a nearby theater in Brooklyn. During the movie, when the heroine fell down a flight of stairs, Grandpa leaped up from his seat to stop her fall. He was loudly shushed by the other moviegoers and we promptly left the theater. He took my hand as we walked home, but didn't say a word. He must have been terribly embarrassed.

My brother "Billy", was once the innocent victim of Grandpa's strict view of the world when he picked an Easter Lily that Grandpa had been growing in his back yard. Billy brought the flower in to give to our mother, but was intercepted by Grandpa who took the flower and admonished him fiercely, causing. Billy to run back into the yard in tears.

James and Sarah's children, circa 1910. Starting left corner clockwise is Flora, Wilson, Betty, Agnes, and baby Margaret center.

Left: Betty Steel, age 14.

I learned later that James Steel had come to America in 1890 as a 20-year-old young man, worked in Atlanta for Coates & Clark, studied accounting at night school, and faithfully corresponded with Sarah back in Paisley. Sarah's father, the Rev. Alexander Wilson, had told James that if he was faithful to Sarah for five years, and made his way in America, he would consent to their marriage. Sarah stayed home in Paisley as an elementary school teacher. She was said to play the piano well and was a good amateur painter.

James was faithful for five years and he did "make his way" in America, returning to Paisley to marry Sarah in 1895. We have a wonderful picture of them on their wedding day. (see previous page)

James and Sarah had five children; my uncle Wilson Steel (1896-1965) who was in the 27th Division in WWI with my father; my mother Elizabeth (Betty) Forrest Steel (1897-1957); and her three younger sisters; Agnes, Flora and Margaret.

James Steel was a classic old-world Scot, a Presbyterian, a thrifty teetotaler, hardworking and mostly quiet, but a righteous and strict man. His strictness alienated his son Wilson who became, like my father; a hard-drinking, hell-raising young man.

Sarah and James Steel on Atlantic city Boardwalk in the 1940s.

Wilson ultimately became a wealthy man, owning the Steel Cadillac-Oldsmobile car dealership for Westport, Bridgeport and Darien, Connecticut during and after World War II. Wilson's life was, however, filled with serious personal difficulties, ending in 1965, after his divorce and remarriage had alienated his family.

My mother, as the eldest daughter, virtually ran the Steel household for her mother Sarah who was frequently ill. Mother was a superb "homemaker" having graduated from Pratt Institute in home economics. Her skills and sense of responsibility carried her through life, making our home a very stable place in spite of my father's difficulties.

Flora, the next eldest daughter, was the object of grandfather's righteous Presbyterian wrath then she announced that she was in love with and wanted to marry Richard Kuebler, also a WWI veteran, but a Roman Catholic. Grandfather refused to allow such a marriage and disowned the young couple. They defied him, eloped and were estranged from the family for some time. A truce was finally arranged and the story of the reunification was told to me by my mother. When Aunt Flora and Uncle Dick came to the house in Bay Ridge, grandfather stood on the front steps and pointed his finger at Flora, saying: "Ye can come in the house, but never forget what his forebears did to yours!" James Steel was pure Scotch Presbyterian, never forgetting the ancestral fears of the past.

My Aunts Flora, Agnes and Margaret were each very loving and good to me and my brother. Flora and Dick never had any children - I'm certain to avoid the religious question. Agnes became a teacher in Brooklyn and never married.

Agnes gave me a beautiful oil portrait of grandfather painted by a professional, artist who was a WWI friend of Wilson's. The portrait now hangs in my office. Every time I look at it I mentally thank Grandpa for his vision and courage to leave Bathgate and come to America. We also have the inscribed heavy silver tray that was given to him when he retired from the banking firm of Hemphill, Noyes after 18 years of service in 1941. He had previously worked for over 30-years at the Guaranty Trust in New York City rising from bookkeeper to Vice President and Head Bookkeeper, then First Auditor and Vault Officer. In 1916 he was "loaned" to the Russian Kerensky government to advise on monetary policy. He died in 1947 and is buried next to his wife Sarah at Greenwood Cemetery in Brooklyn.

Margaret married Thomas Drysdale who unfortunately died rather young and left her with four children, whom she raised well. Their son, cousin Tom, Jr., whom we know the best, married Cathy Ishizuka, the daughter of George and Mary Ishizuka of California, and they have two sons, Noah and Keiji. Cousin Tom and Cathy are wonderful friends of ours. Tom is a professor at New York University and is the genealogist of the Steel family. He has given me most of the following information about the Steels.

James Steel's father was Ebenezer Steel and his grandfather was Eban Steel. Ebenezer was married to Elizabeth Forrest, a daughter of Christian Liddel and Alexander Forrest. Christian Liddel's parents were Mary Couburgh and John

Liddel. Mary Couburgh's parents were John Couburgh of Ellrig, Scotland and Helen Stevenson, married in 1720 and probably born in the 1600s. Eban Steel was born about 1815 and was an iron miner when he married Margaret Sangster, probably about 1835. Eban died in 1885 and is buried with his wife and son in a cemetery in Bathgate, near Edinburgh, Scotland.

Ebenezer Brown Steel (born in 1843) and Elizabeth Forrest Steel had five children: Ebenezer, Alexander, James, William and David who died as an infant. Elizabeth died in 1906 and is buried with Ebenezer in Bathgate. Ebenezer worked as an iron miner and weaver when he was young.

James Steel's parents, Ebenezer Brown Steel b. 1842. Elizabeth Forrest b. 1844.

Family tradition has it that he then, somehow, became the first Prudential Insurance agent in Scotland. He died at Sunnybank, in Bathgate. Bathgate is now a virtual slagheap after many years of mining. I visited there once on a driving trip from Edinburgh to Glasgow. It is a very depressing and poor place.

Grandmother Sarah Wilson Steel's parents were Reverend Alexander Wilson who was born in the parish of Cavers, above Hawick, Scotland in 1840, and Flora Anne MacEwan. Alexander and Flora Anne had seven daughters, including Sarah. Alexander studied first at St. Andrews University and the University of Edinburgh. He became a Presbyterian minister and was among the leaders of church reform in Scotland in the 19th century when the Evangelical Union was established. He preached first in Hamilton, then in Kilwining, and then for 46 years in Paisley, a suburb of Glasgow. He served as chairman of the Evangelican Union in 1903 and retired in 1916 as the senior minister at the New Street E.U. Congregational Church in Paisley. (I have stood in his pulpit as a visitor before the church became an arts and cultural center.)

When Alexander Wilson died in 1920 the Paisley newspaper accounts reported that the Paisley citizens all pulled down their shades in honor of his funeral. He was described as "a man having a singularly Christ

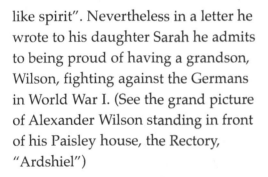

Rev. Alexander Wilson.

Flora Ann McEwan Wilson from Islay.

like spirit". Nevertheless in a letter he wrote to his daughter Sarah he admits to being proud of having a grandson, Wilson, fighting against the Germans in World War I. (See the grand picture of Alexander Wilson standing in front of his Paisley house, the Rectory, "Ardshiel")

By an unusual historical coincidence there was another Alexander Wilson, also from Paisley, born in 1766 and died in 1813. His life was remarkable, beginning as the son of an illiterate Scots distiller, he became a prolific but not a very good poet, then immigrated to America where he became

a teacher, and lastly became a highly skilled and renowned ornithologist. He illustrated and wrote the text for an eight-volume collection of colored engravings of American birds, American Ornithology, and died in 1813. He is buried in the yard of the Swedish Church in Philadelphia. During his unusual life, while he literally walked the length and breadth of America, he met and was befriended by Thomas Jefferson, Thomas Paine, and James Audubon. I mention this other quite famous Alexander Wilson here to spare future genealogists some possible confusion.

Cousin Lady Viola Tait

Violet Wilson, one of Sarah's sisters, married Gavin Hogg who was the manager of the branch of J & P Coats Thread Mills, located in Pressburg, Austria, near Vienna. The Hoggs had two daughters, Isla and Viola. Viola was born in 1911 in Vienna, where Mr. Hogg was posted. Viola became a beautiful and talented young soprano who sang lead roles with the D'Oyly Carte Opera Company. Her career brought her in 1940 to sing in Melbourne, Australia where she met and married Frank Tait, one of seven Australian brothers who were successful impresarios of Australian theaters and musical entertainment. Frank and Viola had three daughters, Isla, Ann and Sally, and Frank was knighted a few years before he died in 1965.

I met Frank and Viola once in 1941 when they came through Chicago in their private railroad car which they used to travel in America interviewing and booking talent for their Australian theaters. My mother took me down to the Chicago Union Station to meet Sir Frank and Lady Viola Tait. Quite a memorable event for a small-town boy in Illinois.

Many years later my wife Josie continued my mother's friendship with Viola and visited her often in both Australia and London where they frequently attended the theater. We have also enjoyed meeting Viola's daughters Isla and Ann in London and her daughter Sally in Melbourne.

Sir Frank and Lady Viola Tait at the Opening of My Fair Lady, *Her Majesty's Theatre, Auckland, New Zealand 1961.*

Viola wrote two books: "A Family of Brothers", (1971), the story of the Tait brothers, and the J.C. Williamson theaters in Australia; and "Dames, Principal Boys...and All That," a history of pantomime in Australia (2001). Combined, these books tell the story of Australian theater and also the extraordinary international theater life of Lady Tait. Viola had a great many theater friends all over the world.

She introduced Josie to the opera stars Joan Sutherland and Luciano Pavarotti during one of her visits to Chicago and I once met Viola at the New York City apartment of Dorothy Hammerstein, the widow of Oscar. And we were Viola's guests at a theater in London at the opening of a revival of No, No, Nannette, starring Dame Anna Neagle. We were assigned the Royal box and as we were being seated at the beginning of the show the audience, honoring tradition, rose and sang "God Save the Queen". Josie, as first in line and wanting to respond appropriately, entered the box and bowed grandly to the audience. We all had a good laugh, and Viola immediately pronounced Josie as "Queen for a moment".

Viola died in 2000 at age 90. She was a most charming, vivacious woman whom we all loved dearly.

Cousin Flora McEwen Lochhead
There was another Scottish cousin, Flora MacEwan Lochhead, who lived in Paisley at her house named "Monimail". Her father had been the publisher of the Paisley Daily Express. She never married and was a great friend of Viola's and loved to travel. As a consequence Josie also became her good friend. When we took our four children to France, Scotland and England in 1978 we visited Flora in Paisley and stayed for a night at her house. She traveled with us as we all toured Scotland for a week in our ten passengers Leyland bus. It was a great trip and the children had a wonderful time getting to know Flora. So much so that our youngest daughter, Julia who was then 10 years old, ultimately named her first child Flora.

Our fondest memory of cousin Flora, who died at age 85 in 1998, was her enthusiastic hiking, usually ahead of us, climbing some of the hills of Scotland. She was a stocky built woman with ruddy cheeks and a ready smile. She was habitually a bit late for dinner at the places we stayed, which she always apologized for by saying she just "had to take a minute to have a wee dram before dinner". Her ruddy cheeks were cheerful evidence of many "wee drams".

I cherish my Scottish ancestry. And we have many, friends who are also descended from Scots and with whom we seem to gather in "clans". Our close friends, Bob and Nancy Gunn, whom we have known since before we or they were married, have shared our family histories. The Gunn's have researched their genealogy and discovered that they intermarried with the Wilson's in Scotland. So, just as it is with so many of the world's people, we are cousins.

Flora McEwan, Robert, Julia, Josie, Betsy and John in Scotland, 1978.

"These immigrants were made of sturdy stuff." AMEN!

THE SEARCH FOR JOSIE'S ANCESTORS

The search or my wife Josie's ancestors has been more straightforward and less serendipitous than the search was for my ancestors. In the first place, Josie's ancestors are all Pennsylvania Dutch and have mostly lived in their present geographic areas for over 250 years. They have regular family reunions, have kept the old family Bibles, buried their ancestors in local cemeteries, and have good local history museums. There has also been a considerable literature created about the history of Pennsylvania and the immigration records of the Pennsylvania German Pioneers are readily available. And Josie's father, Francis Alvin Raymaley, and one of Josie's cousins, Sylvia Hague Raymaley) Duncan, have done excellent work recording their family histories.

Having said all that it must also be said that it has still taken significant effort and interest on our part to learn and interrelate all the available genealogical information into a coherent whole. This brief summary will present an outline of the major elements of Josie's family history, but anyone seriously interested will need to refer to the larger libraries of available information.

Josie's full name is Joann Schaeffer Witmeyer Raymaley Tomes, reflecting the names of many, but not all of her ancestors. Others were named Urich, Yeagley, Schumacher, Burger and Brubaker. All of her ancestors were what we now call "Pennsylvania Dutch", meaning Pennsylvania German. The "Dutch" is an American version of "deutsch", i.e. German.

The Pennsylvania Dutch

The term "Pennsylvania Dutch" generally covers all those immigrants and their descendents who came to America between 1630 and 1900 from the Rhineland countries of what is now Germany, France and Switzerland. This area was generally referred to as the "Palatinate", governed by powerful barons who served as "Electors" of the Emperor. Strictly speaking the Palatinate was the smaller area of Germany bounded on the north by Mainz (on the Rhine, west of Frankfurt am/Main), and Mannheim and Heidelberg on the south, and also spreading many miles east and west of the Rhine. But most of the immigrants coming to America in the 17th, 18th and 19th, centuries were generally referred to as "Palatines", even though they came from a much wider area including Strasbourg and what is now the Alsatian part of France, the central Rhine in Germany, and Switzerland around Basel. Alsace is now in France, but has been historically part of Germany. Many of its towns still bear German names.

In the 17th century this area was plagued by constant wars of religion between Catholic and Protestant contenders and the various duchies vying for control of land and resources. The countryside was laid waste repeatedly and poor farmers and craftsmen were made destitute. They were desperate to escape the endless religious persecution and forced military service, and to improve their economic circumstances.

A great many of these poor people were "Anabaptists", who did not believe in baptizing their new-born infants, but insisting on waiting until their children reached early maturity to make their conscious choice to become baptized Christians. Anabaptists also refused to bear arms or swear oaths. The ruling governments and churches severely punished Anabaptists because of their religious beliefs, and used baptism as a principal means of taking the census of people for levying taxes and for military conscription. The punishment of Anabaptists was literally torture, cutting off ears and noses and tongues, or death by drowning or burning at the stake. The extreme cruelty of this persecution has been forever memorialized in the Mennonite Martyr Book.

The Anabaptists also refused to worship with the ruling Catholic or Lutheran churches, organizing themselves into independent local churches such as the Moravians, Mennonites, Amish, Brethren (Dunkards), Schwenkenfelders, and the communal Protestants of the Ephrata Society. They lived simple church lives, serving as their own pastors and worshipping in unadorned buildings, which they typically built for themselves. They were, accordingly, called "The Plain People".

William Penn
These people were attracted particularly to Pennsylvania because of William Penn's policy of religious freedom and economic opportunity. William Penn Jr. was the son of Sir

William Penn, an aristocrat who had been an Admiral of the English Navy serving first under Cromwell, and later under King Charles II as his Lord High Admiral, (an obviously adept politician). William Penn Jr. grew up as a privileged aristocrat, but because of his extraordinary turn of mind became attracted to the religious teachings of George Fox, the founder of the Quaker religion. Penn became active in defending the Quaker cause and was imprisoned many times, once in the Tower, for refusing to compromise his Quaker principles. One famous case before a notoriously prejudiced judge, resulted in the jury ruling for Penn and his Quaker co-defendant, William Mead. The judge then locked up the jury whose foreman refused to recant. The case was finally overturned on appeal and the jury foreman vindicated and released, thus establishing the independence of the jury in English law.

Penn ultimately became Fox's partner and wrote much of the Quaker theology, known for its pacifism, its refusal to take oaths, and its lack of church hierarchy or creed. During this time the English Parliament passed laws attempting to enforce conformity to the Anglican Church and punishing all "non-conformists" including Quakers. Penn and Fox and all Quakers became constant dissenters, troubling the Crown.

After Sir William Penn died in 1670 William Penn Jr. came into a substantial inheritance, married and continued his pursuit of Quaker freedom. After arbitrating a case for the Crown involving lands in New Jersey Penn began to plan for a Quaker refuge in America. In June 1680 he formally petitioned King Charles II for a grant of 40,000 square miles of American land to compensate him for the 16,000-Pound Sterling debt owed by the King to the late Sir William Penn. The King granted the request in 1681, in part to be rid of dissenting English Quakers. The King also named the huge grant of land "Pennsylvania" in honor of Sir William Penn.

Penn then organized the Pennsylvania government as the Proprietor with an Assembly elected by the vote of all free inhabitants, regardless of whether they were landholders or British subjects. No taxes could be imposed except by law, courts were to be open and juries free to interpret law as they saw fit. Gambling, stage plays, drunkenness, profanity, scandal mongering and lying were all prohibited and the Sabbath was to be devoted to rest and religious observance. Freedom of worship was guaranteed, but no one could hold office unless he "professed his belief in Jesus Christ as the Son of God and Savior of the World."

Penn made only two short visits to Pennsylvania during his life, once in 1682-3 and once more in 1699-1701.

He actively encouraged oppressed people in Europe, particularly Germans along the Rhine, to immigrate to Pennsylvania. In 1681 Penn wrote and distributed widely, in English and German, a pamphlet entitled: "Brief Account of the Province of Pennsylvania," a wonderful model of ethical real estate development.

After his second visit Penn returned to live the rest of his life in England, where he was beset by legal, financial and health problems. He died in 1718 and is buried in England, leaving one-half of Pennsylvania to his son John and the other half divided three ways among the sons of his second marriage.

Thus, Pennsylvania was founded as a remarkably free land, a perfect refuge for not only Quakers, but all other people persecuted and oppressed because of their religion.

The religions of the Quakers and Plain People were similar, particularly in their lack of creed. Benjamin Franklin (1706-1790), when once inquiring of a member of the Brethren church why they did not publish a creed, learned that it was "their modesty and concern for preventing further improvement".

One of my favorite Franklin anecdotes, showing both his admiration for the Brethrens 'modesty and reasonableness, and his own knack for story telling, was this reply:

"This modesty in a sect is perhaps a single instance in the history of mankind. Every other sect, supposing itself in the possession of all truth and that those that differ are so far in the wrong, like a man traveling in foggy weather, those at some distance before him on the road he sees wrapped up in the fog, as well as those behind him, and also the people in the fields on each side, but near him all appears clear, though in truth he is as much in the fog as any of them." (The Pennsylvania Dutch, Klees, 1951, p. 62)

German Immigration To Pennsylvania

The earliest immigration of Germans to Pennsylvania occurred before there was a Pennsylvania, in the 1630s under the auspices of the Swedish King.

But the establishment of the first significant German settlement in Pennsylvania was in 1683, in Germantown near Philadelphia, led by the Mennonite leader Francis Pastorious. Pastorious, with his compatriots, including, one of Josie's Schumacher ancestors, purchased thousands of acres of Pennsylvania directly from Penn.

Fortunately, for us amateur genealogists, the German immigrants left copious records of their arrivals in America. They are, of course not a complete record, but they are remarkable considering the helter-skelter nature of the immigration. They are incomplete in another tragic way since they only rarely record the arrivals of the women and children.

But, even though they are incomplete they are full of fascinating detail. The principal documents are the copies of the ship's registers, compiled as "Pennsylvania German Pioneers," volumes I, II and. III, published by the Pennsylvania German Society in 1934. These records cover the period from 1727 to 1775. The earlier period from 1680 to 1727 is not well documented, but separate records of ship arrivals do exist.

Although the records of Colonial German immigration are incomplete, and sometimes contradictory, the analysis prepared by the Pennsylvania German Society and published in Volume 1 of the Pennsylvania German Pioneers, (1934) gives the following summary:

"Between 1727 and 1775 there were 324 ships bringing German passengers to the port of Philadelphia. In some years there were no ships, in some one ship, in many there were 2 to 10 ships, and in others 10 or more. The most ships arriving in one year were 22 in 1749.

The number of passengers arriving on those ships has to be calculated because only the physically well males were required to sign the oaths of abjuration (swearing loyalty to the Protestant King George II, and deny-ing the right of the pretender James). Sick males and women and children did not sign. From sample records comparing the surviving Captain's lists to the Proprietor's lists yields a ratio of 5 total passengers to each 2-oath signers. This ratio computes to a total number of 65,000 passengers on the 324 ships arriving in Philadelphia from 1727 to 1775. This means an average of 200 passengers per ship during that nearly 50 year period."

It is of course also true that many Germans came to Pennsylvania before 1727 and many others came by way of ports other than Philadelphia, such as New York or Boston.

The trip from Germany to Philadelphia was a very difficult one, usually taking about six months. The first leg was "down" the Rhine, north, from German towns to Holland. The Rhine passage was slow, mostly because of the 26 customs houses, which examined each of the boats and exacted tolls. So the trip "down" the Rhine lasted 4 to 6 weeks, and was very expensive for the emigrants.

When the Rhine boats arrived in Holland they were detained another 5 to 6 weeks for further customs inspections. The passenger's cost of maintaining themselves during these long delays was high and most of the poor passengers would have to spend all they had during this part of the trip.

The second stage of the trip was from Rotterdam, or Amsterdam, to one of the English ports - mostly Cowes on the Isle of Wight off Southampton in the English Channel. Other English ports were London, Deal, Dover, Portsmouth and Falmouth. Some ships also went as far north as Scotland.

"And then, when the Atlantic crossing ships finally set sail for America, "the real misery begins", as reported by one passenger. The Atlantic crossing often took "eight, nine to twelve weeks before reaching Philadelphia. Even with the best of winds the voyage lasted 7 weeks."

"And the trip was marked by much suffering and hardship. The passengers were packed densely like Herrings, without proper food and water and were soon subject to all sorts of diseases, such as dysentery, scurvy, typhoid and small-pox. Children were the first to be attacked and died in large numbers."

"The terrors of disease, brought about to a large extent by poor food and lack of good drinking water, were much aggravated by frequent storms through which ships and passengers had to pass."

One passenger reported, "One day, just as we had a heavy gale, a woman on our ship, who was to give birth and could not under the circumstances of the storm, was pushed through the port-hole and dropped into the sea, because she was far in the rear of the ship and could not be brought forward."

"The misery reaches a climax when a gale rages for two or three nights and days, so that everyone believes that the ship will go to the bottom with all human beings on board. In such a visitation the people, cry and pray most piteously. When in such a gale the sea rages and surges, so that the waves rise often like mountains one above the other, and often tumble over the ship, so that one fears to go down with the ship; when the ship is constantly tossed from side to side by the storm and waves, so that no one can either walk, or sit or lie, and the closely packed people in the berths are thereby tumbled over each other, both sick and well - it will be readily understood what many of these people, none of whom had been prepared for hardships, suffer so terribly from them that they do not survive."

"When at last the Delaware River was reached and the City of Brotherly Love hove in sight, where all their miseries were to end, another delay occurred. A health officer visited the ship and, if any persons with infectious diseases were discovered on the ship; it was ordered to remove one mile from the city."

"The sick passengers on newly arrived ships were further detained in quarantine, first in the countryside and later on a 340 acre island at the junction of the Schuylkill with the Delaware rivers."

"Those passengers who could not pay, or borrow the funds to pay for their passage were "sold" to waiting buyers before they were allowed to disembark. Thus, the ships became a market place for human labor. The buyers made their choices among the arrivals and bargained with them for a certain number of years and days of servitude."

"Some passengers had already sold their servitude to agents who made a business of financing German refugee's passages. These indentures of servitude were then sold to waiting buyers. Since most of the ships arrived in the fall season, the arriving passengers were facing the rigors of the coming winter and were therefore put at a significant disadvantage for negotiating the terms of their indentures."

"But, in spite of the risk and difficulties of the Atlantic passage, the immigrants kept coming. The persecution and deprivation they suffered in their homelands, and the hope for a better life in America, was enough to give them the strength to bear the hardships."

Quoted from "Pennsylvanian German Pioneers," Vol I

"These immigrants were made of sturdy stuff." AMEN!

One of the Pioneer records shows a Hans Nicholas Eisenhauer, the great-great-great grandfather of General and President Dwight D. Eisenhower. Hans arrived at Philadelphia on the ship Europe on November 20, 1741. He settled on land in Bethel Township, now in Lebanon County and had three sons, Martin, Peter and John. "Ike" was descended from Peter.

The Gov. Hunt -
Livingston Manor Scheme
There was a brief period from 1708 to 1710 during which an unusually large exodus of German refugees from extreme oppression fled to England. They were responding en masse to an offer by Queen Anne's government to become British subjects if they would swear fealty to the British government and to become Protestants. The offer also included passage to America and 40 acres of land if they worked off their costs by serving in "The Naval Stores project." It also coincided with the most severe cold winter in Europe's history. They numbered in the thousands and soon became a burden on the English government under Queen Anne. A scheme was therefore proposed by the then Governor of New York, John Hunter, and his colleague John Livingston to transport 3,000 of these refuges to Livingston

Manor along the Hudson river south of what is now Albany, New York to establish a community for the purpose of provisioning the English Navy with lumber, pitch, tar, and turpentine from the forest of New York, "The Naval Stores project."

A convoy of ten ships left England in December of 1709 and arrived in New York City at Governor's Island in July, 1710, after a storm-tossed, illness plagued, deadly voyage. Upwards of 500 souls died during the voyage and many more were fatally ill on arrival. There was no effective medical treatment for the prevalent diseases of the day. Smallpox, cholera, typhus, "consumption" (tuberculosis), influenza and "childbed fever" (septicemia) were simply untreatable, and were usually fatal. One of the ships was lost.

A sign at Tulpehocken acknowledging the pioneers from Schoharie Valley.

The two thousand or so survivors were taken into the wilderness to Livingston Manor to start the provisioning project. They were called "Servants to the Crown" and contracted to repay the Crown the expenses incurred for their trip.

Among these survivors were Johannes Urich and his son Valentine, and Philip Kilmer, each ancestors of Josie, as described in her genealogy to follow.

One of the leaders of the group was John Conrad Weiser whose attempts to represent the group against the hard practices of Livingston failed in a trial back in England, after which he was imprisoned in the Tower. John Weiser's 13-year-old son, Conrad Weiser, who came to America with his father, ultimately became a prominent leader of the Pennsylvania Germans as an adult.

The provisioning project failed and the immigrants were released from their transport payment obligations, but without any place to work or live. They dispersed in small groups during the next ten years. One group of 150 families, including the Urichs and the Kilmers, walked 40 miles overland in December to Schoharie, New York at the invitation of the Mohawk Indians whose Chief they had met during their stay in England. Unfortunately, the Mohawks had previously granted the same land to others, which ultimately required the Pennsylvanians to move once again.

Josie's Parents, Penn State circa 1927

PURE PENNSYLVANIA DUTCH

Josie's Maternal Ancestors
Johanne Urich And His Descendents
Josie's ancestor, Johanne Urich and
his family was among the Conrad
Weiser group of 33 families who left
Schoharie in 1727 and rafted 300 miles
down the Susquehanna River, past
what is now Harrisburg to the
Swatara Creek. They then walked
and pulled their few belongings up
the Swatara to Tulpehoeken Creek,
between what is now Lebanon and
Myerstown, where they settled.

Johanne's son, Valentine, also made
this heroic journey. He is one of Josie's
great (to the fifth power) grandfathers.
He is buried in the cemetery at Zion &
St. John's (Reeds) Lutheran Church at
38 Main Street, in Stouchburg, PA near
Lebanon, just east of Meyerstown.
Valentine was one of the founders
of this church which is still active and
thriving almost 300 years later. His
son, also Valentine Urich, was born
at Tulpehoeken in 1740 and died there
in 1812. He served as a soldier in
George Washington's Army during
the Revolution. His war record is
given in Series 5, Vol. VII, page 182.
Soldiers of the American Revolution

Food for the American soldiers at
Valley Forge and other encampments
was supplied by the farmers of
Tulpehoeken, and iron from the
mine at nearby Cornwall supplied
the mills that made the cannon for
the Revolution. George Washington
also began his development of the
Union Canal at Tulpehoeken.

Valentine's granddaughter, Magdalena
Urich (1808-1888) married Jacob
Schaeffer (1808-1881). Together they
built the house and barn on what
became Josie's family farm on
Halfway Drive between Lebanon and
Myerstown. Magdalena and Jacob's
names are inscribed on a stone
mounted at the peak of the barn roof.
They are buried together in the Union
Church cemetery in Myerstown. The
Tulpehoeken Creek still runs nearby
and the neighboring farm still has
the house built by Valentine Urich.

Phillip Schaeffer
and His Descendents

Jacob Schaeffer was the great-great grandson of Phillip Schaeffer who emigrated from the Palatinate to America in 1744, bought the Halfway Drive Farm in 1755, and died there in late 1758 or 1759. We believe that Phillip came from Alsace since there is still a small village there near Strasburg with the name, "Schaeffer-sheim". It is an ancient village with the barns connected to their houses and narrow streets all leading to the old church.

We found the record of Phillip's emigration to America in the Pennsylvania German Pioneers books. He arrived in Philadelphia on November 2nd, 1744 on the Friendship. He took his Oath to the Government by making his mark in the same way he acknowledged his agreement to purchase the farm by a deed dated 1755. Since he was not literate he was probably also a "redemptioner", owing the cost of his transportation to America to whoever held his indenture. Working off his indenture and saving money probably accounts for the eleven years between his arrival at Philadelphia and his purchase of the farm. What fortitude!

He purchased the farm from the agents of an absentee English land speculator who had purchased the land from William Penn in London.

We have framed this original deed as well as subsequent deeds, which granted portions of the farm to Phillip's sons.

Jacob and Magdalena's son, Isaac Urich Schaeffer, (1839-1915) married Elizabeth Brubaker (1841-1895), whose only surviving adult child was Agnes Rachael Schaeffer (1870-1939), Josie's grandmother. Agnes's sister died of typhus as a young girl. Agnes grew up living on the farm, known as "The Schaeffer Farm", and graduated from a Normal school to become a teacher.

(The surname "Shaeffer" has been spelled many different ways by members of the family. Some used "Shaffer," some "Schaffer," some "Schaeffer." The name is spelled "Schaeffer" on most of the grave-stones and some "Shaffer" on deeds. I have used Schaeffer on the granite memorial to be consistent with the gravestones. But I have dropped the "C" to be consistent with other family usage. Schaeffersheim in Alsace is also spelled with a "C.")

The World, According to Mitchell's Geography, Circa 1841-1847

Among the old books, mostly Bibles, hymnals and arithmetic lesson books, we found in Josie's grandfather Harry C. Witmeyer's (1874-1957) attic in Lebanon, PA, were two editions of Mitchell's School Geography. The two editions are virtually the same, one-dated 1841, with 18 maps, and the other, dated 1847 with 28 maps. The

Josie's grandfather as a young man.

Josie and Grandfather Dr. Harry Calvin Witmeyer

Josie, her mothjer and grandmother,
Agnes Schaeffer Witmeyer

1841 edition lists the American presidents through Martin Van Buren (1837), and the 1847 edition lists presidents through James Polk (1845).

They are fascinating views of the content of public elementary school education in rural Pennsylvania in the 1840's. They audaciously include descriptions of "The WORLD and its five great divisions: America, Europe, Asia, Africa and Oceana, with their several Empires, Kingdoms, States, Territories, etc., embellished by numerous engravings and adapted to the capacity of youth." It is certainly breathtaking in its scope. A young person growing up in rural Pennsylvania in the 1840s could gain a comprehensive, albeit Christian, view of the entire known world by reading these brief geographies.

Although they were published for use in public schools they are expressly and specifically based upon a Christian, Biblical view of history and the "Stages of Society".

"The Stages of Society" are described as; Savage, Barbarous Half-Civilized, Civilized, and Enlightened. The Savage are: Australian aborigines, South-East Asian jungle island natives, North and South American Indians and Eskimos; the Barbarous are: "roving tribes of Tartary, Arabia, Central Africa and the people of Abyssinia"; the Half-Civilized are: "China, Japan, Bunnah, Siam, Turkey, Persia, etc." the Civilized are: "Russia,

Spain, Portugal, Greece, Mexico, etc." and the enlightened are (guess who?): "The United States, Great Britain, France, Switzerland, and some of the German States." The cultural traits of each of these categories are described in mostly pejorative terms.

Religions are also described as: "All races of men, even the most savage, appear to believe in the existence of some invisible being possessed of power superior to man. The various methods in which this faith is manifested, form so many different modes of religion, and exhibit one of the most striking diversities by which nations are distinguished from each other."

The geography goes on to explain, in what are now very politically incorrect terms, that; "The different forms of religion can be divided into true and false religions." "True religion consists in worshiping God, according to his revealed will, and false religion consists in the worship of idols and the rejection of the true God."

"Mahomed" is described as "a religious impostor", "Pagans or Heathens" are described as those who "believe in false Gods and who worship idols, beasts, birds, serpents, etc." and include "Bramins, Buddhists, worshipers of the Grand Lama, etc, and number more than one half the inhabitants of the earth." "Jews are those who believe in the Old Testament, but reject the New, and expect a Savior yet to come".

So rural Pennsylvania at least saw itself as a Christian place, superior to all other religions. Curiously, Mitchell's lists the Protestant "sects" as Episcopalians, Lutherans, Presbyterians, Baptists, Methodists, Friends, etc., but does not list the Anabaptists sects, such as the Mennonites, Amish, Brethren, Schwenkenfelders, Dunkards, Moravians, etc., all thriving in rural Pennsylvania. The religion of William Penn, the founder of Pennsylvania, a Quaker, is listed as the "Friends".

Dr. Harry Calvin Witmeyer

Agnes married Dr. Harry Calvin Witmeyer (1874-1957) who was first a teacher and then became a homeopathic doctor, graduating from Hahneman Medical College. He began his practice as a "horse and buggy" doctor, first in Lickdale, PA and then served his patients out of an office in his home at 500 N. 8th Street in Lebanon, PA. We have his teacher's desk, his office desk and his medical instruments. And we have his window sign reading: "House Calls - One Dollar". Times have changed!

Dr. Witmeyer practiced medicine for many years until his death in 1957 at age 83. Josie lived in the house with her grandfather and mother from the age of 8 until she left for college at age 18. Dr. Witmeyer and Agnes's only child was Elizabeth Schaeffer Witmeyer Raymaley, Josie's mother.

The Witmeyer name is also recorded among the Pennsylvania German pioneers, but we have never been able to trace the Witmeyer ancestors beyond the names of Josie's grandfather's parents, great-grandfather Nathaniel Witmeyer (1849-1928) and Elizabeth Yeagley (1852-1,935), and great-great grand parents, Samuel Witmeyer (1817-1894) and Elizabeth Bross (1821-1900). Yeagley and Bross are also Pioneer names. Josie recalls that they lived on a farm north of Lebanon, near Sand Hill.

We have a circa 1895(?) photograph of the Witmeyer farm at Sand Hill showing Nathaniel and "Lizzie," and their sons, Harry, Howard and Samuel.

Elizabeth Shaeffer Witmeyer Raymaley

Josie's mother, Elizabeth Schaeffer Witmeyer Raymaley (1902-1989) was an accomplished woman for her day. She graduated from Hood College in Frederick, Maryland and was a teacher before she was married to Francis A. Raymaley. After they separated in 1937 she returned to Lebanon with Josie and they lived with Dr. Witmeyer in Lebanon. She encouraged Josie's many interests in reading classics and taking her to Philadelphia theaters and concerts.

The Witmeyer Farm Circa 1895 at Sand Hill

The Halfway Drive Farm

When Mrs. Raymaley moved to a nursing home in 1987, we became the managers of her properties, which included the "Halfway Drive Farm". We soon learned that it had not been well maintained and needed major repair and restoration, which we undertook. The beams holding up the first floor had rotted and were collapsing. The basement was built over a spring and was full of muck. The electricity had been condemned by the fire department because of recurring short-circuit fires. There was no insulation of the brick walls, and the plumbing was mostly inoperative.

The roof leaked. The "smoke house" attached to the main house had become a coal bin and was literally falling down. The tenants who had been living in the house for the past twenty years had done nothing to stem the deterioration and were in fact making it worse day by day.

The barns were in equally bad shape. The roof peak of the main barn, which was a masterpiece of 19th century "ship hull" construction, had parted and was open to the rain and snow. The foundations had been battered by careless tractor drivers. The dairy cow stanchions were broken and wired

Josie's Ancestral Schaeffer Farm on Halfway Drive, Myerstown, PA.

Schaeffer farm 1800s.

back together. One of the smaller side barns was so full of manure that the cows standing on top of the pile were breaking the roof beams.

The obvious question for us was whether to bulldoze the whole place and just sell the land, or to try to repair and restore this once wonderful family farm.

While driving down Halfway Drive one day to visit the Schaeffer farm as we considered these questions, I had what some might call a "vision". It was at least an image in my mind's eye of Phillip Schaeffer, the family's patriarch, sitting by the side of the road with his head in his hands, as if he was saying "How could anyone let my beautiful farm come to this grief?" I couldn't get this image out of my mind for days, and finally, after discussing it with Josie, we decided to try to repair and restore the farm.

It took us ten years with a significant investment and many, many visits. We couldn't have done it without the exceptional skill and help of J. Elvin Horst, a local contractor, whom we learned later is also a Mennonite pastor and bishop.

We completely restored the farmhouse and the barns. We jacked up the floors and installed new iron beams, we excavated and put concrete floors in the basement. We insulated the entire house, put in all new electrical and plumbing systems, replaced the leaky roof, and made the old "smoke house" into an attached but separate two-bedroom residence with a two car garage. We did all the necessary repair work on the barns, removing the old stanchions and turning it into a large feeder barn. And we repainted and restored all the interiors to like new condition. Then, since we did not want to live there ourselves, we leased the house and barn. We had previously leased the farmland to a neighboring farmer with whom we began a program to restore the land to a more productive condition.

From then on, when we drove down Halfway Drive toward the farm we saw a better image of Phillip Schaeffer, now standing by the side of the road smiling and waving his hand as if to thank us for restoring his farm. We hope we have met our obligation to the memory of Phillip Schaeffer.

Restored Schaeffer Cemetery
During the ten-year restoration period we also concluded that since neither we nor anyone in our family wanted to continue owning or maintaining the farm, we would sell it. Before we sold however we also restored the small family cemetery that still stands at the top of a cornfield hill on the farm. The ancient gravestones had receded into the ground or had been broken and the cemetery wall had collapsed. We rebuilt the wall, lifted and remounted the stones, and installed a simple granite monument reciting Josie 's genealogy from Phillip Schaeffer to the present. We also had the cemetery reconsecrated by our contractor and, by then, good friend, Elvin Horst.

The dedication inscribed on the monument is:

"This Sacred Plot of Ground is dedicated to the Memory of

Phillip Schaeffer and his descendents"

"Phillip emigrated from the Palatinate to America on the Friendship and arrived at Philadelphia in 1744. He acquired the 500 acres on the Tulpehoeken Creek that included this farm in 1755 and was the founder of the family that continued in ownership until 1997.

"Many of Phillip Schaeffer's descendents are buried here; including his son, Isaac Sr., his grandson Isaac Jr., and his wife Elisabeth, and their sons Jacob, and the Rev. John Schaeffer and his wife Catherine Bamberger, and their first son John.

"Their second son Jacob, and his wife Magdalena Urich, built the present farmhouse and barn in 1854

Top: From left to right, J Elvin Horst, Verna Horst, Josie Tomes and Jim Tomes. Bottom: Schaeffer Cemetery Plot at the Schaeffer Farm

and are buried at Union Cemetery in Myerstown. Their five-year-old son Jacob is buried here.

"My Grandmother, Agnes Rachael Schaeffer, lived at this farm until she married. She, my grandfather, Harry Calvin Witmeyer, and my mother Elizabeth Shaeffer Witmeyer Raymaley, are buried at nearby Kimmerlings Cemetery.

"My husband, James Steel Tomes, and I rebuilt and restored this farm and cemetery beginning in 1987.

Joann Schaeffer Witmeyer Raymaley Tomes March 31, 1997"

When we sold the farm in 1997, to the dairy-farming, good Mennonite family of Lester and Esther Martin,

we reserved the perpetual right to maintain and visit the cemetery. The Martins have recently sold the farm's development rights to the Commonwealth of Pennsylvania so it is now dedicated for exclusive farm use in the future. The Martin's "Halfway Holsteins" farm was designated as one of the eight Dairy of Distinction farms in Pennsylvania in 2003.

So, we have been able to document and memorialize Josie's maternal ancestry as pure Pennsylvania Dutch, and restore the family homestead to its original purpose. The heritage of the heroic Phillip Schaeffer and Josie's maternal ancestry should have a long future.

Valentine Urich House

Josie's and her father.

JOSIE'S PATERNAL ANCESTRY

**Remelis, Burgers,
Nahliqs and Schumachers**
Josie's father was Francis Alvin
Raymaley (1903-1973) who was born
in a log cabin in Penn Township,
Westmoreland County (western
Pennsylvania - near Pittsburgh) in
1903. He borrowed money, which
he repaid, from a man who wanted to
help him, and worked his way
through college. He graduated from
Penn State University in agriculture
in 1926 and married Josie's mother
Elizabeth Witmeyer in 1929. "Ray",
as he was known by his friends, was
a very gregarious and industrious
man. He was a high school teacher,
a County agricultural agent, and a
Naval officer in World War II from
1942 to 1946. He served with a food
mission in New Zealand and the
South Pacific. He retired with the rank
of commander, two U.S. Navy com-
mendations, a Bronze Star, and a
citation from the United Kingdom
Ministry of Food for his wartime
achievements. In 1946 he became an
executive with Seabrook Farms and

later with American Cyanamid
Company. In 1973 as Director of
the Division of Rural Resources of
the State of New Jersey he received
the highest citation from the U.S.
Department of Agriculture, its
Distinguished Service Award, signed
by President Nixon and presented
to him by the U.S. Secretary of
Agriculture.

Ray was divorced from Josie's mother
in 1952, remarried in 1955, and died in
1973 at age 70. He was given a Quaker
memorial service at his request and is
buried in Fernwood Cemetery north
of Bridgeton, New Jersey, near the
graves of his long-time friends and
mentor Mr. and Mrs. Frank App, also
a Pennsylvania German Pioneer name.

On July 19, 2007 we attended the
funeral of Susanna Grace Raymaley
Hague, Josie's father's youngest and
last remaining sibling. "Grace", as she
was known to all, was born in 1914
and was 93 when she died. She was
the beloved matriarch of a large fam-

Susanna Grace Raymaley Hague with Josie

ily, including three daughters, Sylvia, Joyfa, and Brenda; many grandchildren, and a few great-grandchildren, plus a large circle of friends who considered themselves part of Grace's extended family. She always gave generous help to family and friends in need, in spite of the fact that she was crippled by polio as a young girl. Grace was buried at Woodlawn Cemetery at Denmark Manor Reformed Church, alongside her husband, Henry Hague, and near many of her ancestors. Many relatives and friends came from far and wide to attend her funeral in Harrison City, Pennsylvania. She was truly an "Amazing Grace", one of her favorite

hymns, which was sung by all at her memorial service.

Our record of Ray's ancestry begins in Germany, in what is now the Alsatian part of France south of Strasbourg, with Nicolas Remeli (1678-1748). One of Nicolas's sons, George Remaley, also came to America from Alsace and fought in the Revolutionary War. Family tradition tells us that Georges' son, also named George, carried water to the wounded American soldiers after the battle of Brandywine.

Nicolas was born and died in Germany, but his son Ambrose (1702-1776) immigrated to America in 1749. The Pennsylvania Pioneers records

Grace with the Raymaley women discussing their ancestry.

A gathering of the Raymaley ladies at Grace's memorial Service.

Jacob Remeli's Saw Mill, near Harrison City, PA.

show that he arrived in Philadelphia on the ship Lydia on October 9th, 1749. Ambrose made the voyage with his wife Anna Catherine Schick and three sons, Michael (Josie's ancestor), George and John, and two daughters. They settled in Northampton County, north of Allentown, Pennsylvania.

Ambrose got a land warrant of 500 acres of forestland, with the help of Benjamin Franklin in Heidelberg Township. George (Jurg), Michael and John settled around Egypt, Emmaus and Slatington in Northampton County. Ray left a note dated October 29, 1960 saying that "Jurge's

farm RN #1 Egypt north of Allentown, PA is owned by James Frantz, a potato farmer - Jurge's name is on the eaves of the house and springhouse - dated 1756."

Sylvia Hague Duncan (daughter of Grace Raymaley Hague), one of Josie's Raymaley cousins and the Raymaley family genealogist, also reported that the three Remeli sons operated a sawmill, which they brought from Germany and became pioneer builders in Northampton County. It is believed Ambrose is buried in Heidelberg cemetery in Slatington, PA.

Sylvia Duncan also reported, "Nine of our Raymaley ancestors were enrolled in the American Revolution which started on April 19, 1775. John Adams, President of the Continental Congress proposed special awards for Ambrose Remeli who was called "Soldier of the Revolution". A "Soldier and Ranger on the -Front Line in Philadelphia" award was given to Jacob Remeli. To George Remeli the honor "Soldier of the Pack Horses" was given for transporting war supplies from Carlisle Fort to Pittsburgh, a very dangerous undertaking." (Raymaley genealogy, July 17, 1999)

Michael Remeli Sr. (1731-1792) and his brother John moved to Westmoreland County (near Pittsburgh) in 1767 after the Battle of Bushy Run, which ended the Seven-Year War between the British and French. Pontiac, the Iroquois Indian leader of the great League of Indians (aka "The Indian Conspiracy") had previously kept the whole region unsafe for settlement. When he was defeated at Bushy Run on August 13, 1763 by British Colonel Bocquet and the Militia, the Indian League fell apart and ended the Seven Year French and Indian War. Bushy Run battlefield is now a State Park worth visiting, 3 miles from the old Burger homestead.

Michael Remeli Jr. (1773-1820) purchased a 149-acre farm from his uncle John and married Susannah Margaretha Schaeffer. Their son, Michael Remeli III (1801-1870), married Mary Rupright (1807-1840). They had seven children; Jacob, Susannah, William, Catherine, Richard, Noah and Mary. They are both buried in Olive Cemetery at the Old Hills Church near Murrysville, PA. Michael's second wife, Katherine Best, had four more children by Michael; May, Daniel, Caroline and Elizabeth.

Jacob Remeli (1829-1914) married Susannah Rose Cutshall (1840-1925) in 1861 and had seven children; William, Murray, Ida Mae, Parmenus, Mary Belle, Chalmers and Maria. Jacob and Susannah are buried in the cemetery of the Presbyterian Church in Murrysville, PA.

Many old cemetery records are lost or incomplete, so amateur genealogists must be prepared to tramp between the rows of gravestone in old cemeteries until you find the names. You must also be prepared for the creative spellings that history gives to family names. Raymaley is spelled R-a-m-a-1-e-y, Remeli, Remeleigh, Ramli, etc. Parmenus Alvin Raymaley (1868-1945) changed the spelling of his family name by adding another "y" to Ramalcy because he believed people would pronounce it more correctly.

Lydia Cline b. 1812.

Parmenas Cutshall b. 1802. d. 1888

Susannah Rose Cutshall b. 1840 d. 1925

Jacob Remeli b. 1829 d. 1914

Jacob and Susannah Ramaley with their children: From left to right: Murray, Ida,
Parmenas, Molly Chalmers, Blanche Edwin, and Michael

1915 or 1916. Taken at the Old Raymaley Homestead in Franklin WP Allegheny County Near
Murraysville. Back Row left to right: Charles and Margaret Lintner, Joseph and Ida Kifer, Murray and
Sadie Raymaley, Parmenis Alvin Raymaley Angeline Burger Raymaley, Chalmers and Nora Raymaley.
Front Row: Lillian and Edward Raymaley, Seated: Jacob Raymaley and Susannah Cutshall Raymaley,
Alonzo and Blanche Beacom, kneeling in front: Mike Raymaley.

Parmenas Alvin Raymaley b. 1868 d. 1945

Angeline N. Burger Raymaley b. 1869 d. 1924

Abigail Neleigh Burger b. 1825 d. 1906.

Philip Burger b. 1820 d. 1900.

Parmenus married Angeline Neighly Burger (1869-1924) (Neighly is also spelled Nahlig, Nelig, Ne1ich, Neely) Angeline's ancestry also goes way back to Colonial days, starting with Nicholas Nahlig, who was the son of John Frederick Nahlig from Wurttemberg, Germany. Nicholas arrived in Philadelphia from Germany on the ship Neptune on October 4, 1752. Nicholas took the oath of allegiance to King George II at the Philadelphia Courthouse on the day of his arrival.

His signature is on the passenger list. He also went to Egypt in Northampton County and joined the Egypt Reformed Church. Nicho1as's son John Paul Neligh, who was born in 1759, is buried in the Denmark Manor Church Woodlawn cemetery, with a Revolutionary War marker beside his grave. He is listed in Soldiers of the American Revolution as Nicholas Neallich, a private, 6th Class, in the 8th Company, 4th Bn, 1781.

Angeline Neighly (Nelig) Burger Rayma1ey was born July 29, 1869 to Abigail Neighly and Philip Burger. She was born in the log cabin built by Philip Burger. The land where the cabin was built was a section of Denmark Manor purchased by Nicholas Neighly after he arrived in Westmoreland County from Northampton County. This cabin was enlarged and sided by Phillip Burger and Parmenus Raymaley. It later became known as the "Raymaley House." Angeline, "Angie" was born,

had ten children, and died in the same room of this house. (Josie's father, "Ray" Raymaley was also born in this log cabin house.) Angie died in 1924 and is buried at Woodlawn cemetery at Denmark Manor.

George Gottfried Ephriam Burger
Angie's mother and father were Philip Burger (1820-1900) and Abigail Neighly Burger (1825-1906). Philip Burger's father was George Gottfried Ephriam Burger (1791-1861), born in Landenberg, Germany and died in Harrison City, PA, and buried in Woodlawn Cemetery at Denmark Manor Church. George was a very unusual man for his time, or for any time.

He was educated at Heidelberg University spoke five languages and, at age 22, was the Provincial Rentmeister. He immigrated to Harrison City in 1812 and was a schoolteacher at Holtzer's School near the ancestral Burger farm. He also preached at Denmark Manor Reformed Church. He was Westmoreland County Clerk where his written work is still displayed for its beautiful script. We have three marvelous specimens of his work- illuminated manuscripts, "Frakturs," recording the birth, baptism and marriage of family members. His Frakturs are noted in collector's encyclopedias. We also have his restored, handmade, long rifle, which he carried across the Alleghenies in 1812. And we have the desk he made from a walnut tree he

Log Cabin Built by Philip Burger, Josie's Great Grandfather. Grandmother, Angeline Burger on steps
Great grandmother, Abigail Neighly Burger, at the fence.

House Built by John Martin Neighley.

Cabin Built by Nicholas Neighley.

Barn Built by Nicholas Neighley.

felled and made in 1834. He owned a farm where McCullough Village now stands near Harrison City. His grave and that of his wife are well marked in Woodlawn Cemetery at the Denmark Manor Reformed Church.

George's wife, Elizabeth Schumacher Burger (1790-1863) is also descended from Colonial Pennsylvania Germans. Her father, William Schumacher, was an officer in George Washington's Army, and one of her ancestors came to America in 1683 with Pastorious to the original Germantown.

Thus, we have traced Josie's paternal ancestry, from the earliest immigration to Pennsylvania until the present. Both Josie's mother and father were 100% Pennsylvania Dutch.

The Inheritance
These groups of immigrants made an unusually significant contribution to the founding of America. They settled the land, and through their exceptional skills and capacity for hard work built farms and villages and cities that continue to exist and thrive until the present. Their religious practices, were mostly peace loving and private. Their churches continue until the present. They supported and risked their lives and fortunes in the American Revolution against the English colonists. They formed egalitarian, democratic local govern-

Josie Tomes on Raymaley Road Harrison City, PA.

ments. They built roads and canals, Conestoga Wagons, and, ultimately, railroads. They pioneered the American way toward the west. And they left us a heritage for which we and our descendents will be forever grateful.

As the only child of an only child Josie has inherited many beautiful things acquired or made by her ancestors These include furniture; such as Dutch cupboards, desks, blanket and bride's, chests, chairs; beds, spinning wheels, yarn counting wheel, dough trays, chairs, rockers, a cradle, and a chiming tall case "grandfather" clock that still keeps time. Josie also has a collection of Pennsylvania Dutch pottery, cooking and eating utensils, quilts and blankets, frakturs, and

Some of Josie's ancestral Frakturs, Done by George Gottfried Burger.

Bibles and schoolbooks. And we have a large, handmade wooden box full of Josie's ancestors' carpenters and farm tools, which were used to make some of the furniture.

One of the reasons we believe that Josie's ancestors came from Alsace is that the Musee Unterlinden in Colmar has displayed many of the same things that have come down to Josie through her family. The construction and designs are identical. The evidence is very compelling.

It is Josie's intent to pass on these treasures from the past to our four children as reminders of their heritage.

JOSIE'S PENNSYLVANIA GERMAN GENEALOGY

Because Josie's ancestry is 100% Pennsylvania German and extends back about 300 years, and includes many families who typically had many, many children, I have prepared the following simplified set of charts showing mainly the direct line of descent and leaving out the collateral siblings. These charts relate directly to the narrative in the book "Serendipity".

SHAEFFER (Shaeffer also spelled Shaffer and Schaeffer within family)

Philip Shaffer (1710 ? – 1759 ?)

Came to America on the "Friendship," 1744. Bought the Halfway Drive farm in 1755

Son – Isaac Schaeffer, Sr. (1738 – 1784)

Grandson – Isaac Schaeffer, Jr. (1760 -1801)
    Married – Elizabeth ? Schaeffer (1754 – 1831)

Great - grandson – John Schaeffer (1780 – 1851)
    Married – Catherine Bamberger (1780 – 1845)

Great- great - grandson - Jacob Schaeffer (1808 -1881)
    Married – Magdelena Urich (1808 – 1888)

    Jacob built present Schaeffer farm in 1854

Great - great - great - grandson – Isaac Urich Schaeffer (1839 – 1915)
    Married – Elizabeth Brubaker (1841 – 1895)

Great - great - great - great - granddaughter – Agnes Rachel Shaeffer Witmeyer
    Married – Harry Calvin Witmeyer (1874 -1957)

Great - great - great - great - great - granddaughter –
Elizabeth Shaeffer Witmeyer Raymaley (1902 – 1990)
    Married – Francis Alvin Raymaley (1903 – 1973)

Great - great - great - great - great - great - granddaughter –
Joann Shaeffer Witmeyer Raymaley Tomes (1929 ---)
    Married – James Steel Tomes (1927 ---)

NEIGHLY, NALIG, etc.

John Frederick Nalig (CA 1710 - ?)

Nicholas Neighly (1730 – 1812)
   Married – Anna Margaretha Fabian Neighly (1740-1816)

   Nicholas came to America on ship Neptune, 1752.

John Martin Neighly (1773 -1849)
   Married – Catherine Long Neighly (1781 -1861)

Abigail Neighly Burger (1825 -1906)
   Married – Plhilip Burger (1820 – 1900)

   (see Burger line and George Burger's frakturs)

SCHUMACHER

Jost Schumacher (1716 - ?)
   Married – Anna Elizabeth ? (? - ?)

   Jost came to America on ship St. Andrew, 1738.
   Another Jost Schumacher came to America with Pastorious in 1683.

William Schumacher (1766 - ?)
   Married - Catherine ? (1766 – 1830)

Elizabeth Schumacher Burger (1790 – 1861)
   Married – George Gottfried Ephriam Burger (1790 – 1861)

Philip Burger (1820 -1900)
   Married - Abigail Neighly Burger (1825 -1906)

   (see Burger line)

RAYMALEY
Nicolas Remeli (CA 1678 — CA 1748)

Ambrose Remeli (1702 -1776)
    Married — Anna Catherine Schick (1697 — 1776)

    Ambrose came to America in 1749 on ship Lydia.

Michael (Johann Michael) Remeli Sr. (1731 — 1792)
    Married — Anna ? (1737 — 1784)

    Michael was soldier in Revolution w/brother George

Michael Remely Jr. (1773 — 1820)
    Married — Susanna Margaretha Schaeffer Remely (1774 — 1825)

Michael Remely III (1801 - ?)
    Married — Mary ? (1807 - ?)

Jacob Ramaley (1829 — 1914)
    Married - Susannah Cutshall (1840 — 1925)

    Susannah father was Parmenus Cutshall.

Parmenus Alvin Raymaley (1868 — 1945) (added "y" to spelling of Raymaley)
    Married — Angeline Burger (1869 — 1924)

Francis Alvin Raymaley (1903 — 1973)
    Married — Elizabeth S.Witmeyer (1902 — 1990)

Joann S.W. Raymaley Tomes (1929 --)
    Married — James Steel Tomes (1929 --)

        Robert Steel Tomes (1960 --)
        Married - Cynthia Zeltwanger (1960 --)

        Elizabeth Austin Tomes Sandbo (1962 --)
            Married — Scott Edwards Sandbo (1961 --)
                Elizabeth Austin Sandbo (1994 --)
                John Edwards Sandbo (1996 --)

        John Wilson Tomes (1962 --)
            Married - Jennifer Harringon (1966 --)
                Alexander Steel Tomes (1995 --)
                Katherine Harrington Tomes (1996 --)

URICH

Johannes Urich (? — 1758)
    Married - ?

    Johannes came to America with son Valentine in 1710 as part of "Naval Stores
    Project" from England to New York. When the project failed, they moved overland to
    Schoharie, NY, then, with 33 other families, rafted down the Susquehanna river to
    the Swatara Creek, and then to the Tulpehoeken Creek where he settled.

Valentine Urich   (1700 ? - ?)
    Married — Maria Margarette Volsin,

    Valentine was one of founders of Christ Lutheran Church in Stouchburg. Maria
    was a French Huguenot.

Valentine Urich (1740 — 1812)
    Married -Susanna Hain (1750 — 1791)

    Valentine was soldier in American Revolution in Lancaster County Militia. They had
    ten children.

Michael Urich (1782 — 1844)
    Married — Eva Margaret Kilmer (1783 — 1847)

Magdelena Urich (1808 -1888)
    Married Jacob Shaeffer (1808 - 1881)

Isaac Urich Shaeffer (1839 — 1915)
    Married — Elizabeth Brubaker(1841 — 1895)

Agnes Rachael Shaeffer (1870 — 1939)
    Married - Harry C. Witmeyer (1874 — 1957)

Elizabeth S.W. Raymaley (1902 — 1990)
    Married - Francis A. Raymaley (1903 — 1973)

Joann S.W. Raymaley Tomes (1929 ---)
    Married — James S. Tomes (1927 --)

WITMEYER

Samuel Witmer (1720 - ?) Came to America 1747 on "Bilander Vernon"
   Married - ?

Unknown Witmer/ Witmeyer (1750 ? - ?)
   Married - ?

Unknown Witmer/ Witmeyer (1780 ? -?)
   Married - ?

Samuel Witmeyer (1817-1892)
   Married – Elizabeth Bross ((1821 – 1900)

Nathaniel Witmeyer (1849 -1930)
   Married – Elizabeth Yeagley ((1852 – 1935)

      1st son, Harry Calvin Witmeyer (1874 – 1957)
         Married – Agnes Rachel Shaeffer (1870 – 1939)

      2nd son, Samuel Witmeyer (1876 ?- ??)

      3rd son, Howard Witmeyer (1889 – 1985)
         Married Edna Peterson (1891-1958)

Elizabeth S. W. Raymaley (1902 – 1990)
   Married – Francis A. Raymaley (1903 – 1973)

Joann S.W. Raymaley Tomes (1929 --)
   Married – James S. Tomes (1927 --)

BURGER

Johann Wilhelm Burger (1760 -
        Married – Maria Helmschmidt Burger (1764 - ?)

George Gottfried Ephriam Burger (1790 -1861)
        Married – Elizabeth Schumacher Burger (1798 – 1863)

        George was born in Langenberg, Germany. Came to America in 1816,
        made Frakturs, Recorder of Westmoreland County, PA

Phillip Burger (1820 – 1900)
        Married – Abigail Neighly Burger (1825 – 1906)

Angeline Neighly Burger Raymaley (1869 – 1924)
        Married – Parmenus Alvin Raymaley (1868 – 1945)

Francis Alvin Raymaley (1903 – 1973)
        Married – Elizabeth S. W. Raymaley (1902 – 1990)

Joann Witmeyer Raymaley (1929 --)
        Married – James S. Tomes (1927 --)

The Internet has expanded the reach of genealogical research enormously and The Newberry Library provides users with ready access to these resources.

THE NEWBERRY LIBRARY'S GENEALOGY COLLECTION

The best possible place to begin a genealogical search is at The Newberry Library. I began there on my search in 1959 and its services and resources are vastly enhanced now in 2008. The best way to see what is available is to view the library's website, www.newberry.org. It covers (1) an overview of its Genealogy Collections, (2) Beginning Genealogy, (3) Bibliographies of Important Sources, and (4) Genealogical Research on the Internet. Suffice it to say that The Newberry has one of the best genealogy collections in the world and has a very user-friendly staff, well managed by Jack Simpson, Curator of Local and Family History, to help beginners learn the ropes. The library also has a series of ongoing courses that help beginners become acclimated.

The library has, for instance, over 17,000 genealogies, especially covering colonial America and the British Isles. The Local History Collection covers county, city, town, church and other local histories from all regions of the United States, as well as from Canada and the British Isles.

The Newberry's federal census holdings are complete for the entire country from 1790-1850 and for other parts of the U.S. through 1920-1925. The Newberry also has a significant collection of probate, deed, court, tax and cemetery records for the area of the Mississippi Valley to the Eastern Seaboard.

The Newberry also collects roster and pension reference works covering the colonial wars through the Civil War and Civil War unit histories. It also has complete runs of many state historical and genealogical journals, as well as passenger lists Revolutionary War veteran lists, etc.

The library also has a number of genealogy guidebooks and specialized, ethnic resources, such as Pennsylvania German Pioneers (detailed ships registers of thousands of German, Alsatian and Swiss immigrants who came to Pennsylvania in the 1700s); and Scottish and English and African-American genealogies.

The Internet has expanded the reach of genealogical research enormously and The Newberry Library provides users with ready access to these resources. Genealogical Cooperatives, Databases and Links Pages are powerful entrees into research, including very specialized areas such as Jewish (Jewish Gen) and African-American (Afri Geneas) genealogy.

The Mormon Family History Library is also accessible via the Internet on their FamilySearch.com website. The Mormon church, (The Church of Jesus Christ of Latter Day Saints) (LDS), has compiled an extraordinary database of genealogical data – over two billion names! – accessible via the Internet.

The Mormon Church continues every day to add to this enormous database. Many adult church members and many young members perform their two-year mission projects by searching out and recording genealogical information all over the world. It is truly a religious mission for Mormons. The 19th century founder of the Mormon Church, Joseph Smith, took the teachings of Saint Paul in I Corinthians, 15:29, literally. It refers to baptism of the dead, and Smith began himself to provide surrogate baptisms for deceased persons who had not been baptized during their lives. The Mormon Church has continued the tradition begun by Smith.

There is a considerable literature about Joseph Smith and the founding and growth of the Mormon Church available at The Newberry Library in Chicago. Their website catalog can be found at www.newberry.org.

The Mormon diligence at ferreting out remote genealogical records proved quite beneficial to us when we learned of my great-great-great grandmother's, Sarah Hawk's, family history from the Mormon churches microfilmed record of that family's baptismal record in the Anglican Church in Shipston-on-Stour in the English Cotswolds. We had previously been to that small church, but had been unable to find the records. The Mormons did - and made it available in electronic form!

There are also various commercial websites, such as that are Ancestry.com and Lineages.com and Everton.com available for nominal charges.

Fortunately for the Tomes clan -there is a highly skilled amateur genealogist in our family. He is retired Major Ian Tomes, MC, OBE, who now lives in Somerset, England. It was Ian who, after he was contacted by his uncle, the sadly recently deceased Colonel "Dick" Tomes, broke through the blank wall that blocked me from probing the past beyond my great grandfather, Dr. Robert Tomes. Brief biographies of both Ian and Dick are included in the biographical section of this book.

OUR GENEALOGY

THE FAMILY HISTORY AND PEDIGREE
OF THE FAMILY OF TOMES
OF BROADWAY, BIDFORD AND CAMPDEN (ENGLAND)
AND
NEW YORK (UNITED STATES OF AMERICA)

The Family Crest ('Coat of Arms')
(Shield) *Ar. a garb betw, four cornish Choughs ppr.* **(Crest)** *A cornish Chough volant ppr.*

Compiler:

Major (Retd) I M Tomes MBE, MC *(Ian)*
Sparrow Hill Farm
Upper Weare
AXBRIDGE
Somerset BS26 2LN
ENGLAND
email: tomestome@btinternet.com

Edition 6   As at: 18 November 2005

TOMES OF BROADWAY, BIDFORD, CAMPDEN & NEW YORK

Generation

(1)   COOPER : ········· = ?

Benjamin = Elizabeth
TOMES/TOMS | MAIDS
(m 3 Feb 1702, Campden, GLS)

(surmised)

(2) Thomas
COOPER
of Ullington
'will did
1791'

Mary = Peter
| WESTON
: Of Ullington
(m 25 Sep 1746,
Chipping Campden)

Johanne/John = Ann/Anna HALE
TOMES/TOMS
bap 17 Feb 1703,
Broadway, WOR
(m 27 Dec 1720, Broadway)

(surmised)

Ebenezer
bap 29 Oct 1705,
Broadway

Thomas
bap 9 Nov 1707,
Broadway

Anne
bap 5 Mar 1709,
Campden

Benjamin = Elizabeth
TOMES/TOMS | MILWARD
bap 3 Feb 1711, Barford [2] Of Bidford, bc 1711
Of Alcester at mar d 28 Jan 1784,
'Sadler of Bidford' bur Bidford
d 9 May 1786, aged 75,
bur Bidford
(m 28 Jan 1734, St Mary's, Warwick)

(3) Thomas
WESTON

Jane = Thomas
TOMES   BEZLEY
bap 22 Oct
1721,
Broadway
(m 26 Sep 1744, Willersey
or Western Subedge) [3]

Ann
bap 29 Oct
1723,
Broadway

Maria
bap 11 Jul
1728,
Broadway

Elizabeth
bap 20 Feb
1732,
Broadway

William
bap 13 Feb
1735,
Broadway

Benjamin = Mary, WESTON
TOMES d 13 Jan
bc 1733 [1] 1795
d 1793 (m 1792)

Ann = Job
BOSSARD
bap 30 Jan 1735,
Bidford
(m 29 Jul 1751, by Licence,
Bidford on Avon)

John
bap 28 Mar 1737,
Bidford

Thomas
bap 16 Sep 1739,
bur 1 Jan 1740,
both Bidford

Jane
bap 19 Oct 1740
later of Bromsgrove
a Oct 1807

(4) Hannah
TOMES

The Church of St James, Chipping Campden

Bidford on Avon Church

[PAGE 2]

Notes:
[1] Benjamin: bap not traced.
[2] Barford: Barford lies 3 miles NE of Stratford on Avon. However the entry (from the IGI) could be a transcription error and should be Bidford - there being no other family connections known with Barford
[3] Jane: Possible one: Willersey & Weston Subedge are villages close to Broadway.

- i -

(1)

Richard = Elizabeth HODGES

Charles = Elizabeth OLDACRE ; bc 1710
Of Stratford on Avon & ; a miller in Cleeve Prior ; d 10 Oct 1780,
d 16 Mar 1776, aged 65, ; aged 70,
bur Cleeve Prior [1]

(2)

<[PAGE 1]

Richard = Sarah HAWKS
bap 1 Mar 1745, Of Shipston
Bidford on Stour

Edward = Elizabeth OLDACRE
HODGES [her 1st man]
bap 15 Apr 1735, Bidford bap 20 Nov 1742,
Landlord of 'The Lion' d 10 Jan 1802,
in Bidford bur 13 Jan,
(m, 1st, 2 Aug 1792, Bidford
Cleeve Prior, WOR)

Ebenezer =
bap 2 Sep 1751,
Bidford
d 20 Sep 1788,
bur 2 Oct,
Bidford
(W) Will dated 20 Jan 1786,
Est: 'under £300'
(m, 2nd, 5 Jan 1783,
Bidford on Avon)

Matthew,
bap 7 Feb 1787,
Bidford
di, bur 16 Jan
1787, Bidford

Francis = ?
bap 23 Apr 1785,
Bidford
d aged 28 in
Jamaica
Given £100 in his
father's Will [2]

Benjamin
TOMES
bap 21 Mar 1784,
Bidford
dii, bur 13 May
1786, Bidford

Francis
TOMES
b in Jamaica
came to England [2]

(3)

Thomas
TOMES
bap 2 May 1742,
bur 1 Apr 1743,
both Bidford

William
bap 14 Aug 1743,
bur 13 Jan 1745,
both Bidford

Elizabeth
bap 28 Apr 1747,
Bidford
d um, bur
20 Aug 1807, aged
60, Bidford
(W) Will dtd
22 Jul 1797,
Est: 'under £200'

Susannah/Susan
bap 2 Jun 1749,
bur 20 May 1752,
both Bidford

[PAGE 2/A]

Edward = Elizabeth
HODGES CHAIR
Of Welford Of Sambourne
Pasture
(m 29 Apr 1802, Arrow, WAR)

Thomas = Hannah
HODGES HANCOCK
Of Welford Pasture Of Little Dorrington
(m 20 Feb 1843, Kidderminster, WOR)

(4)

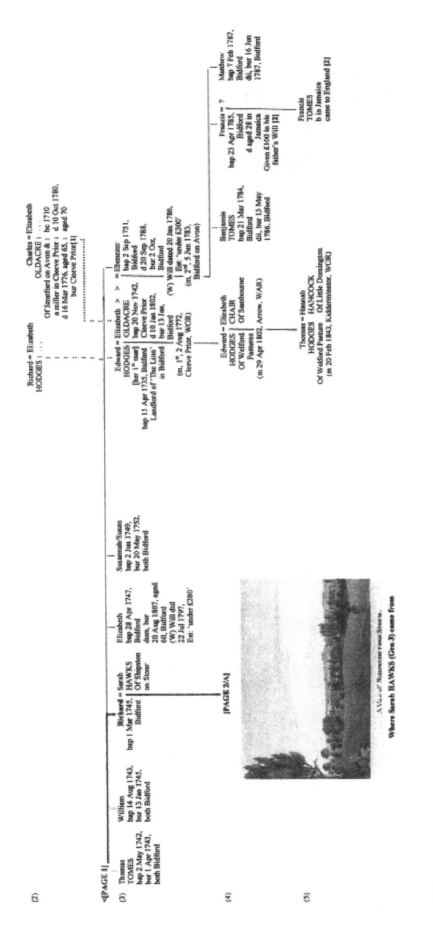

(5)

A View of Shakespeare's Birth Street.

Where Sarah HAWKS (Gen 3) came from

Notes:
[1] **Charles & Elizabeth** As well as Elizabeth (Gen 3) they had ' 7 other children, of which 5 died in infancy'
[2] **Francis** *'Francis TOMES was apprenticed to a printer named HEMMING of Stourbridge, from whom he ran away and went to Jamaica. He died in good circumstances early in life, leaving a son by a woman in Jamaica, who was brought to England at his father's death and apprenticed to a brass founder in Birmingham, from whom he ran away and came to no good'.*

-2-

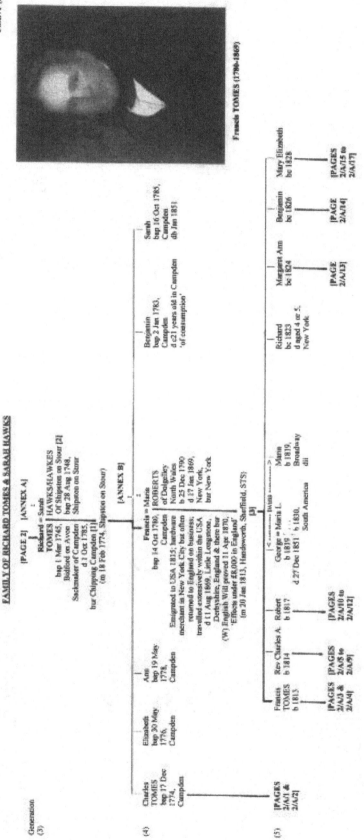

Francis TOMES (1790-1869)

FAMILY OF RICHARD TOMES & SARAH HAWKS

Generation
(3)

[PAGE 2]   [ANNEX A]

Richard = Sarah
TOMES   HAWKS/HAWKES
bap 1 Mar 1745,   Of Shipston on Stour [2]
Bidford on Avon   bap 28 Aug 1748,
Sackmaker of Campden   Shipston on Stour
d 1 Oct 1785,
bur Chipping Campden [1]
(m 18 Feb 1774, Shipston on Stour)

[ANNEX B]

(4)

| Charles TOMES bap 17 Dec 1774, Campden | Elizabeth bap 30 May 1776, Campden | Ann bap 19 May 1778, Campden | Francis = Maria bap 14 Oct 1780, Campden | | Benjamin bap 2 Jun 1783, Campden d c21 years old in Campden 'of consumption' | Sarah bap 16 Oct 1785, Campden db 3 Jan 1851 |

Francis = Maria ROBERTS
of Dolgelley
North Wales
b 25 Dec 1790,
d 17 Jan 1869,
New York,
bur New York
Emigrated to USA 1815; hardware
merchant in New York City but often
returned to England on business;
travelled extensively within the USA.
d 11 Aug 1869, Little Longstone,
Derbyshire, England & there bur
(W) English Will proved 31 Apr 1870,
'Effects under £8,000 in England'
[m 20 Jan 1813, Handsworth, Sheffield, 873]

[3]

(5)

[PAGES 2/A/1 & 2/A/2]

| Francis TOMES b 1813 | Rev Charles A. b 1814 | Robert b 1817 | George = Maria L. b 1819 | | Richard bc 1823 d aged 4 or 5, New York | Margaret Ann bc 1824 | Benjamin bc 1826 | Mary Elizabeth bc 1828 |

George = Maria L.
b 1819
d 27 Dec 1851
Maria
b 1819,
Broadway
dll
b 1830,
South America

[PAGES 2/A/3 & 2/A/4]   [PAGES 2/A/5 to 2/A/9]   [PAGES 2/A/10 to 2/A/12]   [PAGE 2/A/13]   [PAGE 2/A/14]   [PAGES 2/A/15 to 2/A/17]

Notes:
[1] Richard 'Inscription on top of a tomb in Campden Churchyard, north of the church, the following 'To the memory of Richard Tomes who died Oct 1, 1785'. This recorded by Robert Fisher TOMES (of LONGM Pedigree) in the late 1860s. However a visit by the compiler in 1983 to the churchyard revealed no trace - and indeed most of the 18th Century headstone inscriptions there were then so weathered they were quite unreadable.
[2] Shipston on Stour. Lies 7 miles east of Chipping Campden.
[3] Issue of Francis & Maria First two children born in England, the rest in the USA.

- 2/A -

FAMILY OF CHARLES TOMES & ELIZABETH WILLIAMS [1]

[PAGE 2/A2]▷
[PAGE 2/A2]▷
[PAGE 2/A2]▷
[PAGE 2/A2]▷

Generation (3)

Charles TOMES = Elizabeth WILLIAMS
bap 17 Dec 1774, Campden | bc 1772
Solicitor, Attorney & Notary, Oxford 1812; Clerk of | d 19 Jun 1852, 3 Providence Row,
arraigns & indictments on Oxford circuit, based at 50 Lincoln's Inn Fields, | Hackney, London, aged 79
London 1835; Attorney in Oxford & London 1836; 'For upwards of 20 | (W) died 16 Nov 1847, proved
years, Clerk of the Indictments on the Oxford Circuit' | London, 16 Mar 1852
d 9 Jun 1857, Hackney, London

(4)

(5) **Francis TOMES** | **Charles = Caroline Elizabeth Stratton** | **Eliza**
bap 25 Jun 1802, | bap 30 Apr 1804, | JAMES | bap 13 Jun 1804,
St Peters Le Bailey, | St Peters Le Bailey, | bc 1802, Oxford | St Peters Le Bailey,
Oxford | Oxford | dr O-D 1898, aged 96, | Oxford
A surgeon | An attorney | Wandsworth, London, Dist
d 9 Jun 1854, aged 51, | d 23 Aug 1846, aged 47
Beverley, Essex | Observatory St,
 | St Giles, Windsor

(6) **Caroline Elizabeth Stratton TOMES** | **Emily = Joseph** | **Mary Jane = Joseph**
bc 1835 [4], Oxford | b 12 Feb 1840 | CHIPPERFIELD
Dressmaker (81c); 'living on own means' (01C) | Walton Place, | b 29 Mar 1843,
dum 19 Mar 1918, aged 83, 163 Northcote Rd, | St Thomas, Oxford | Walton Place,
New Wandsworth, SW18, Surrey | dr O-D 1869, | St Thomas,
(W) Est £321 11s 4d | Hackney Dist, | Oxford
 | aged 28 [5]

(7) **[6] Alice Mary = Frederick**
CHIPPERFIELD | GOODERHAM
br A-J 1867, |
Hackney, London, Dist

Henry ("Harry") = Mary Barton = Mary Ann/Anna
bc 1810, b Oxford | (1st), DYER | (2nd) CREAK
d 2 Nov 1874, | | Sep 12 Feb 1812, Jamaica Row
Acock's Green, Birmingham, ENG | | Independent Ch, Bermondsey, SRY [3]
'formerly of Brooklyn, New York,' | | d 21 May 1888,
Major US Army and merchant | | New York, USA
(W) Will dated 30 Oct 1874 & | | (W) Will dated 10 Apr 1885,
proved 22 Mar 1875 [2] | | with Codicil of 18 Sep 1885
St Andrews, Philadelphia, USA) | (m, 1st, 26 Mar 1832,
 | | (m, 2nd, 25 Aug 1856,
 | | St James, Bermondsey, London)

**Dr H.K. = Jane S
CHAPMAN**

Elizabeth Waters = William | **Chapman** | **Sarah = Arthur J.** | **Matilda J.**
TOMES | CHAPMAN | George | Isabella | um in 1874
bc 1839, Brooklyn | bc 1839 | a 1874 | PLYMPTON
d 11 Jan 1925, aged 86 | d 14 Feb 1898, aged 59 | | a 1874

Hiram = Alice | **Augusta = William Henry**
CHAPMAN | CARRUTH | b 12 Oct 1865 | BURGER
b 2 Aug 1883 | d 12 Dec 1946 | b 28 Jun 1860
d Aug 1976 | | d 4 Dec 1922

Frank Tomes = Dorothy | **Sybil** | **Norman = Margaret**
CHAPMAN | b 14 May 1913 | BURGER | b 12 Sep 1897 | ROBERTS
b 9 Jan 1905 | | b 18 Jun 1893 | d 18 Feb 1929
d 29 Oct 1978 | | d 3 Sep 1912

Anne C. = TULLAR | **Sybil** | **Gloria Whitney = George Chapman**
b 25 Apr 1943 | BURGER | b 27 Oct 1924 | SINGER
 | b 18 Apr 1927

(10) **John Tomes** | **Alice** | **Tera** | **Christopher** | **Lynda Karen Pam** | **Lauren Rob Meg**
CHAPMAN | TULLAR | b 4 Mar 1970 | b 24 Feb 1973 | BURGER | SINGER
b 15 May 1945 | b 16 Nov 1973

(11) **Ava Dorothy** | **Lydia Madeleine** | **Evan Allistar**
TULLAR | TULLAR | b 24 Jun 2003
b 14 May 2001 | b 9 Dec 1998

Notes:

[1] **The Family:** See content of the 'SOME HISTORICAL NOTES ON THE EARLY GENERATIONS' pages, for detailed notes on individuals in this family group.

[2] **Henry's WILL** A 'G W. TOMES of Acock's Green' was a witness to Henry's Will, but has not been traced. Acock's Green lies some 2 miles South East of Birmingham City Centre.

[3] **Mary Ann/Anna.** Her bap details, including the name of her father, have been extracted from the IGI, but would seem to fit.

[4] **Caroline.** Appears to have had the same names as her mother. When she was born is not clear, viz. (81C), aged 38, is bc 1843; (01C), aged 64, so bc 1837; dr, aged 83, so bc 1835. There is through no GRO br, so a birth around 1835-37 seems most probable.

[5] **Emily.** A probable dr

[6] **Alice Mary.** Caroline (Gen 2) in her Will names 'my niece Alice GOODERHAM wife of Frederick GOODERHAM' & from her br she would have been a dau of Mary Jane & Joseph.

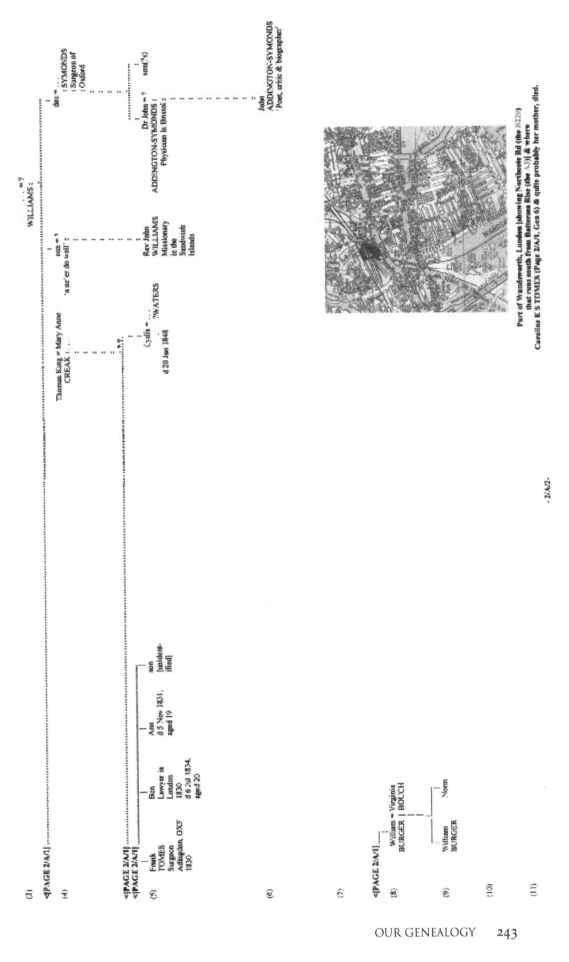

WILLIAMS = ?

dau = : SYMONDS : Surgeon of : Oxford

son(?s)

Thomas King = Mary Anne CREAK

son = ? 'a ne'er do well'

Dr John = ? ADDINGTON-SYMONDS : Physician in Bristol

Rev John WILLIAMS Missionary in the Sandwich Islands

John ADDINGTON-SYMONDS 'Poet, critic & biographer'

(3)

<[PAGE 2/A/0]

(4)

<[PAGE 2/A/1]
<[PAGE 2/A/1]

Lydia = ? ?WATERS d 20 Jan 1843

(5)

Frank TOMES Surgeon Arlington, OXF 1830

Ben Lawyer in London 1830 d 6 Jul 1834, aged 20

Ann d 5 Nov 1831, aged 19

son [unidentified]

(6)

(7)

<[PAGE 2/A/1]

(8)

William = Virginia BURGER | BOLCH

(9)

William BURGER

Norm

(10)

(11)

Part of Wandsworth, London (showing Northcote Rd (the 8E19) & where that runs south from Battersea Rise (the AB)) & where Caroline E S TOMES (Page 2/A/1, Gen 6) & quite probably her mother, died.

Shewborough House, nr Tewkesbury?
The home of Arthur Windham BALDWIN & Joan Elspeth TOMES (Gen 7)
[Photo taken by the Compiler Apr 1994, when then an old peoples' residential home]

(5)

<[PAGE 2/A/3]

(6)
Isabel Hosden
TOMES
b 2 Apr 1859, New York
d 7 May 1925
[#]

Rosalie = Frank HALPIN
b 3862, CT
d 1939

<[PAGE 2/A/3]

(7)
Joan Elspeth = Arthur Windham   [ANNEX D]
TOMES   BALDWIN
b 2 Jun 1901, b 22 Mar 1904, London
Natn. SCT   3rd Earl Baldwin of Bewdley
d 24 Jul 1980, d 5 Jul 1976,
Tewkesbury, ENG Tewkesbury,
(m 26 Aug 1936, Westminster, London)

Eleanor = ... STEARNS
HALPIN
b 1892

John = ?
b 1894

Murrey = ?

Joe = ?
STERNS

Issue   Issue   Issue

(8)
Edward Alfred Alexander = Sarah MacMurrie
b 3 Jan 1938, Astley, WOR   ('Sally') JAMES
4th Earl Baldwin of Bewdley b 16 Apr 1942
d 22 Jun 2001,
Oxford
(m 19 Dec 1970)

(9)
Benedict Alexander Stanley   Hon James Conrad   Hon Mark Thomas Maitland
BALDWIN   b 13 Mar 1976,   b 24 Jul 1980,
b 28 Dec 1973, Oxford   Oxford   Oxford
Viscount Corvedale

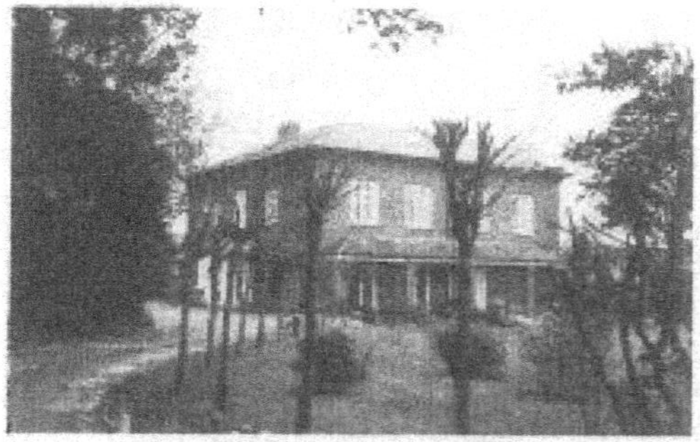

Notes:
[#] Buried. Bur in family plot, Greenwich, CT

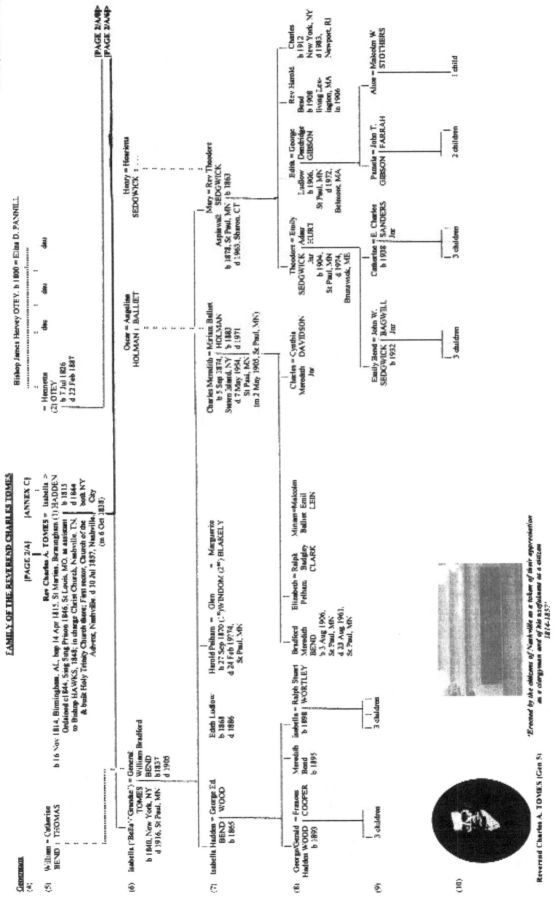

FAMILY OF THE REVEREND CHARLES TOMES

Reverend Charles A. TOMES (Gen 5)

"Erected by the citizens of Nashville as a token of their appreciation
as a clergyman and of his usefulness as a citizen
1814–1857"

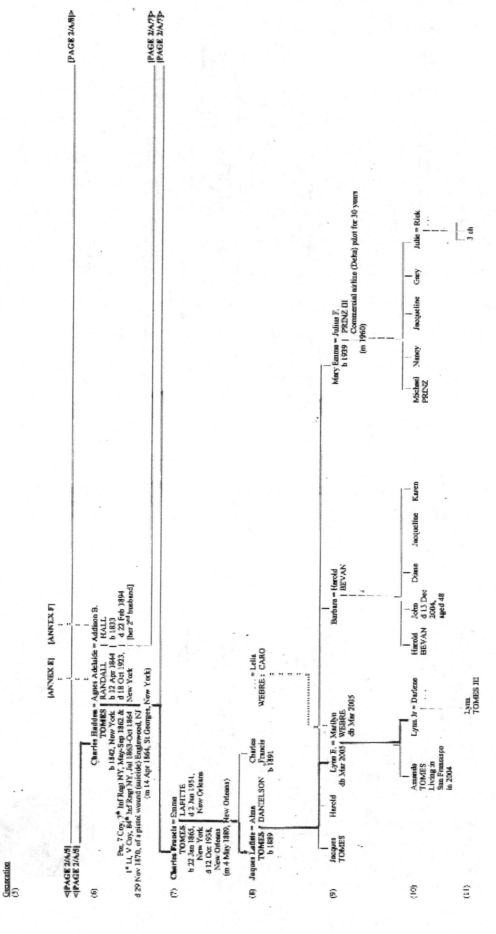

Generation
(5)

<PAGE 2/A/5]
<PAGE 2/A/5]

[ANNEX E]   [ANNEX F]

[PAGE 2/A/5]
[PAGE 2/A/5]

(6)

Charlie Haddon = Agnes Adelaide = Addison B.
TOMES | RANDALL | HALL
b 1842, New York | b 12 Apr 1844 | b 1833
| d 18 Oct 1923, | d 22 Feb 1894
| New York | [her 2nd husband]

Pte. 7 Coy, 1st Inf Regt NY, May-Sep 1862 &
1st Lt, V Coy, 84th 3rd Regt NY, Jul 1863-Oct 1864
d 29 Nov 1870, of a pistol wound (suicide) Englewood, NJ
(m 14 Apr 1864, St Georges, New York)

(7)

Charles Francis = Emma
TOMES | LAFITTE
b 22 Jan 1865, | d 2 Jun 1951,
New York | New Orleans
d 12 Oct 1938,
New Orleans
(m 4 May 1889, New Orleans)

(8)

Jacques Lafitte = Alma   Charles   = Leila
TOMES | DANIELSON   Francis   WEBRE = CARO
b 1889   b 1891

(9)

Jacques   Harold   Lynn E. = Marilyn   Barbara = Harold   Mary Emma = Julius F.
TOMES   dh Mar 2005 WEBRE   BEVAN   b 1939 | PRINZ III
                              dh Mar 2005   Commercial airline (Delta) pilot for 30 years
                                                                        (m 1960)

(10)

Amanda   Lynn Jr = Darlene   Harold   John   Diane   Jacqueline   Karen   Michael   Nancy   Jacqueline   Gary   Julie = Rick
TOMES   BEVAN   BEVAN   PRINZ
Living in   d 13 Dec
San Francisco   2004,
in 2004   aged 48

3 ch

(11)

Lynn
TOMES III

Generation
(5)

<PAGE 2/A5>

(6)

[PAGE 2/A8]>

August = Amelia
OLSON : OLSON
b 1857 ; b 1858,
Sweden ; Sweden,
d 1930, ; d 1899,
Duluth, MN ; Duluth, MN

Oscar = Anna Maria
OLSON : JOHNSON
b 4 Apr 1856, ; b 23 Nov 1857,
Sweden ; Sweden,
d 10 Jul 1924, ; d 9 Mar 1938,
Duluth, MN ; Duluth, MN

<PAGE 2/A8>

<PAGE 2/A6]
<PAGE 2/A6>

Fred Oscar = Anna Amelia
OLSON : OLSON
b 13 Dec 1889, ; b 31 May 1886,
d 7 Aug 1979, ; W. Duluth, MN,
both Duluth, MN ; d 12 Dec 1959

Emily Randall = Frederick A.
b 5 Sep 1869, FLAGG
Englewood, NJ d 1916

(7)

John Randall = Hulda Maria
b 8 Nov 1867, TENTELIN
New York City b 2 Sep 1881,
d 15 Dec 1932, Jssasjärvi, Finland
Aurora, MN d 15 Jun 1946,
Aurora, MN

Helen Adele = Clifford
b 31 Aug 1913 Henry
d 5 Dec 1988 LAKOSKY
(m 1936)

Arthur ('Art') Charles = Beverly Lois
b 28 Dec 1920, OLSON
Aurora, MN b 7 Jan 1922,
Bomber Pilot (Capt.) Duluth, MN
Far East, WW2
(m 20 Dec 1947, Duluth, St Louis, MN)

John Randall = Karen Ann
b 10 Nov 1958 HANSON
b 1 Aug 1959,
Grand Forks, ND
[2]

John Randall = Dorthea
('Jack') TOMES HELENIUS
b 2 Jun 1910 b 1 Mar 1909
d 30 Jun 1994 d 18 Jun 1983
(m 15 Jun 1945)

Susan Adele = Daniel John
b 25 Jan 1957 CACICH
b 26 Dec 1957
(m 15 Apr 1983)
(div 5 Mar 2001)

Jennifer Marie
TOMES
b 23 May 1982

Randall Allen
b 29 May 1985

Joseph Charles
b 30 Sep 1987

Mary Elizabeth = Gary Arthur
b 22 Sep 1955 YANAGITA
(m 20 Dec 1986)

Nichole Adele
CACICH
b 21 Nov 1986

Danielle Jean
b 19 Jun 2000

Bryan Tomes
YANAGITA
b 5 Apr 1992

David Tomes
b 23 Jul 1994

Agnes Adelaide = Arthur Winchester
b 17 Sep 1866, CHILDS
New York Of Boston
b 29 Mar 1859
(m 28 Oct 1885, St Michaels, Brattleboro, VT)

Charles
Kamner
Randall
b 15 Jul 1898,
Brattleboro, VT

(8)

Walter Haldon = Lynder
CHILDS COURSER
b 1 Apr 1888, b 13 Jan 1891
Brattleboro, VT d 13 Jun 1985
d 23 Oct 1963

Helen
Louise
Randall
b 30 Apr 1890,
Brattleboro, VT

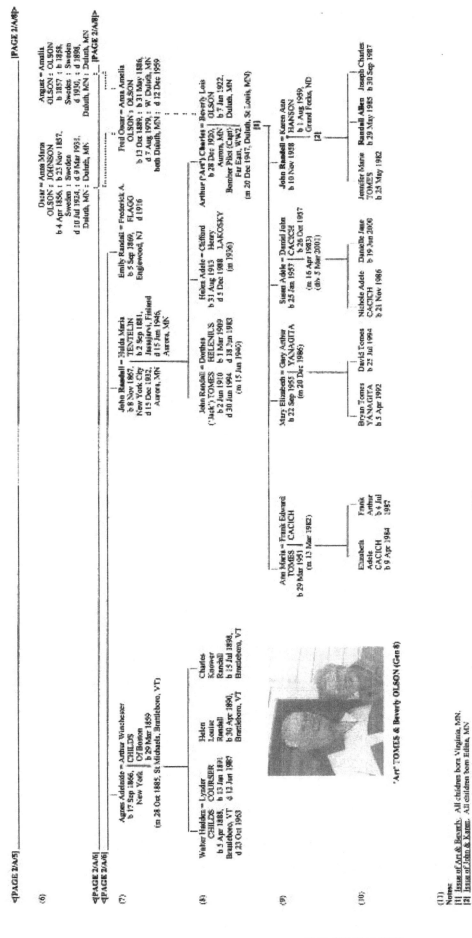

(9)

Ann Maria = Frank Edward
TOMES CACICH
b 29 Mar 1951
(m 13 Mar 1982)

(10)

Elizabeth
Adele
CACICH
b 9 Apr 1984

Frank
Arthur
b 4 Jul 1987

"Art" TOMES & Beverly OLSON (Gen 8)

(11)
Notes:
[1] Issue of Art & Beverly: All children born Virginia, MN.
[2] Issue of John & Karen: All children born Edina, MN

- 2/A7 -

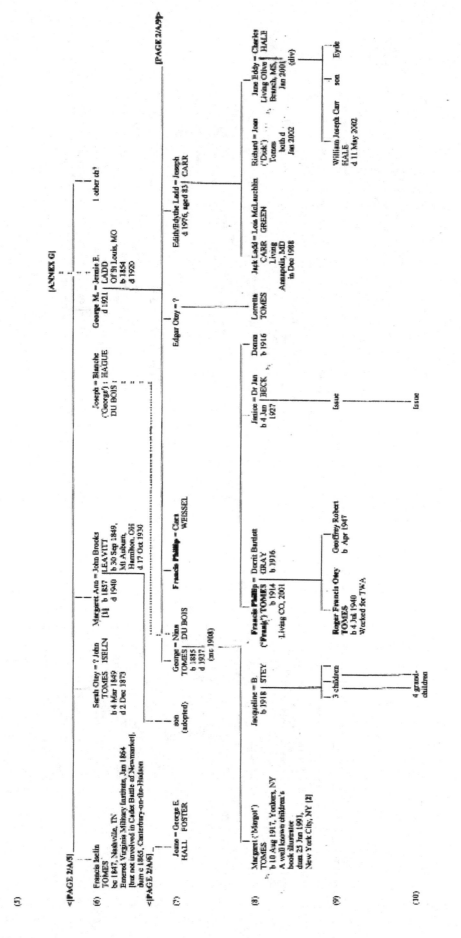

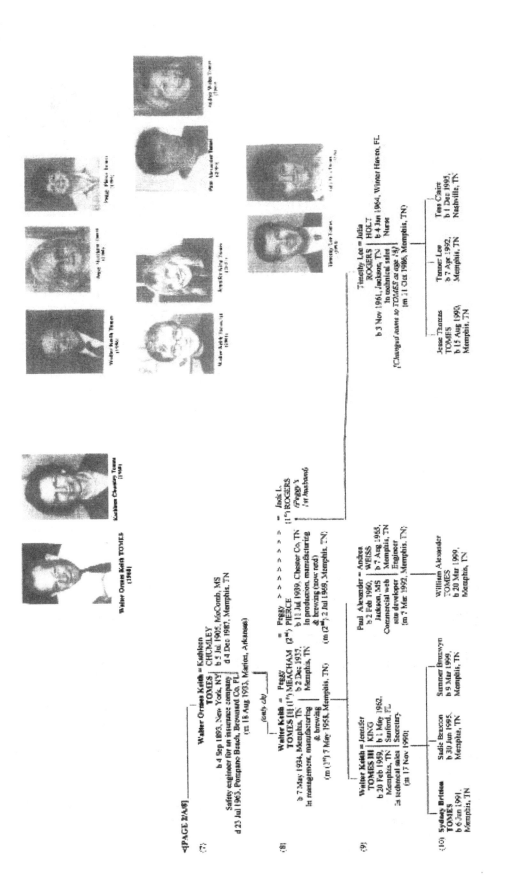

Walter Ormes Keith TOMES (1960)

Kathleen Chumley Tomes (1960)

Walter Keith Tomes (1960)

Janet Maitland Tomes (1960)

Douglas Pierce Tomes (1961)

Walter Keith Tomes III (1961)

Angela Kristin Tomes (2007)

Ryan Alexander Tomes (2009)

Timothy Lee Tomes (2001)

[PAGE 248]

(7) Walter Ormes Keith = Kathleen
    TOMES   CHUMLEY
    b 4 Sep 1893, New York, NY | b 5 Jul 1905, McComb, MS
    d 23 Jul 1963, Pompano Beach, Broward Co, FL | d 4 Dec 1987, Memphis, TN
    Safety engineer for an insurance company
    (m 18 Aug 1933, Marion, Arkansas)

(8) Walter Keith = Peggy > > > > > > > > = Jack L.
    TOMES III | (1st) MEACHAM (2nd) PIERCE   (1st) ROGERS
    b 7 May 1934, | b 2 Dec 1937,   (Peggy's
    Memphis, TN | Memphis, TN   1st husband)
    In management, manufacturing   b 13 Jul 1939, Chester Co, TN
    & brewing   In production, manufacturing
    (m (3rd) 7 Mar 1958, Memphis, TN)   & brewing (now red)
        (m (2nd) 2 Jul 1959, Memphis, TN)

(9) Walter Keith = Jennifer   Paul Alexander = Andrea   Timothy Lee = Julia
    TOMES | KING   b 2 Feb 1960, | WEISS   ROGERS | HOLT
    b 30 Feb 1959, | b 1 May 1962,   Jackson, MS | b 7 Aug 1965,   b 3 Nov 1961, Jackson, TN | b 4 Jan 1964, Winter Haven, FL
    Memphis, TN | Sanford, FL   Commercial web | Memphis, TN   In technical sales | Nurse
    In technical sales | Secretary   site developer | Engineer   (Changed name to TOMES at age 19)
    (m 17 Nov 1990)   (m 7 Mar 1992, Memphis, TN)   (m 31 Oct 1986, Memphis, TN)

(10) Sydney Britton   Sadie Braxton   Summer Bronwyn   William Alexander   Jesse Thomas   Tanner Lee   Tess Claire
    TOMES   b 30 Jun 1995,   b 9 Mar 1999,   TOMES   TOMES   b 7 Apr 1992,   b 1 Dec 1995,
    b 6 Jan 1991,   Memphis, TN   Memphis, TN   b 20 Mar 1999,   b 15 Aug 1990,   Memphis, TN   Nashville, TN
    Memphis, TN   Memphis, TN   Memphis, TN

Notes:
[1] Walter Keith (Gen 8)   Provided the Pedigree information on this page

- 249 -

FAMILY OF ROBERT TOMES AND CATHERINE FASNET

Generation

(5)

[PAGE 2/A]

Robert = **Catherine**
TOMES | FASNET (nee FASSNACHT)
b 27 Mar 1817, New York | Of Wiesbaden, Germany
| b 28 Jun 1839
| d 11 Aug 1923

Doctor, writer publisher & literary patron, Friend of author H. Melville & Evert Duyckinck. Lived in Wiesbaden, Germany, in his later years d 28 Aug 1882

(m 1860)

[PAGE 2/A/1]▶

(6)

Catherine M Fasnet TOMES
b 25 Sep 1860
than 22 Sep 1920,
New York City

Arthur Lloyd = James F.
TOMES | SCHACHE
b 11 Apr 1863, Williamsburg, VA, | b 20 Feb 1877,
Lawyer in 'Tomes, Shell & | New York, NY
Palmer' in New York | d 10 Oct 1959,
d 17 Aug 1922, Brooklyn, NY | Taunton, MA

(m 12 Aug 1901)

Thomas Pelin = Elizabeth = Thomas
| LEWRY : DUNKLEY | FITZ-
Of Brooklyn | PATRICK
b Jan 1873 : | Of
d 3 Aug 1913 : | Brooklyn
(m 14 Nov 1898) | (Her 2nd
| husband)

[PAGE 2/A/1]▶

(7)

Margaret Earlie = Edward Thomas
TOMES | LEWRY
b 6 Dec 1903, | b 13 Jan 1900,
Brooklyn, NY | New York, NY
d 28 Mar 1984, | d 14 Feb 1982,
Taunton, MA | Taunton, MA

(m 12 Oct 1923)

(8)

Robert Edward = Eugenia ('Jeanne') = Robert B.
LEWRY | BUTLER | STILLWELL
b 5 Jul 1922, | b 28 Dec 1931, | [her 2nd
Brooklyn, NY | Taunton, MA. | husband]
d 24 Nov 1993, |
Taunton, MA. | (m 18 Jan 1997)

(m 12 Oct 1948)

Jeanne Margaret
b 1 May 1935,
Taunton, MA

Richard Tomes = Michele
b 11 Mar 1939,
Taunton, MA.
(m 30 May 1982)

[PAGE 2/A/1]▶

(9)

David Edward = Kathleen Doe;
LEWRY | LEWRY
b 10 Jul 1949, | b 1 Aug 1951,
Taunton, MA. | Taunton, MA.

(m 5 Jun 1971)

Carol Jean = Daniel = Josie
b 28 Sep 1951, (1st) RAPOZA (2nd) FRAUSE
Taunton, MA. | b 28 Jul 1931
| Taunton, MA.

(m. 1st, 14 Sep 1975) (m. 2nd, 23 Oct 1997)

Lori Jean
RAPOZA
b 23 May 1979,
Taunton, MA

Noel Antoinette LEWRY
b 21 Jan 1985,
Taunton, MA

Nicholas Robert Tomes
b 8 Aug 1997,
Taunton, MA

b 4 Nov 1965,
Taunton, MA

(10)

Jennifer = David M
LEWRY | NICOL
b 1 Sep 1973,
Taunton, MA

(m 30 Jun 1996)

Kathleen
b 17 Aug 1977,
Taunton, MA

(11)

Skya Maureen NICOL
b 24 Sep 2001

Justine Amber LEWRY
b 17 Oct 1996,
Taunton, MA

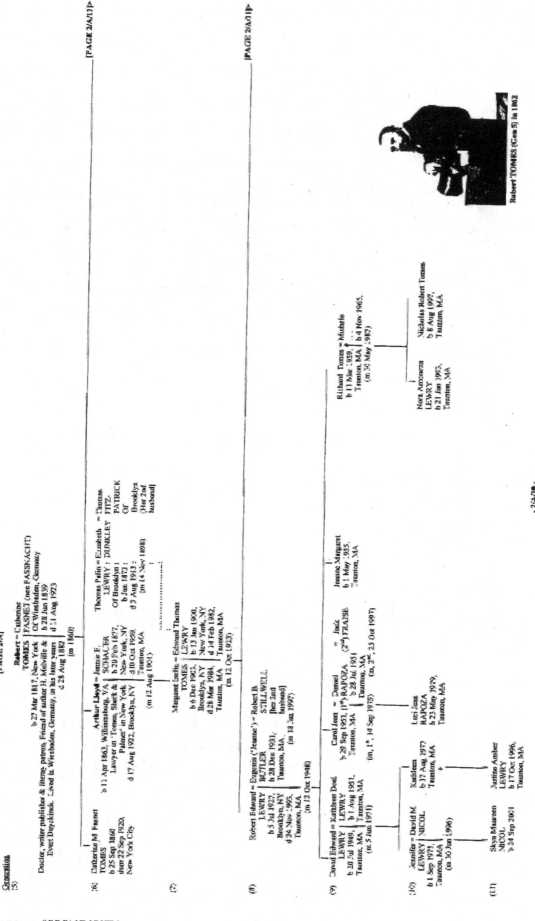

Robert TOMES (Gen 5) in 1862

Generation
(5)

<[PAGE 2/A/10]

(6)

[ANNEX F]

William Austin = Julia> > > = Gertrude
TOMES (1st) HALL [2nd]
b 14 Feb 1863, Williamsburg   b 1870, Boonsboro
A better   d 1945,
d 28 Jun 1920, Brooklyn, NY   Evanston, IL
(m 1st, 1887)   (m. 2nd 1919?)
(div 1908)

[PAGE 2/A/12]P

Yvonne = ...   Valerie = Arthur
TOMES | BOWEN   LETHBRIDGE

Issue   issue

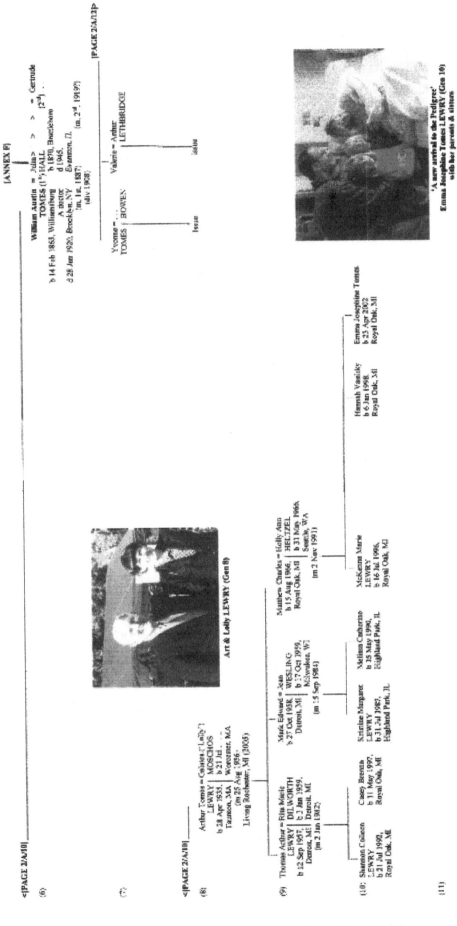

'A new arrival to the Pedigree'
Emma Josephine Tomes LEWRY (Gen 10)
with her parents & sisters

Art & Lelly LEWRY (Gen 8)

<[PAGE 2/A/10]

(7)

<[PAGE 2/A/10]

(8)

Arthur Tomes = Celeste ("Lelly")
LEWRY | MOSCHOS
b 28 Apr 1933,   b 21 Jul ...
Taunton, MA   Worcester, MA
(m 25 Aug 1956;
Living Rochester, MI (2005)

Matthew Charles = Holly Ann
LEWRY   HELTZEL
b 15 Aug 1966,   b 31 May 1966,
Royal Oak, MI   Seattle, WA
(m 2 Nov 1991)

Mark Edward = Jean
LEWRY | WESLING
b 27 Oct 1958,   b 17 Oct 1959,
Detroit, MI   Milwaukee, WI
(m 15 Sep 1984)

(9)

Thomas Arthur = Rita Marie
LEWRY | DILWORTH
b 12 Sep 1957,   b 3 Jan 1959,
Detroit, MI   Detroit, MI
(m 2 Jan 1982)

Hannah Vassiliky   Emma Josephine Tomes
b 6 Jan 1998,   b 23 Apr 2002,
Royal Oak, MI   Royal Oak, MI

McKenna Marie
LEWRY
b 16 Jul 1996,
Royal Oak, MI

Melissa Catherine
b 25 May 1990,
Highland Park, IL

Kristine Margaret
LEWRY
b 31 Jul 1987,
Highland Park, IL

(10)

Shannon Colleen
LEWRY
b 21 Jul 1992,
Royal Oak, MI

Casey Steven
b 11 May 1997,
Royal Oak, MI

(11)

- 2/A/11 -

(5)

(Rear) Robert Steel TOMES, Cynthia ZELTWANGER, Josie RAYMALEY, John Wilson TOMES,
Jennifer HARRINGTON, Elizabeth Austin SANDBO, Elizabeth Austin TOMES, Scott Edwards SANDBO.
(Front) Julia Hall TOMES, Jim TOMES
(Jun 1994 picture)

(6)

<[PAGE 2/A/11] _____   [ANNEX H]

(7)

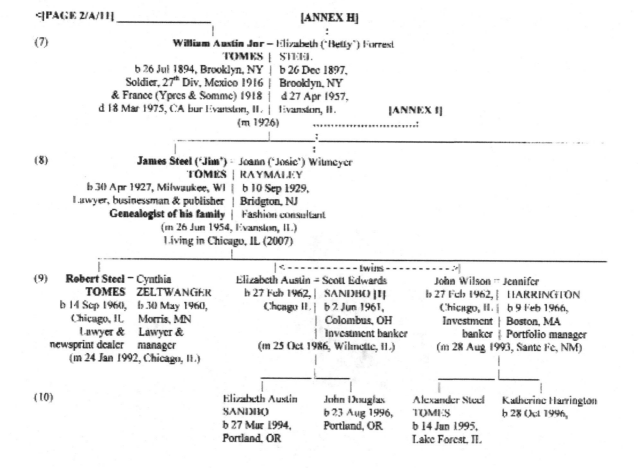

William Austin Jnr – Elizabeth ('Betty') Forrest
TOMES | STEEL,
b 26 Jul 1894, Brooklyn, NY | b 26 Dec 1897,
Soldier, 27th Div, Mexico 1916 | Brooklyn, NY
& France (Ypres & Somme) 1918 | d 27 Apr 1957,
d 18 Mar 1975, CA bur Evanston, IL | Evanston, IL.   [ANNEX I]
(m 1926)

(8)

James Steel ('Jim') – Joann ('Josie') Witmeyer
TOMES | RAYMALEY
b 30 Apr 1927, Milwaukee, WI | b 10 Sep 1929,
Lawyer, businessman & publisher | Bridgton, NJ
Genealogist of his family | Fashion consultant
(m 26 Jun 1954, Evanston, IL.)
Living in Chicago, IL (2007)

(9)

Robert Steel – Cynthia	Elizabeth Austin = Scott Edwards	John Wilson = Jennifer
TOMES ZELTWANGER	b 27 Feb 1962,	SANDBO [1]	b 27 Feb 1962,	HARRINGTON
b 14 Sep 1960, b 30 May 1960,	Chicago IL.	b 2 Jun 1961,	Chicago, IL.	b 9 Feb 1966,
Chicago, IL Morris, MN		Colombus, OH	Investment	Boston, MA
Lawyer & Lawyer &		Investment banker	banker	Portfolio manager
newsprint dealer manager	(m 25 Oct 1986, Wilmette, IL.)	(m 28 Aug 1993, Sante Fe, NM)
(m 24 Jan 1992, Chicago, IL.)		

|< - - - - - - - - - twins - - - - - - - - - >|

(10)

Elizabeth Austin	John Douglas	Alexander Steel	Katherine Harrington
SANDBO	b 23 Aug 1996,	TOMES	b 28 Oct 1996,
b 27 Mar 1994,	Portland, OR	b 14 Jun 1995,	
Portland, OR		Lake Forest, IL.	

Note:
[1] Scott SANDBO. His grandparents came from England & Norway

_____|PAGE 2/A/12 |ADDN 1|>

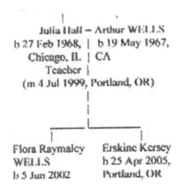

Julia Hall ─ Arthur WELLS
b 27 Feb 1968, | b 19 May 1967,
Chicago, IL | CA
Teacher |
(m 4 Jul 1999, Portland, OR)

Flora Raymalcy   Erskine Kersey
WELLS   b 25 Apr 2005,
b 5 Jun 2002   Portland, OR

Generation

(5)

(6)

(7)

<[PAGE 2/A/12] _____

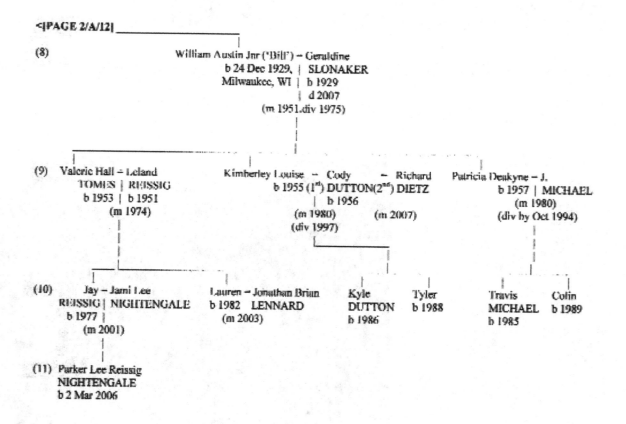

(8)
                    William Austin Jnr ('Bill') — Geraldine
                    b 24 Dec 1929, | SLONAKER
                    Milwaukee, WI | b 1929
                                  | d 2007
                        (m 1951,div 1975)

(9) Valerie Hall = Leland   Kimberley Louise — Cody   — Richard   Patricia Deakyne — J.
     TOMES | REISSIG   b 1955 (1st) DUTTON(2nd) DIETZ   b 1957 | MICHAEL
     b 1953 | b 1951 | b 1956   (m 1980)
        (m 1974)   (m 1980)   (m 2007)   (div by Oct 1994)
                                      (div 1997)

(10) Jay — Jami Lee   Lauren — Jonathan Brian   Kyle   Tyler   Travis   Colin
      REISSIG | NIGHTENGALE   b 1982   LENNARD   DUTTON   b 1988   MICHAEL   b 1989
      b 1977 | (m 2003)   b 1986   b 1985
        (m 2001)

(11) Parker Lee Reissig
     NIGHTENGALE
     b 2 Mar 2006

2/A/12 [ADDN 1]

FAMILY OF MARGARET ANN TOMES & JOHN ISELIN

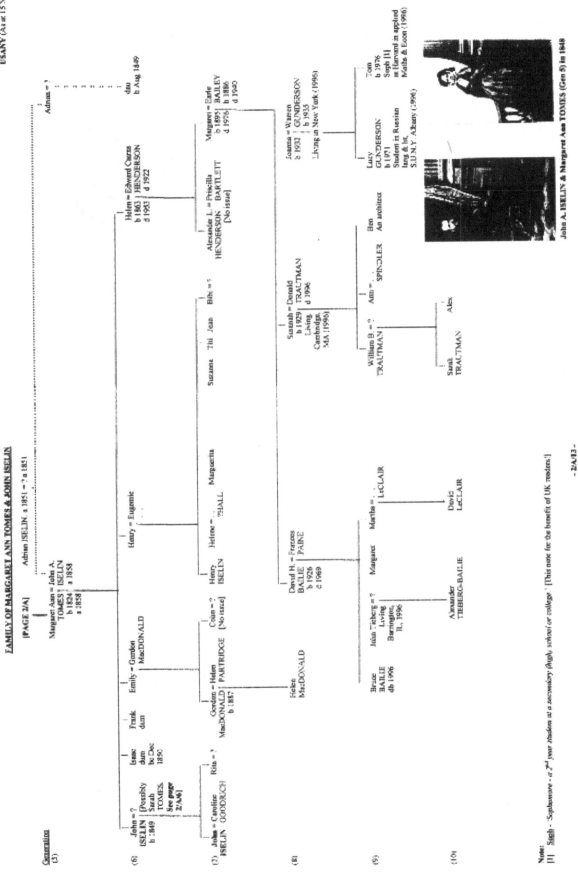

Generation
(5)

Adrian ISELIN. a 1851 = ? a 1851

[PAGE 2/A]

Margaret Ann TOMES = John A. ISELIN
b 1824 b 1858
a 1858

Adrian = ?

dau
b Aug 1849

(6)

John = ? ISELIN [Possibly Sarah TOMES See page 2/A/6] b ?849

Isaac dau bc Dec 1850

Frank dau

Emily = Gordon MacDONALD

Henry = Eugenie

Helen = Edward Cairns HENDERSON d 1922 b 1863 d 1951

(7)

John = Caroline ISELIN GOODRICH

Rita = ?

Gordon = Helen MacDONALD PARTRIDGE b 1887

Colin = ? [No issue]

Henry ISELIN

Helene = ...HALL

Suzanne Til Jean Bibs = ?

Margaretta

Margaret = Earle b 1891 BAILEY d 1976 b 1888 d 1960

Alexander L. = Priscilla HENDERSON BARTLETT [No issue]

(8)

Helen MacDONALD

Donald H. = Frances BAILIE PAINE b 1926 d 1969

Susanah = Donald b 1929 TRAUTMAN Living d 1996 Cambridge, MA (1996)

Joanna = Warren b 1932 GUNDERSON b 1935 Living in New York (1995)

(9)

Bruce BAILIE db 1996

Margaret = John ...ieberg = ? Living Barrington, IL, 1996

Martha = ...LeCLAIR

William B. = ? TRAUTMAN

Ann = ? SPINDLER

Ben An architect

Lucy GUNDERSON b 1971 Student in Russian lang & lit, S.U.N.Y. Albany (1996)

Tom b 1976 Soph [1] at Harvard in applied Maths & Econ (1996)

(10)

Alexander TIEBERG-BAILIE

David LeCLAIR

Sarah TRAUTMAN

Alex TRAUTMAN

John A. ISELIN & Margaret Ann TOMES (Gen 5) in 1848

Note:
[1] Soph - Sophomore - a 2nd year student at a secondary (high) school or college.' [This note for the benefit of UK readers!]

- 2/A/13 -

John C. ZIMMERMAN = Louise HALBACH
b 28 Dec 1786, Eibenhagen, Grand Duchy of Berg, Germany / Remscheid, Germany   (m 1825)
d 28 Feb 1857, New York, NY   d 20 Sep 1863, New York, NY
[PAGE 26A]
[1] .....

Generation (5):

Benjamin = Marie Louise = Rosalie E. M.
TOMES (1st) ZIMMERMAN (2nd) ZIMMERMAN
b 27 Sep 1825   b 17 Nov 1829,   b 14 Sep 1836,
d 1 Jun 1895 [2]   Buenos Ayres   Buenos Ayres
(m2 Oct 1849)   d 27 Sep 1900 [2]

Generation (6):

Louise TOMES d/um

Anna Zimmerman ('Annie'?) b 18 Sep 1853 d/um 29 Feb 1920 [2]

Mary Elizabeth b 23 Jun 1855 d/um 1 Jan 1890 [2]

Benjamin Langspoon ('Benito'?) TOMES b 23 Oct 1859 d 30 Oct 1937 [2]

Edward b 18 Oct 1860 d/um 25 May 1939 [2]

Helen R. b 16 Oct 1863 d/um 30 Dec 1954 [2]

Leonora b 8 Nov 1865 d/um 3 Feb 1941 [2]

Isabella = Rev Frederick A. MacMILLAN [No issue] d 22 Dec 1943 [2]

Margaret = Rev B. Duvall CHAMBERS [No issue] d 11 Nov 1928 [2]

Generation (7)

Generation (8)

Generation (9)

Benjamin TOMES (Gen 5) in 1866

Notes:
[1] ZIMMERMAN Family. All that had originally been known was that Benjamin mar, 1st, Louisa ZIMMERMAN, c Oct 1849 and second Rosalie ZIMMERMAN, b 1836, d 27 Sep 1900. The additional details shown were subsequently extracted in 2002, from the web site, www.ancestry.com. This seemingly shows that Benjamin's wives were sisters & both born in Buenos Ayres. One can though only perhaps conjecture that Marie died & Benjamin then married her sister. One wonders what the law on this was in the USA at that time. The web site though only shows Louisa's husband was Benjamin & gives no marriage or death details for her. The site gives no details of a spouse of Rosalie. [2]

a. Benjamin (Gen 5), his second wife, Rosalie, and all his children (except the first, Louisa), are buried in the same plot in Trinity City cemetery, New York City. Curiously the grave markers for Isabella & Margaret (which gives no date of birth), records them under their maiden name of TOMES & stating they were the 'wife of' the husbands shown - so why were they not buried under their married names and with their husbands?

b. The main memorial though at the site shows, only partially readable, "Hermann ZIMMERMANN [two 'N's] 28 Apr 1802 aged 79 years and his wife Mary E. ZIMMERMANN died 2 Dec 1913 in her 87th year,' but they have not been identified.

- 2/3/16 -

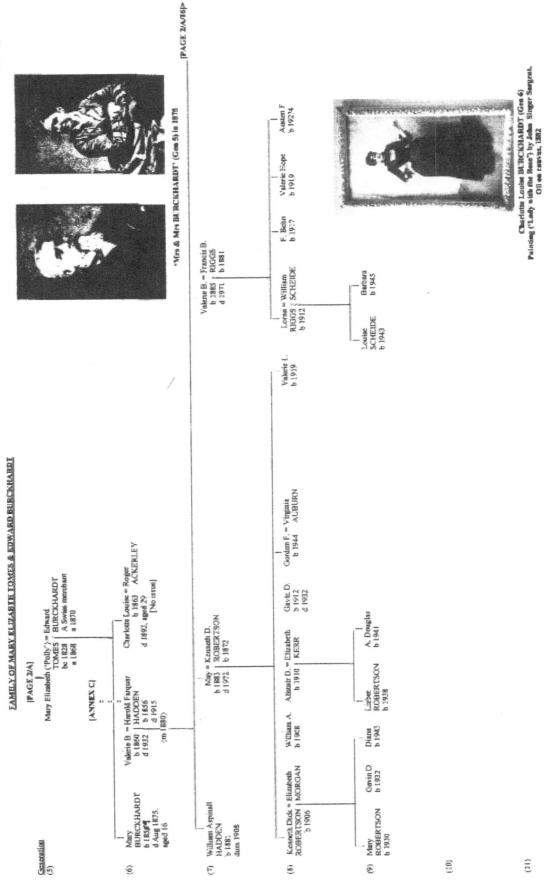

FAMILY OF MARY ELIZABETH TOMES & EDWARD BURCKHARDT

[PAGE 2/A]

Generation
(5)

Mary Elizabeth ("Polly") = Edward
TOMES | BURCKHARDT
bc 1828 | A. Swiss merchant
d 1868 | d 1870

[ANNEX C]

(6)
Mary
BURCKHARDT
b 185[?]
d Aug 1875,
aged 16

Valerie B. = Harold Farquar
b 1860 | HADDEN
d 1922 | b 1856
 | d 1915
(m 1880?)

Charlotte Louise = Roger
b 1863 | ACKERLEY
d 1892, aged 29
[No issue]

Valerie B. = Francis B.
b 1885 | RIGGS
d 1971 | b 1881

"Mrs & Mrs BURCKHARDT' (Gen 5) in 1875

[PAGE 2/A/6P>

(7)
William Aspinall
HADDEN
b 1881
d.un 1908

May = Kenneth D.
b 1883 | ROBERTSON
d 1951 | b 1872

F. Bein
b 1917

Valerie Hope
b 1919

Austen F
b 192?4

Lorna = William
RIGGS | SCHEIDE
b 1912

(8)
Kenneth Dick = Elizabeth
ROBERTSON | MORGAN
b 1906

William A.
b 1908

Alastair D. = Elizabeth
b 1910 | KERR

Gavin D.
b 1912
d 1932

Gordon F. = Virginia
b 1944 | AUBURN

Valerie L.
b 1919

Louise
SCHEIDE
b 1943

Barbara
b 1945

(9)
Mary
ROBERTSON
b 1930

Gavin D
b 1932

Diana
b 1943

Lizbet
ROBERTSON
b 1938

A. Douglas
b 1941

(10)

(11)

Charlotte Louise BURCKHARDT (Gen 6)
Painting ('Lady with the Rose') by John Singer Sargent,
Oil on canvas, 1882

- 2/A/15 -

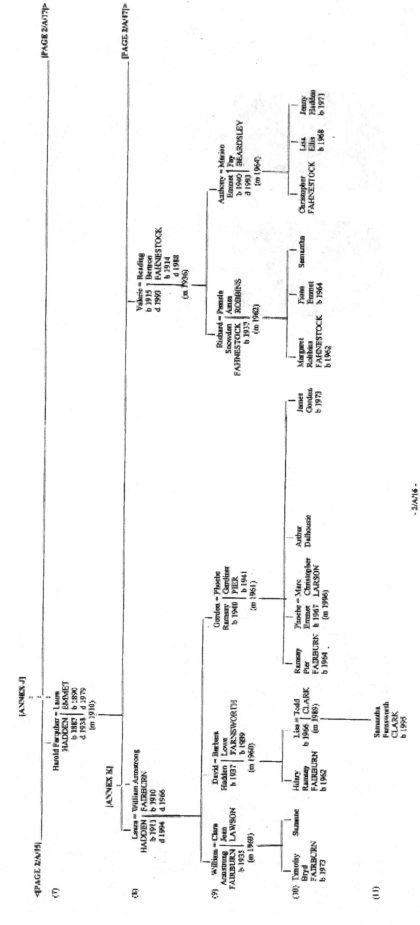

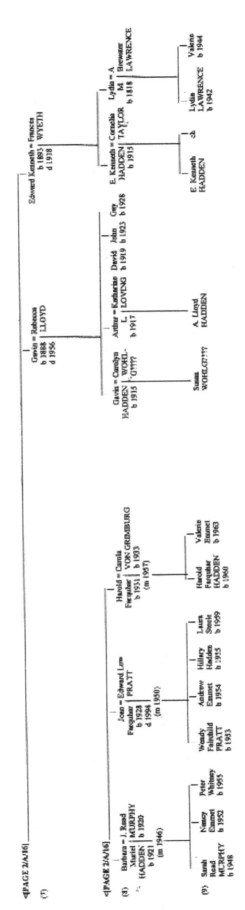

Edward Kenneth = Frances WYETH
b 1893
d 1918

Gwin = Rebecca LLOYD
b 1888
d 1956

E. Kenneth = Cornelia HADDEN TAYLOR
b 1915

Lydia = A. Brewster M LAWRENCE
b 1818

Lydia LAWRENCE
b 1942

Valerie
b 1944

E. Kenneth HADDEN
db

Arthur = Katharine L. LOVING
b 1917

David b 1919   John b 1923   Guy b 1926

A. Lloyd HADDEN

Gavin = Carolyn WOHLGT???? HADDEN
b 1915

Susan WOHLGT????

Harold = Carola VON GRIMBURG Farquhar
b 1931   b 1933
(m 1957)

Harold Farquhar HADDEN
b 1960

Valerie Emmet
b 1963

Joan = Edward Lom PRATT Farquhar
b 1928
d 1994
(m 1950)

Wendy Fairchild PRATT
b 1953

Andrew Emmet
b 1954

Hillary Hadden
b 1955

Laura Steele
b 1959

Barbara = J. Reed MURPHY Muriel HADDEN
b 1921   b 1920
(m 1946)

Sarah Read MURPHY
b 1948

Nancy Emmet
b 1952

Peter Whitney
b 1955

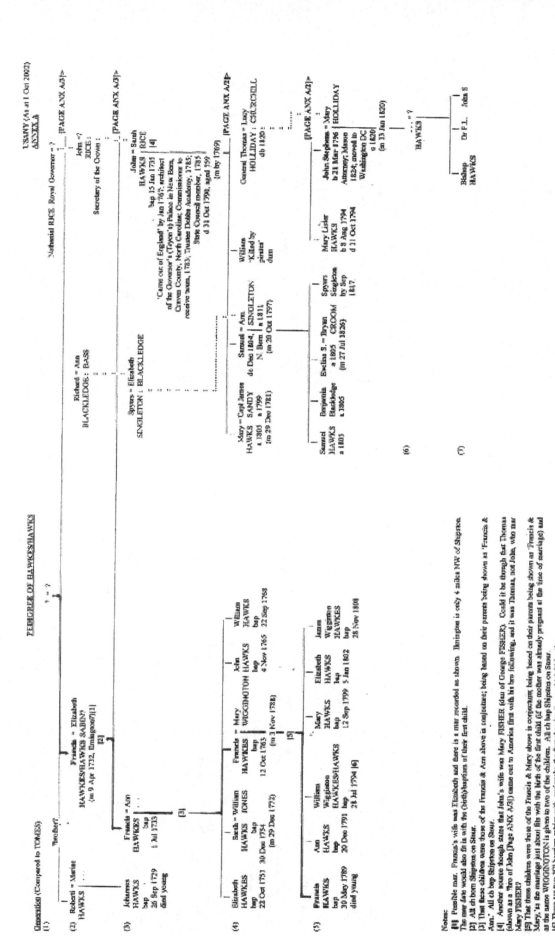

PEDIGREE OF HAWKES/HAWKS

USANY (As at 1 Oct 2002)
ANNEX A

Generation (Compared to TOMES)

(1) ? = ?   "See Bury?"

Nathaniel RICE, Royal Governor = ?   [PAGE ANX A3]>

(2) Robert = Maurice? HAWKES | Francis = Elizabeth HAWKES/HAWKS : SABIN? (m 9 Apr 1732, [linksgood?]) [1]

Richard = Ann BLACKLEDGE : BASS

John = ? RICE : Secretary of the Crown :   [PAGE ANX A3]>

(3) Johanna HAWKS bap 26 Sep 1729 died young | Francis = Ann HAWKES bap 4 Jul 1733 [3]

Spyers = Elizabeth SINGLETON : BLACKLEDGE

John = Sarah HAWKS RICE Sep 15 Jan 1735 [4] 'Came out of England' by Jan 1765; architect of the Governor's (Tryon's) Palace in New Bern, Craven County, North Carolina; Commissioner to receive taxes, 1783; Trustee Dobbs Academy, 1785; State Council member, 1785; d 31 Oct 1790, aged 59 [m by 1769]

General Thomas = Lucy HOLLIDAY : CHURCHILL db 1820 :   [PAGE ANX A2]>

(4) Elizabeth HAWKS bap 22 Oct 1751 | Sarah = William HAWKS JONES bap 30 Dec 1754 (m 29 Dec 1772) | Francis = Mary HAWKES WIGGINGTON bap 12 Oct 1763 (m 3 Nov 1788) [5] | John HAWKS bap 4 Nov 1765 | William HAWKES bap 22 Sep 1768

William "Killed by pirates" dsm | Mary = Capt James HAWKS SANDY n 1803 n 1799 (m 29 Dec 1781) | Samuel = Ann de Dec 1804, SINGLETON N. Bern n 1811 (m 20 Oct 1797)

Mary Lisler HAWKS b 8 Aug 1794 d 31 Oct 1794

John Stephens = Mary HAWKES HOLLIDAY b 21 Mar 1796 Attorney; Mason 1824, moved to Washington DC o 1820 (m 13 Jun 1820)   [PAGE ANX A3]>

(5) Francis HAWKS bap 30 May 1789 died young | Ann HAWKS bap 29 Dec 1791 | William Wigginton HAWKES/HAWKS bap 28 Jul 1794 [6]

Mary HAWKS bap 12 Sep 1799 | Elizabeth HAWKS bap 5 Jun 1802 | James Wigginton HAWKES bap 28 Nov 1809

Samuel HAWKS n 1805 | Benjamin Blackledge n 1805 | Evelina S. = Bryan CROOM (m 27 Jul 1826) n 1805 | Spyers Singleton by Sep 1817

HAWKS = ?

Bishop HAWKS | Dr F.L. | John S

(6)

(7)

Notes:

[1] Possible mar. Francis's wife was Elizabeth and there is a mar recorded as shown. Ilmington is only 4 miles NW of Shipston. The mar date would also fit in with the (birth)baptism of their first child.

[2] All ch born Shipston on Stour.

[3] That these children were those of the Francis & Ann above is conjecture; being based on their parents being shown as 'Francis & Ann.' All ch bap Shipston on Stour.

[4] Another source though states that John's wife was Mary FISHER (dau of George FISHER). Could it be through that Thomas (shown as a 'bro of John [Page ANX A3]) came out to America first with his bro following, and it was Thomas, and John, who mar Mary FISHER?

[5] That these children were those of the Francis & Mary above is conjecture, being based on their parents being shown as 'Francis & Mary, 'In the marriage just about fits with the birth of the first child (if the mother was already pregnant at the time of marriage) and as the name WIGGINGTON is given to two of the children. All ch bap Shipston on Stour.

[6] There are two JOII baptism entries with, curiously, the first showing it as an 'Adult' baptism.

- ANX A/1 -

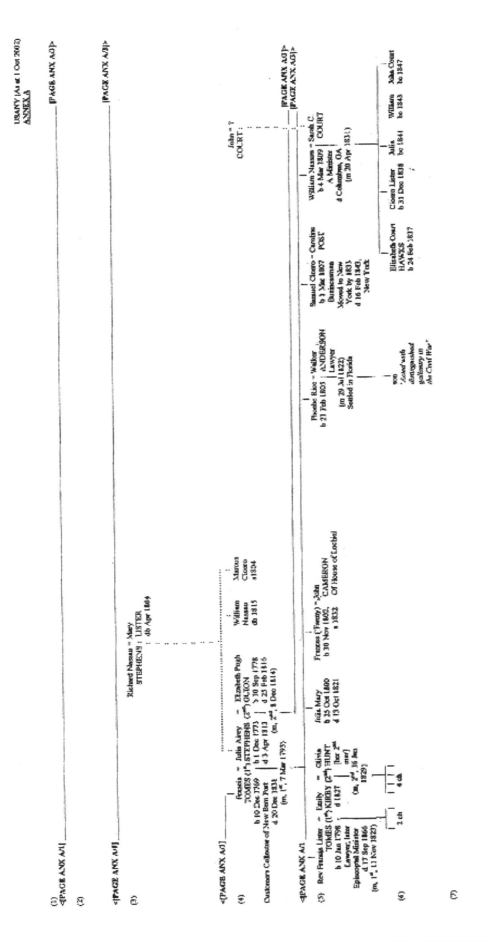

(1)

<PAGE ANX A/1]

(2)

<[PAGE ANX A/2]

(3)

'brother?' 'brother?' 'sister*' 'brother?'

John = Elizabeth
HAWKES
....

Mary = John
HAWKES BOWLER,
[1] + (m 9 Feb 1752,
Shipston on
Stour)

William = Sarah

John   Martha   Mary
HAWKES   HAWKES   HAWKES   James
bap   bap   bap   HAWKES
20 Jan 1734,   5 Mar 1736   3 Jul 1746
Shipston   Shipston   Shipston   Mary
on Stour   on Stour   on Stour   HAWKES
                                        [Illegitimate]   bap
                                                                         18 Sep 1772
                                                                         Shipston
                                                                         on Stour

Samuel = Mary
HAWKES ....
bap 21 Jan 1737
Shipston on Stour

Ann   Elizabeth = William   Sarah = Richard   Thomas = Mary
bap 1 Feb   bap 1 Jan 1744,   CLARK   bap 28 Aug 1759   ....
1736(39?)   Shipston   1743   in USA,
Shipston   on Stour   Shipston on   db Nov 1772
on Stour   (m 12 Aug 1773,   Stour   [3]
                    Shipston on Stour) [2]

                                             [PAGE 2/4]   Mary   John   Ann   Richard
                                                                 HAWKS

(4)

Dr Hugh = ?   James
JONES :   HAWKES
                      bap 22 Sep 1769,
                      Shipston on Stour
                      [4]

<[PAGE ANX A/2]
<[PAGE ANX A/2]

(5)

Cicero Stephen = Ann   Susannah Airey   Infant
HAWKS   JONES   b 2 Apr 1813   (stillborn)
b 26 May 1811   (her mother died 1½   3 Jan 1816
Bishop of Missouri,   hrs after her birth)
1844-68   dum 3 Sep 1843,
d 1868   Columbus, GA
(m 20 Feb 1835)

(6)

(7)

Notes:

[1] Mary. PRes shows Mary, dau of Mary Hawkes, was born illegitimate. It is possible the mother later married John BOWLER.

[2] Elizabeth & William. Their marriage is conjecture.

[3] Thomas. Possibly a son. See also Note [4] on Page ANX A/1.

[4] James. It is supposition he was the son of Samuel & Mary.

A View of Shipston upon Stour.

A Print of c 1796

- ANX A/3 -

262   SERENDIPITY

Map showing locations of Bathgate & Whitburn in Scotland
[From: 1:63,660 map of 1963]

The Parish Church of Whitburn (but known as the South Church since 1929)
Opened in 1731, a cross shaped kirk & the only listed building in the town.
Quite probably where family members were baptised, married and buried.

PEDIGREE OF STEEL [1]

Notes:

[1] The original source material (supplied by Jim TOMES in 1994), showed 'Ebenezer TOMES (Gen 5) born Bathgate, SCT, who married Elizabeth FORREST, with only one son, James, b 1873, Bathgate' with no further details about him and his family. The details now shown of their other children (including James, but born in 1870) and Ebenezer's ancestors have been taken from www.familysearch.com). They seem to tie in exactly with the information previously known. The only variation is that the IGI shows Whitburn throughout, whereas the original source named Bathgate. These two towns are though only some 3 miles apart (see map) and it seems highly probably that the two were (& are) closely linked. Both towns lie about midway between Glasgow & Edinburgh.

- ANN H/1 -

OUR GENEALOGY   263

Fortunes of War, by Robert Tomes, 1864 Harper's Magazine

List of Books Authored by Dr Robert Tomes

Eulogy of Alexander Hadden Tomes, Jr. by Jim Tomes

Himeji Address by Art Tomes

Where Are the Christians? by Jim Tomes

Complete Hawks Family Genealogy

APPENDIX

The Fortunes Of War
How They Are Made And Spent
*Reprinted in Harper's 150th
Anniversary Edition 2000*
July 1864

By Robert Tomes

The strangest and most frequently repeated boasts – for boasts we make, such is our national vanity, on all occasions whether of prosperity or adversity - is that we don't feel this war. Above the shock of battle, the groans of the wounded and dying, he sobs of the bereaved, the murmurs of defeat, and the shouts of victory, rises the triumphant exclamation, we don't feel it! Is this insensibility? Is it the delight in ruin? Is it indifference to failure or success? No! It is worse than either of these, for it embraces them all; it is the chuckling of gain over its pockets filling with the treasure of the country, while our brave soldiers are pouring out their blood in its defense.

We don't feel the war! Is the exulting cry of the contractors, moneychangers, and speculators, whose shouts of revel stifle the tearful voice of misery. It is in our large cities especially where this boasted insensibility to the havoc of war is found. It is there in the market place and exchange, where fortunes are being made with such marvelous rapidity, and in the haunts of pleasure, where they are being spent with such wanton extravagance, that they don't feel this war. They are at a banquet of abundance and light, from which they are not to be unseated, though the ghosts of the hundreds of thousands of their slaughtered countrymen shake their gory locks at them.

While the national wealth has been poured out with a profuse generosity in behalf of a cause dear to the national heart, there have been immense fortunes made by enterprising money-getters, seeking only to fill their own pockets.

When the war suddenly burst upon the nation, and before it was able to arouse its gigantic energies, the Government was so helpless that it besought aid at any cost. It was then, as our brave fellow-citizens came forward in multitudes to defend their country, there arose an urgent command for arms, clothing, and subsistence. Every thing required for the use and consumption of the soldier was wanted, and wanted at once. Tents and blankets to protect him from the weather-clothes, from cap to shoe, to dress him - bread and meat and all the varied necessaries of the daily ration, even to the salt, to feed him-the knapsack, haversack, belt, and cartridge box, to equip him - muskets, pistols, cannon, swords, sabers, powder, shot, and percussion caps to fight with horses and mules, wagons, railways, steam and sailing vessels of all kinds, for transportation.

A hundred thousand men or more in the immediate and continued want, not only of all the ordinary necessaries of life, but of the many additional requirements for war, were to be provided for without delay. The Government with a commissariat organized only for an army of some sixteen thousand soldiers, and suddenly called upon to clothe, arm, and subsist more than six times the number, could do nothing but appeal to the enterprise of trade to supply its pressing necessities. The appeal, with the treasure of the whole nation to sustain it, was not made in vain. Another army - the army of contractors-then came forward no less promptly than the hundred thousands of citizen soldiers.

These with their lives as their offering asking nothing in exchange, and-receiving only a bare subsistence; the former, no less liberal of the contents of their docks, ships, fields, stables, granaries, warehouses, and shops, demanding a great price, and getting it.

Think of the immense activity with which trade was inspired by the numerous and multifarious demands of the Government! Contractors for meat, contractors for bread, contractors for tents, contractors for clothing, contractors for arms, contractors for ammunition, contractors for equipments, contractors for wagons, contractors for horses, contractors for mules, contractors for forage, contractors for railway conveyance, contractors for steamers, contractors for ships, contractors for coal, contractors for hospitals, contractors for surgical instruments, contractors for drugs, and contractors for every thing else required for human use and consumption in order not only to sustain life but to destroy it, suddenly started into existence. The Government, pressed by a necessity, which admitted of no hesitation in regard to time, character, quantity, quality, and cost, accepted almost every offer, and paid almost any price. It is true, that political allies and social friends and relatives were favored with the earliest information and the best places in the general race and scramble for the national treasure. That eager partisans and devoted brothers, cousins and brothers-in-law, having taken the shortest road, should come in. ahead and grasp the first and biggest prizes, was not unnatural. There was one of these lucky favorites who made a fortune of a hundred thousands dollars or more as easily as these words which state the fact are written. Having secured a contract or agency for the purchase of transport steamers and other vessels, he fulfilled it with no more cost to himself than a cigar or two over the preliminary negotiation, and no greater effort than signing his name. The fortune was made by a minimum of personal labor given and a maximum of pay received.

The contractors of all kinds, with their contracts signed and sealed, hastened to pocket the profits. In many cases, with a mere dash of their pens, they transferred their bargains at an advance, and made snug fortunes, without the labor of an hour or the expense of a shilling. In other instances they fulfilled their contracts in a way more prof¬itable to themselves than useful to the Government. The quality of the article they heeded little, provided it bore the name and the semblance of the thing, and could be had for almost nothing, or for much less than they were to receive for it. Thus shoddy, a villainous compound, the refuse stuff and sweepings of the shop, pounded, rolled, glued, and smoothed to the external form and gloss of cloth, but no more like the genuine article than the shadow is to the substance, was hastily got up,

at the smallest expense, and supplied to the Government at the greatest. Our soldiers, on the first day's march, or in the earliest storm, found their clothes, over-coats, and blankets, scattering to the winds in rags, or dissolving into their primitive elements of dust under the pelting rain. Splendid looking warriors today, in their brand new uniforms! Tomorrow, in their rags and nakedness more pitiful objects than the ragged regiment of Falstaff, without a whole shirt among 'em! Shoddy, with the external gloss and form of a substantial thing but with the inherent weakness and solubility of its reflected image, has ever since become a word, in the vocabulary of the people, always quick in their forcible and incisive rhetoric to catch and appropriate a simple and expressive figure to represent a familiar idea. [...]

It was not only in the contracts for clothing, but in those for almost every other supply that Government paying for the substance was mocked by the shadow. For sugar it often got sand; for coffee, rye; for leather, something no better than brown paper; for sound horses and mules, spavined beasts and dying donkeys; and for serviceable muskets and pistols the experimental failures of sanguine inventors, or the refuse of shops and foreign armories. There was, it is true, a show of caution on the part of the authorities in the form of a Governmental inspection; but the object of this was often thwarted by haste, negligence, collusion, or favoritism. [...]

There were fifty millions of dollars spent by the Government in a few months, at the beginning of the war, for arms alone. Out of this a dozen or more contractors enriched themselves for life. Poor men thus became rich between the rising and setting of the same day's sun; while the hundreds of thousands of dollars of the wealthy increased to millions in the same brief space of time. It is said that one of our great merchant princes gained from his transactions with Government two millions of dollars in a single year.

The proprietors of coalmines came in for a large share of the national treasure. One company made such enormous profits from its supplies of coal to the Government, and the general rise in price in consequence of the increased demand, that it was enabled to declare, in a single year, dividends that, in the aggregate, amounted to two-thirds of its capital. Its stock, which a few years since could hardly tempt a purchaser at ten dollars a share, has arisen since the war to more than two hundred dollars, and is eagerly caught up at that price. One shareholder, in a twelve month, received in dividends no less than a hundred and fifty thousand dollars for a stock which cost him less than that sum, but which he could now sell for a million.

The "good time" of the contractors has, however, now gone. The Government, with the experience of three years war, and with its commissariat thoroughly organized, is no longer at the mercy of the fraudulent and extortionate. In fact, it is said that in some later contracts the Government, more thanks to its luck than shrewdness: has, with the depreciation of the currency and the consequent rise in prices, got the best of the bargain.

As fortunes can be no longer made in a day out of the national treasury the eager money-seekers have taken to the stock exchange to make them out of each other. The rage of speculation - excitement is too mild a word- which has seized the community, and is fast making us a nation of stockjobbers, has never been equaled since the days of John Law during the French regency of the Duc d'Orleans. The city exchanges and their approaches are already crowded with a frenzied throng of eager speculators; as was the Rue de Quincampoix of old. [...] The stranger goes to look at the speculators at the hour of exchange as he does at a collection of wild beasts at feeding-time, and comes away with the same impression, namely, that. in their hunger to get their fill they are ready to devour each other. The prudent citizen turns the street, and shuns the place as dangerous - to his morals and his person. If not tempted to risk his fortune, he is sure to be so hustled by the unruly crowd as to spoil his temper or his clothes, and perhaps endanger his limbs or life.

The passion for stock gambling is fast extending to very class of society. Merchants, mechanics, and traders of all kinds are abandoning their counting houses, their workshops, and their stalls, and thronging into Wall Street. The daily industry, the constant self-denial, the vigilant prudence, the patient expectation necessary to acquire a decent competence are scorned for the chances of making a fortune in a day. The number of brokers has more than quadrupled in a few months; such has been the enormous increase of stock jobbing. Their aggregate business, in the city of New York alone, has arisen from twenty-five to more than a hundred millions a day. The transactions of several sum up to the amount of millions each in a morning, with a profit in commissions alone of more than a thousand dollars daily. There would be a cause of congratulation if this enormous business was an indication of the increased productive wealth of the nation; but it is nothing of the kind. It is only a proof of the passion for buying and selling, with the hope of benefiting by the fluctuations of price. [...]

The mania of speculation is wondrously contagious, especially among a people so gregarious and sympathetic as we are. What touches one is apt to be felt by all. As men of every class, age, and business are already thronging Wall Street, it may not be long before our women shall be seen,

as in the times of John Law in France, and of the South Sea bubble in England, trailing their silks and satins in the dust of the exchange, and raising their voice in its din of excited barter. Already the spirit of speculation so pervades the community that the rise and fall of stocks is the most common topic of daily conversation, in our houses during the hours of leisure, if hours of leisure we can be said to have when they are filled with the thoughts and talks of business. Some of our women are already infected with the prevailing passion of moneymaking, as they have been long with that of spending it. "What's the price of gold today, my dear?" escapes from the pretty mouth of your wife before she has impressed the habitual kiss of connubial welcome upon your expectant lips. If you are a speculator, as you probably are in common with most of your fellow-citizens at this moment, and have made a good day of it, you answer blandly and don't complain of the loss of the conjugal embrace. If you have been unlucky and want consolation, and seek what you have a right to expect but don't find, you mourn over the loss, and conclude probably, with St. Paul, that money, or rather the love of it, is the root of all evil. [...]

It is obvious that when all are seeking to make their fortunes at others' expense that most will be disappointed. Each one, however, thinks that it will be his neighbor until he awakes some morning and finds it is himself who is ruined. There are some seductive examples undoubtedly of great success, of the rise of poverty to wealth in the course of a few weeks. There will be, too, with no less certainty before long, many striking instances of a fall from riches to beggary. [...]

The old proverb says: "That which comes easy goes easy." The suddenly enriched contractors, speculators, and stockjobbers illustrate its truth. They are spending money with a profusion never before witnessed in our country, at no time remarkable for its frugality. Our great houses are not big enough for them; they pull them down and build greater. They, like the proud and wanton Caligula, construct stables of marble at a fabulous cost, in which their horses are stabled (some, doubtless, to be fed on gilded oats), with a luxury never hitherto indulged in by the most opulent of our fellow-citizens. Even the manure heaps lie upon more resplendent floors than are swept by the silken trains of our proudest dames. So magnificent are these structures that their proprietors have not hesitated to assemble within them "the best society" they could command of fine gentlemen and finer ladies, to, hold a, carnival of pleasure. The playing of Comedies, it is said, was a part of the, program, as if the presence of the beau monde, seeking pleasure in a stable, was not in itself a sufficiently sorry farce. [...]

These Sybarites of "shoddy" buy finer furniture than was ever bought before, and dress in costlier cloths and silks than have been hitherto imported. No foreign luxury, even at the present enormous prices, is too dear for their exorbitant desires and swollen pockets. The importations of the country have arisen to the large amount of thirty millions of dollars a month, chiefly to satisfy the increased appetite for luxurious expense.

The ordinary sources of expenditure seem to have been exhausted, and these ingenious prodigals have invented new ones. The men button their waistcoats with diamonds of the first water, and the women powder their hair with gold and silver dust.

As excess, overflowing the natural channels of enjoyment is always sure to take an irregular and perverted course for the indulgence of its unchecked vagaries, it is not surprising to find the boundless extravagance of the times assuming forms at variance with propriety and taste. Paris, provoked to excessive folly and wild extravagance by an imperial court willing to enervate the people by debauchery that they may become too languid for resistance to tyranny, has, among other forms of dissipations, invented a grotesque kind of fancy ball. In this the guests represent things instead of persons. For example, one presents herself as a kitchen, with her person hung all over with pots and kettles, wearing a saucepan for a helmet, like Sancho Panza, brandishing a shovel and tongs, and playing the part of a kitchen wench with probably a dishcloth hanging to her tail. Another of a more sentimental turn is a flower garden, festooned with roses and bearing a spade and rake. A third is a pack of playing cards, bedizened all over with clubs, diamonds, and hearts, and so on with every possible transformation of the human spiritual being (supposed to be rational) into the senseless, material thing.

This absurdity has been imported by our wealthy New Yorkers, together with other Parisian extravagances. Last winter, during which, high carnival was held by our nou-veaux riches, a dame who has traveled, and had the honor of fainting in the arms, it is said, of Imperial Majesty, in the course of which embrace she probably imbibed her high appreciation of imperial folly, got up one of these grotesque fancy balls. She herself appeared on the occasion as music, and bore upon her head an illuminated lyre supplied with genuine gas, from a reservoir and fixtures concealed somewhere under her clothes. "We don't feel this war," they say. We believe them. Nothing, we

fear, while they are stupefying themselves in this whirl of absurd folly would bring them to their senses short of a shower of Greek fire. [...]

Are we deluding ourselves with the idea that this war is to be a continued carnival of abundance and pleasure? If so, we had better awaken at once to the fact that it is a sacrifice demanding the utmost effort of patient endurance. No noble cause, such as we are struggling for, was ever won by men while besotting themselves with excess and dallying pleasure. We must feel this war, and feel it resolutely, or we shall never triumph. Are we willing to prove ourselves worthy to triumph?

LIST OF BOOKS AUTHORED BY DR. ROBERT TOMES

Year	Title	Publisher
1853	The Black Man, written by Herman Burmeister, translated from the German by Robert Tomes	W.C. Bryant & Co.
1853	The Bourbon Prince	Harper & Brothers
1854	Richard the Lion Hearted	
1855	Panama in 1855 (An Account of the Panama Railroad)	Harper & Brothers
1857	The American in Japan (an abridgement of the Narrative of Commodore Perry's Expedition to Japan)	D. Appleton & Co.
1861	Battles of America By Sea and Land (With Biographical Sketches of Naval and Military Commanders 3 volumes – second edition 1878)	Virtue & Co.
1864 to 1867	War With The South (3 volumes – also published in German in 2 volumes)	Virtue & Yorston
1867	The Champagne Country	Hurd & Houghton
1870	The Bazar Book of Decorum	Harper & Brothers
1875	Bazar Book of the Household	Harper & Brothers
1878	Youth's Health Book	Harper & Brothers
1880	My College Days	Harper & Brothers

Harper's New Monthly Magazine

1. Tomes, Robert	About Cold
2. Tomes, Robert	About Heat
3. Tomes, Robert	Americans on Their Travels
4. Tomes, Robert	Before, At, and After Meals
5. Tomes, Robert	Dickens' Second Visit
6. Tomes, Robert	The Fortunes of War
7. Tomes, Robert	Houses We Live In
8. Tomes, Robert	Preachers and Preaching
9. Tomes, Robert	To Majorca
10. Tomes, Robert	Woman's Beauty: - How to Get and Keep It
11. Tomes, Robert	Woman's Form
12. Tomes, Robert	Your Humble Servant
13. Tomes, Robert	Dr. Wiesbaden, Reformed
14. Tomes, Robert	Making the Most of One's Self

Memorial Service
Alexander Hadden Tomes, Jr.
(1931-1997)
Christ Church,
Greenwich- Connecticut

Remarks by James S. Tomes,
September 30, 1997
When Ham Forster asked if I would say a few words today I felt both honored and awkward. Honored because of my friendship, love and respect for Hadden. Awkward because I am one of the most recently admitted members of the greater Tomes-Hadden family.

Hadden and I shared great-great grandparents, Francis and Maria Tomes. Hadden's great-grandfather, Francis Tomes, Jr. and my great-grandfather, Dr. Robert Tomes, were brothers. Hadden's extraordinary knowledge of our family genealogy requires that I begin these remarks by defining our family relationship.

Hadden's English first cousins, Lord Edward Baldwin and his wife Lady Sarah (Sally), and Georgina Hamilton-Weston, and her mother, Mrs. Hamilton, also asked that I express their affection in remembrance of Hadden today. They are holding an informal personal memorial service today in England at this very time. They gave the beautiful flowers in the narthex and will soon be visiting here to honor Hadden's memory in person. Edward Baldwin's mother was Joan Elspeth Tomes, the youngest sister of Hadden's father.

As everyone who knew Hadden well realized, he was a very gifted, bright, articulate and generous person who was also beset by some difficult afflictions. But his indomitable spirit never yielded to the afflictions and, with his brave heart, he strove constantly to overcome them.

I feel blessed to have known Hadden if only for the three brief years since 1994. Hadden's generosity and knowledge of the Tomes-Hadden family has literally given me my family heritage and put me in touch with many other cousins, whom I otherwise would never have known.

I will never forget the first time we actually met in New York City in the summer of 1995. We had been previously introduced via mail by Edward Baldwin, whom I had located through another English cousin and amateur genealogist, Major (now retired) Ian Tomes, and Hadden and I had arranged to meet in New York.

I would like to tell you briefly now about the two days we spent together in 1994 in New York City and Tuxedo, plus another day we spent together just last month as guests of cousins Gordon and Phoebe Fairburn in New Canaan, and here at this church, as a way of remembering Hadden's exceptional life.

We met on a hot summer day in 1994 at the Racquet Club in Manhattan. I was told at the entrance that Hadden was waiting for me in the member's lounge, but when I entered that cavernous room which was filled with large chairs there was no one to be seen. I called out Hadden's name and he appeared from behind one of the chairs, six feet six inches tall, wearing a baseball cap, old clothes and. running shoes, and carrying his trademark seven iron golf club. He greeted me with a wide-open smile and we shook hands warmly. He gave me a tour of the club, showing me his and his father's squash, billiard and pool trophies and talking about our shared genealogy all the while. By the time we left the club in less than an hour it seemed as if we had known each other and had been good friends for a long time.

We then walked to Saint Thomas Church at 53rd and Fifth Avenue. Hadden's Scottish great-great-grandfather was David Hadden who was one of the founding Vestryman in 1823 and then Warden from 1824 to 1856. Coincidentally, one of our other shared ancestors, The Rev. Francis L. Hawks, was also the third Rector of Saint Thomas Church from 1831 to 1843. Hadden showed me the baptismal font that David Hadden had given the early church. We then walked from the church to pick up a car I had rented for the trip to Tuxedo.

En route to Tuxedo we visited the Manhattan Trinity Church cemetery annex where my direct ancestors are buried, at 153rd Street and the Hudson River, just south of the George Washington Bridge. The land for this cemetery annex was given to Trinity by James Audubon, the ornithologist, who was a member of Trinity in the 1840s and who then owned a farm along the Hudson River. It was there that I showed Hadden the only thing I knew about the family that he hadn't previously known; that next to the Tomes plot there is the Hadden plot where David Hadden and other members of his family are buried. Incidentally, the Astor family plot is on other side of the Hadden plot, which I have recently learned from Gordon Fairburn, is logical since the Haddens and the Astors were also next door neighbors on Lafayette Street in New York City.

Hadden and I then drove to Tuxedo Park where we had lunch at the golf club, met some of Hadden's friends, saw the many golf trophies won by Hadden and his father, and then visited the tennis club where we met more friends and of course saw many more trophies. The tennis club pro pulled me aside and told me that Hadden was still a legend there and was surely one of the best court tennis players ever. As remarkably skilled as Hadden was in tennis, golf, pool and squash, he would always dismiss any compliments I offered as merely the result of good genes for eye-hand coordination.

Hadden also showed me the tennis clubrooms that he and his family had lived in for a while after the 1929 Crash, which devastated his father's financial resources. I was beginning to learn about some of the difficulties that Hadden and his family had suffered through.

On the way to Hadden's house on West Lake Road he pointed out the large house on the hill that was his birthplace. As soon as we got into his present house he began showing me various books, photographs and documents of family history. Among the mail that had arrived that day was a package of some items from the estate of his Aunt Lelia, one of his favorite people. In the package was a large 350 page, old book with a broken cover, entitled "Our Great-Grandfather". It was a book of letters, mostly from Francis Tomes, written from 1840 to 1873, to his daughter, Mary Elizabeth Tomes. Burckhardt, and published later by her for her grandchildren. Hadden handed me the book saying "You have one of these, don't you?" and when I said no he said "Take it, I have another." I would learn later that this was simply an expression of his natural and spontaneous generosity.

Hadden also handed me a stack of the original notebook journals of Francis Tomes far the years 1837 to 1839. They were quite dilapidated and badly deteriorated, but legible. These handwritten journals contained over three hundred pages and covered

four transatlantic sailing ship trips and one seven month overland business trip via horseback, stage coach, river boat, wagon, and primitive railroad through what Francis called "the Southwestern United States", meaning from New York to Chicago, Nashville, New Orleans, Macon and back to New York. I was amazed to see and hold these original journals, which I had not previously known about. My immediate reaction was to offer to restore them so they didn't fall into ruin. Hadden just as quickly agreed and there began our joint Tomes writings restoration and publishing project, which continues still. As many of you I know, we have since transcribed the Francis Tomes and Robert Tomes' journals, with considerable help from Arthur Tomes and Arthur Tomes Lewry and his wife Lolly, and reprinted "Our Great-Grandfather." Hadden and other cousins have donated their original and now restored copies to The Newberry Library in Chicago for safekeeping in perpetuity. We have made copies of all these publications available to all branches of the family.

Among the many photographs that Hadden showed me that day were pictures of his mother and father in pre World War I and subsequent years and also of his lovely sister Elizabeth who had such later misfortune. There were also photograph albums of nineteenth century Hong Kong where Hadden's grandfather, Charles Alexander Tomes had established a trading business and where Hadden's father and aunts and uncles were born.

The discovery of these pictures solved a personal mystery for me that began thirty years ago when I was doing frequent business in Hong Kong. I was asked by the chief executive of Hutchison's, one of the largest trading companies there, if I was related to one of the founders of Shewan, Tomes, a predecessor to Hutchison's. Since I then knew nothing of this part of my heritage I said I didn't know, but there in Hadden's living, room was the answer, Hadden's grandfather was that Tomes.

Hadden also gave me copies of his cousin Jean Crawford's genealogical charts of my side of the Tomes family which led me to be in touch with cousins Arthur Tomes Lewry, Arthur Tomes, Mary Tomes Prinz, Joan Tomes Beck, Francis P. Tomes, The Rev. Harold Bend Sedgwick, Gordon Fairburn, Joanna Gunderson and others. It was through each of these cousin's generous help that we have found, transcribed and published Robert Tomes's journals and restored the monument built by the city of Nashville to our shared great-uncle The Rev. Charles Tomes.

Going through the papers Hadden gave me that evening I learned that Hadden was a graduate of St. Mark's prep school, Harvard University and the Harvard Law School. I also found a copy of an eighty-two page memoir written by Hadden, entitled "Summer Holiday, 1953". It is a very well written piece about the trip Hadden took to England, Scotland and Ireland with his parents in 1953. It also includes a short side trip to Paris Hadden took with Jean Crawford and Edward Baldwin. There are of course descriptions of many golf games played by Hadden and also his hole-by-hole description of the 1953 British Open won by Ben Hogan at Carnoustie. It is a first-rate journalist's report of that classic game, ranking with the best golf writing I have ever read. I will be happy to make copies of the memoir available to those who would like one.

After our two-day meeting in 1994 Hadden and I had weekly telephone discussion and exchanged many letters following up on the projects we had started. Then just one month ago, on August 28th, Hadden and I met again at the home of Gordon and Phoebe Fairburn in New Canaan, Connecticut. We had a wonderful dinner prepared by Phoebe and blessed by Hadden who recited his favorite Bobbie Burns blessing in Scottish brogue. Family discussion continued until late in the evening and after a hearty breakfast the next morning Hadden and I drove to Greenwich where he showed me this church and the Tomes-Higgins house next door.

Fred Sibley gave us a complete tour of the house and also introduced us to Bill Clark who is here today. Hadden's and my genealogical search was surprisingly rewarded once again when Bill responded to meeting two Tomeses by saying that he too was a Tomes descendent!

It was true - Bill is a descendent of the Thomas Welles who was the first governor of the Connecticut Colony and "who was married to Alice Tomes in England before coming to America in the mid 1600s. Alice was one of the direct ancestors of Ian Tomes's branch of the family. Bill is in fact a past president of the Welles-Tomes Family Association. Hadden and I agreed that morning to give Bill and Fred two copies of our family genealogy and publications, which I will deliver to Bill after this service.

And so these stories must now end back here today. But the memory of Hadden will certainly continue with all of us who knew and loved him. We will miss him. We are all blessed to have known him and to have been the recipients of the gifts of his generous and brave heart.

May God rest his soul.

**Himeji Address Commemorating
The 50th Anniversary Of WWII**
*Given by Art Tomes, July 1, 1995,
in Himeji, Japan*

Mayor Totani, Professor Shigeo Imamura, Himeji Air Raid 50th Anniversary Committee Against Future Wars, Himeji City International Association, members of our 504th Bomb Group Association, our sons, daughters and grand daughters, ladies and gentlemen.

This is a very special day for me, and I am sure that I also reflect the feelings of my 504th colleagues, those who are here with me, and those who are with us in spirit. Back in the year 1945, when war raged between our two nations, who among us would have ever imagined a meeting such as this, a meeting dedicated to peace. Among those of you who experienced the bombing raid here on the night of July 3, 1945, who might have been operating the searchlights or antiaircraft guns or defensive aircraft who could have imagined it? Among those of us who were in our B-29s overhead, performing our assigned mission, who would have imagined it? The war, which had raged for so long over so much of the earth, was still taking a costly toll, a toll of our lives and your lives. And the war had been going for such a long time, so long in fact, that it was hard to imagine what peace would be like. Peace had an unreal quality, like a distant, unattainable dream.

But peace came at last, and our two nations set upon a long road of reconciliation. And here we are, half a century later, looking back on a period of war that now has an almost unreal quality. Yet, we know that the war occurred and exacted a cost to us all, that we must never forget. As we honor our own countrymen who perished in that war, so we know that you also honor your fallen countrymen. And as we honor them, recognize that our shared obligation to all of them, and indeed to all the world, is to study the history of the war with a scholar's unbiased eye. And analyze the causes of such conflicts, and thus to help provide our two nations, and all nations, with the means of averting future wars. Biased, slanted presentations of history tear people apart and provoke wars, but fair, comprehensive studies bring peoples together and foster peace. I credited the latter practice here in Himeji, an even - handed pursuit of history, with creating the spirit that has brought us together today in a context of peace and harmony. My prayer today is that I am correct in this assessment, and that our gathering here represents an important, positive step toward a fair and equitable peace that lasts.

But as has been suggested to me, I will share some of my personal recollections of 50 years ago. The 504th Bombardment Group was one of 4 groups (about 60 B-29s per group) of the 313th Bombardment Wing, which was one of 5 Wings of the 21st Bomber Command (1200 B-29s and growing) of the 20th Air Force under the command of Gen. Curtis LeMay. He had the responsibility of bringing the war to the Japanese homeland. It was the 313th Wing over Himeji that night in 1945 with about 100 B-29s. I was the pilot of one of them. Others here were overhead 50 years ago as well.

We covered much of Japan at that time. We took part in the horrendous conflagration in Tokyo on March 10, 1945 and the subsequent torching of Nagoya, Osaka and Kobe. These four cities were hit hard first before turning onto the smaller cities of Japan. Most of these cities were warned before hand by leaflets dropped urging evacuation. The 313th Wing was assigned the task of dropping mines into the harbors and waterways. We saw Tokyo Bay harbors along the Inland Sea, Shiminoseki Straits, and even Rashin and Seishin in northern Korea, eighty miles from Vladivostok Russia.

I was mighty lucky during my 35 missions for never having been wounded. And our B-29, named "Big Boots", was able to run the gauntlet each time successfully and returned to Tinian. We took our share of hits from flak, fighter's bullets, phosphorous bombs, but none were fatal, again lucky for us. The closest I came to being hit was from a piece of flak's shrapnel that came through the plane about yea far from my backside. Many others were

not so fortunate. A feared weapon used against us was, what we called the "baka bomb". Baka means "fool" I understand, a "fool bomb". It had a 1000-pound warhead, wings, 5 minutes of rocket power and was piloted by a man. It was flown aloft under a twin-engine bomber that we named the "Betty bomber", and released at altitude. At night it was particularly fearful, because of the fire from the rocket motor. One night my tail gunner had one in his sights and fired at it, and fired, with no luck. No wonder. It was the moon coming up on the horizon.

My second daughter, Mary, is married to Gary Yanagita. He is a sansei, third generation Japanese-American, a handsome six foot tall American who, unfortunately, doesn't speak a word of Japanese. They have two beautiful young boys, my grandsons, Bryan 3, and David 10 months. Little Bryan, when first learning to talk, formed the word for grandfather, me, as "Baka". A probable genetic breakthrough. His other grandpa didn't much like it.

Professor Imamura searched for us very diligently. He wanted to know if your ancient Himeji Castle in the center of the city was spared on purpose or not. He was assured that it was purely accidental that it was missed. In fact we probably didn't even know it was there. The fact that the castle escaped bombing is a cause for celebration, now, by all of us. The bombing was done by radar, which was quite primitive then. It required land contrasting with water to show on the scope, the area in which to drop the bombs. At a different port city a thunderstorm happened to be alongside. The city and the storm looked alike on the radar screen, we mistakenly went through and bombed in the thunderstorm!!! There probably hasn't ever been another lightning bolt like that.

As I said, I was extremely lucky to have escaped the wrath of flak, search lights, small arms, fighter's gun fire; baka bombs, phosphorus bombs and all the hell that went on up there. Others were not so lucky... Capt Worde and his crew of 11 were shot down, all parachuted safely and were held prisoner at the infamous, in our opinion, Kempei-Tai prison in Tokyo. Happily they are all alive and well today. On the other hand, 158 others died during the combat. The 504th alone lost 28 B-29s to all causes, combat and operational, during the nine months of its campaign. A heavy toll.

You must wonder why we bombed cities. We were engaged in a bitter war. You did everything you could to win it. We did everything we could to win it. Justification used to bomb cities in 1945 was that much of the key industrial production for the military took place in Japan's crowded urban residential neighborhoods. We could see the fires but could not see the people. In that respect air battles are different from ground battles. It's

impersonal. The only Japanese person that I ever saw occurred high over East Kanoya, Shikoku. We had 9 B-29s flying abreast each with 6 forward firing 50 caliber guns. Here comes a single Zero fighter, head-on. He and the formation were firing away at each other, and at a combined rate of closure of about 600 miles per hour. He had to roll sideways to get past. I had the briefest glimpse of him in his cockpit. He wore helmet and goggles, so I know I'd never recognize him if I met him on the street. It was a tremendous display of bravery on his part. I would like to know him. No one got hurt, but he should have been powdered like a clay pigeon by 54 guns firing at him. Another reason we could do and endure such things was because of our youth, I was 24 at the time, the "old man", the others on board were 19.

The best day of 1945 was September 2. This day officially ended the hostilities forever. General McArthur had ordered the last show of force of 1000 B-29s to circle over Tokyo. Below in Tokyo Bay was the battleship Missouri, (those mines sterilized themselves by then). On board were the dignitaries of Japan and the Allies signing the peace. It was a great day. My part was to fly the photo plane, a reconnaissance B-29, with extra window ports for the three combat photographers to record the event on film. We flew mast high by the Missouri several times, we flew high alongside

the formations, we flew low recording the awful devastation of Tokyo.
It was an unforgettable experience.
Another last flight over Japan was to
drop a bomb bay load of food, clothing and supplies to our haggard prisoners of war, alongside their prison
camps. They were a happy group
about to be released.

I went to the National Archives in
Washington DC hoping to find these
films and others of the 504th. I was
disappointed. I found a large group of
our men with the backs of their heads
showing, looking at Gen. Hap Arnold
on the stage. I found 2 of my men in
our plane, but not me, I had fallen to
the cutting room floor.

And now in closing I am very encouraged by the thought that this occasion
is not merely a looking back on divi-
sive events of the past but also a
building of bonds of understanding
that brighten the future. It is on that
note of good expectations that I end
my remarks. I and all my colleagues
express our appreciation to all of
you here today who had a part in
planning this observance, to my
friend, Professor Shigeo Imamura in
particular. For the occasion, for your
invitation to us, and for your gracious
welcome and generous hospitality,
we say thank you.

Reconciliation, Not Renunciation
Where Are The Christians?
April 26, 1985

As a private citizen, I find myself increasingly dismayed and troubled by President Reagan's ill-conceived attempts to explain or adjust the itinerary of his forthcoming trip to Bitburg, Germany to accommodate the justifiable outrage of the world's Jewish community.

I find myself even more dismayed and troubled, as a person raised in Christianity, by the silence of the world's Christian community.

One of the greatest political sins of omission in recent human history was the failure of Europe and America to stop Hitler before it was too late. A significant part of that failure was the silence and lack of aid from predominantly Christian nations on behalf of the Jewish and non-Jewish victims of Nazi tyranny. As Max Dimont says in his Jews, God & History" because the Nazis shouted 'Kill the Jews', the world blinded itself to the murder of Christians." So it seems to be again.

An outrageous affront has now been made to the Jewish community by the President of the United States, and the Christian churches are once again silent. Why are the Jews left again to fight alone for a principle that affects all mankind? Why is Elie Weisel left standing alone to plead with the President?

My own life-long experience with Germany, beginning in 1945, tells me that most German people want reconciliation, but my own experience also tells me that they do not expect the renunciation of the past, which has been attempted by President Reagan. Both West German Chancellor Kohl and President Von Weiszsaecker have publicly acknowledged Germany's "historical responsibility for the crimes of the Nazi tyranny."

But now we are confronted by President Reagan's March 21st White House press conference statement that:

"The German people have very few alive that remember even the war and certainly none of them who were adults and participating in any way...", and "..they have a feeling and a guilt feeling that's been imposed upon them, and I just think it's unnecessary."

These statements are so astonishingly false that it is hard to respond to them rationally.

How does one deal with this kind of ignorance? One could ignore it I suppose, but when it is spoken by the President of the United States, it becomes an American ignorance, unless and until it is corrected.

President Reagan's attempt to forget, or bury the basic historical facts of our time, to confuse the responsibility of

Nazi Germany for World War II, and to arrange the "balancing" of a visit to the graves of Nazi SS soldiers by a visit to the graves of SS victims, are not steps toward reconciliation. Such renunciations of the recent past are, instead, fundamental barriers against reconciliation.

The whole world knows that Naziism, supported by virtually the whole of the German people, made war on all of Europe and committed unspeakably heinous crimes against all humanity, for which most of the Nazi leader and many others were tried and found guilty, by due process of law. Chancellor Kohl himself acknowledges a "never-ending German shame and historical responsibility" for the events.

I was raised as a member of a Christian church in a small town in Illinois. As an eighteen-year-old GI, I saw released victims of concentration camps in Germany in 1945. I remained in Germany as a member of the 82nd Airborne Division Occupation Forces in Frankfurt, until November of 1946. I have since returned to Germany many times as a businessman beginning in 1962. I have many friends who are German nationals. Some are contemporaries, or older, who were members of the German armed forces. Others were too young to have fought, but they also clearly remember World War II and "Der Schrechlicke

Zeit", the Terrible Time, which followed the wartime death and devastation for more than five years after the end of the War.

There are more than 15 million Germans now alive who were at least 12 years old in 1945 and who remember the War and the Terrible Time thereafter. Chancellor Kohl was 15 years old then and he remembers. President Von Weizsaecker was a twice-wounded Wermacht infantry officer.

Reconciliation can only occur when there is understanding. Understanding cannot occur without knowledge and memory. The German government itself knows this. The memorial at Dachau which our President, of all people, must some day visit, is maintained by the State of Bavaria, albeit on the initiative and according to the plans of the International Dachau Committee.

There are two walls at Dachau on which are proclaimed two messages, in French, English, German and Russian, for all to see. The first is: "Never again" and second is:

"May the example of those who were exterminated here between 1933-1945 because they resisted Naziism help to unite the living for the defense of peace and freedom and in respect of their fellow men. "

Dachau, as the first of the hundreds of concentration camps, was organized by Hitler as the place to put his political enemies, whether they were Christian, Jew, Gypsy or otherwise. Hitler's anti-Semitism was only a part of his tyranny. World War II was not fought by the Nazis only to exterminate the Jews; it was fought between the Nazis and most of the civilized world. Surely, the Jews suffered the most proportionately, and were the only people who suffered purely because of their ethnic heritage. But, in fact, more non-Jews than Jews were killed in concentration camps and by Einsatzgruppen extermination and firing squads.

A relatively few brave German Christian clerics did resist Naziism and were severely punished or killed. Two of these, one Protestant and one Catholic, who were imprisoned in Dachau, and somehow survived, wrote words that are instructive now, perhaps more than ever before. The first, Pastor Niemoller, who had been a German submarine commander in World War I, and later became a Lutheran clergyman and was imprisoned by the Nazis, said after his release in 1945:

"In Germany, they came first for the Communists, and I didn't speak up, because I wasn't a Communist. Then they came for the Jews, and I didn't speak up because I wasn't a Jew. Then they came for the Trade Unionists, and I didn't speak up because I wasn't

a Trade Unionist. Then they came for the Catholics, and I didn't speak up because I was a Protestant. Then they came for me, and by that time no one was left to speak up."

The other, a Catholic priest, Johann Neuhausler, imprisoned first in Sachsenhausen and then in Dachau until the end of the War, quoted the dying wish of a fellow prisoner:

"If the miracle should happen, that you live to tell the tale, write it down and tell the world what they did to us."

Father Neuhausler, later the Bishop of Munich, also wrote:

"Forgive, but do not forget. Dachau can and shall be a lesson! Therefore, we dare not be silent about it, although the memory of it is sad and grievous."

We must also never forget that neither the German or other Christian churches, or the universities, proved to be any bulwark against the rise and terror of Naziism.

The predominantly Christian countries of Europe and America hold most of the economic and military power and responsibility in this world. It is the Christians who must not forget the lessons of World War II. The Jews cannot forget.

The risk that the meaning of World War II and the deaths of all the victims of Naziism may be distorted or even lost on the 40th Anniversary of the end of the War, because of unanswered untrue statements by the President of the United States, compels a profound memorial.

President Reagan should be leading a true reconciliation, on this 40th Anniversary of the end of the War, in a memorial of the liberation of Germany, as well as the rest of the world, from Nazi tyranny. And Chancellor Kohl should be at his side, and they should both stand on the sacred ground of prayer and atonement at Dachau, hand in hand with Christians and Jews and Gypsies and every other kind of man and woman.

And, if President Reagan and Chancellor Kohl can't summon the common sense to rearrange their meeting schedule for such a memorial, would it be too much to ask that the leaders of the world's Christian churches hold their own 40th Anniversary ceremony at Dachau.

"Those who cannot remember the past are condemned to repeat it."

Where are the Christians?
Written on April 26, 1985 by:

James S. Tomes
714 Washington Ave.
Wilmette, Illinois 60091
312 251 0947

Published by The Sentinel, Chicago, Illinois May 2, 1985.

1   Francis Hawks b: Abt. 1711 in Warwick, England
.... +Elizabeth Sabin b: 1710 in England d: March 12, 1772 in Shipston-upon-Stour, Warwick, England m: April 9, 1732
.. 2   Francis Hawkes b: July 1, 1733 in Shipston-upon-Stour, Warwick, England
.... +Ann French b: Abt. 1736 in Warwick, England m: October 15, 1750
.... 3   Elizabeth Hawkes b: October 22, 1751 in Shipston-upon-Stour, Warwick, England
.... 3   Ann Hawkes b: June 22, 1753 in Shipston-upon-Stour, Warwick, England
.... 3   Sarah Hawkes b: December 30, 1754 in Shipston-upon-Stour, Warwick, England
.... 3   Francis Hawkes b: October 12, 1763 in Shipston-upon-Stour, Warwick, England
.... +Mary Wigginton b: Abt. 1765 in Warwick, England m: November 3, 1788
.... 4   Francis Hawks b: May 30, 1789 in Shipston-upon-Stour, Warwick, England d: Abt. 1796 in Shipston-upon-Stour, Warwick, England
.... 4   Ann Hawks b: December 20, 1791 in Shipston-upon-Stour, Warwick, England
.... 4   William Wigginton Hawks b: July 23, 1794 in Shipston-upon-Stour, Warwick, England
.... 4   Mary Hawks b: September 12, 1799 in Shipston-upon-Stour, Warwick, England
.... 4   Elizabeth Hawks b: January 5, 1802 in Shipston-upon-Stour, Warwick, England
.... 4   John Hawks b: August 25, 1805 in Shipston-upon-Stour, Warwick, England
.... 4   James Wigginton Hawks b: November 28, 1808 in Shipston-upon-Stour, Warwick, England
.... 4   Francis Hawkes b: January 27, 1797 in of London, London, England
.... 3   John Hawkes b: November 4, 1765 in Shipston-upon-Stour, Warwick, England
...... 3   William Hawkes b: September 22, 1768 in Shipston-upon-Stour, Warwick, England
.. 2   John Hawks b: January 15, 1734/35 in Shipston-upon-Stour, Warwick, England d: October 31, 1790 in New Bern, N.C. Occupation: Architect & Builder Tryon's Palace
.... +Sarah Ann Rice b: August 1, 1743 Occupation: Grndtr of Gov Nathaniel Rice m: 1768
.... 3   Francis Cicero Hawks b: December 10, 1769 in New Bern, NC d: December 20, 1831 in New Bern, NC Occupation: Customs Collector, New Bern
.... +Julia Airay Stephens b: December 1, 1773 d: April 3, 1813 in New Bern, NC Occupation: Mother - 9 children m: March 7, 1793 Event 1: Died during childbirth
.... 4   Mary Lister Hawks b: August 8, 1794 d: October 11, 1794 Event 1: October 10, 1794 Baptized by Rev. Solomon Halling. Died next day.
.... 4   John Stephens Hawks b: March 21, 1796 in New Bern, NC d: October 16, 1865 in Washington, NC Occupation: Lawyer Event 1: May 18, 1796 Baptized by Rev Solomon Halling
.... +Mary Holliday b: Abt. 1799 m: 1820
.... 4   Francis Lister Hawks b: June 10, 1798 in New Bern, N.C. d: September 27, 1866 in New York City Occupation: Clergy, author, Pres Tulane Univ Event 1: October 4, 1798 Baptized by Rev Thomas Pitt Irving
.... +Emily Kirby b: November 19, 1803 in New Haven, CT d: July 12, 1827 Occupation: Mother - 2 children m: November 11, 1823
.... 5   Julia Ann (Susannah) Hawks b: October 16, 1825 in New Haven, CT
.... +Eaton Pugh Guion b: Abt. 1823 m: March 4, 1845
.... 5   William Walter Hawks b: 1827 in New Haven, CT
.... *2nd Wife of Francis Lister Hawks:
.... +Olivia Trowbridge b: August 11, 1798 in Danbury, CT Occupation: Mother - 6 children m: Abt. 1830
.... 5   Emily Hawks b: Abt. 1831
.... +Richard Oakley b: Abt. 1827
.... 5   Olivia Hawks b: Abt. 1833
.... +Edward Bogart b: Abt. 1829
.... 5   Francis Tomes Hawks b: June 9, 1832 in New York City Event 1: October 7, 1832 Baptism by Dr. Milnor
.... +Hannah Manly b: Abt. 1839 Occupation: dtr of Judge Wm Gaston & Hannah McClure
.... 5   Josephine Hawks b: Abt. 1837 in New York? d: Abt. 1902 in New York?
.... +James Pott b: 1827 in New York City d: February 8, 1905 in New York Occupation: Publisher, James Pott & Co.
.... 6   James Pott b: Abt. 1861 Occupation: Publisher
.... +Katherine Maud Mason
.... 7   Eleanor Pott b: 1886
.... 7   Josephine Pott b: 1889
.... 7   Helen Mason Pott b: May 26, 1892 in Greenwich, CT d: January 1972 in Roxbury, CT
.... 6   Kate Pott b: Abt. 1862
.... 6   Francis Lister Hawks Pott b: February 22, 1864 in New York, NY d: March 7, 1947 in Country Hospital, Shanghai, China Occupation: Clergyman, President St. John's Univ
.... +Susan N. Wong b: Abt. 1867 in China d: May 11, 1918 in Shanghai, China Occupation: Headmistress, St. Mary's School m: August 23, 1888

.... 7 James Hawks Pott b: February 9, 1891 in Shanghai, China d: December 15, 1979 in Honolulu, Hawaii Occupation: Missionary teacher

.... +Nancy Yang b: February 3, 1894 in Sinti, Hupeh Province, China d: May 8, 1946 in Pomona, CA Occupation: Homemaker m: February 9, 1920)

.... 8 William Lister Pott b: November 25, 1920 in Anking, China d: November 10, 1944 in Burma Occupation: U.S. Army Air Corps Service Pilot

.... 8 Olivia Kate Hawks Pott b: March 20, 1925 in Shanghai, China d: December 12, 2002 in Long Beach, CA Occupation: Librarian, Musician, Homemaker

.... +Roy Bishop Weathered b: August 19, 1911 in Norwich, Kansas d: September 7, 1972 in Barstow, CA Occupation: Physician, Radiologist m: May 1, 1959

.... 8 James Thomas Pott b: February 28, 1927 in Shanghai, China Occupation: Civil Engineer

.... +Lois Jane Donaldson b: September 11, 1929 in Galt, Ontario, Canada Occupation: Registered Nurse, Homemaker m: July 16, 1955

.... 9 Nancy Louise Pott b: April 10, 1956 in San Francisco, CA Occupation: Homemaker, Registered Nurse

.... +Samuel Allen Booth b: February 27, 1952 in Portland, Oregon Occupation: Emergency Physician m: May 21, 1978

.... 10 Samuel Hawks Booth b: May 5, 1981 in Minneapolis, MN Occupation: Student

.... 10 Brianna Kate Booth b: November 25, 1982 in Minneapolis, MN

.... 10 Vincent James Booth b: August 19, 1984 in Wenatchee, WA Occupation: Little Leaguer

.... 10 Kevin Skuln Booth b: February 10, 1987 in Yakima, WA

.... 9 Catherine Lynn Pott b: April 10, 1956 in San Francisco, CA Occupation: Homemaker, Physiotherapist

.... +David Robert Plocki b: September 12, 1957 in Natrona Heights, Pa Occupation: Oral & Maxillofacial Surgeon m: June 18, 1983

.... 10 Adam James Plocki b: December 11, 1987 in Fallbrook, CA

.... 10 Erik Thomas Plocki b: April 24, 1991 in Fallbrook, CA

.... 9 Margaret Hawks Pott b: December 19, 1963 in Palo Alto, CA Occupation: Advertising, Performing Arts

.... +Richard Scott Hartwell b: June 4, 1962 in Fullerton, CA Occupation: Shop Suprv, Otis School of Design m: April 1, 1989 Marriage ending: December 10, 1996 in Los Angeles

.... 10 Galen Vashti Hartwell b: April 3, 1994 in Culver City, CA Occupation: Baby

.... *2nd Husband of Margaret Hawks Pott:

.... +Joshua Daniel Abramson b: January 24, 1962 in New York, NY m: July 28, 2002

.... 8 Robert Graham Pott b: January 19, 1938 in Shanghai, China d: January 31, 1989 in San Marino, CA Occupation: Attorney

.... +Eleanor (Pepper) Brown b: May 30, 1940 in Long Beach, CA Occupation: Certified Financial Analyst m: August 6, 1966

.... 9 Andrea Christine Pott b: October 12, 1969 in Los Angeles, CA Occupation: Dep Dist Atty, USC Law

.... +John Edward Albin b: May 30, 1966 m: June 3, 2000 Marriage ending: May 2003

.... 9 James Sumner Pott b: August 12, 1971 in Los Angeles, CA Occupation: Cefrtified Financial Analyst

.... *2nd Wife of James Hawks Pott:

.... +Agnes Strasburg b: December 3, 1905 in Minnesota d: June 25, 1986 in Honolulu, Hawaii m: 1946

.... 7 William Sumner Appleton Pott b: December 24, 1892 in New York, N.Y. d: November 7, 1967 in Berkeley, CA Occupation: President, Elmira College

.... +Eleanor Frances Welsh Paul b: December 1, 1892 in Bloomsburg, Columbia Co., PA d: May 1977 in Berkeley, CA m: December 30, 1931

.... 7 Walter Graham Hawks Pott b: January 20, 1895 in Shanghai, China d: February 1982 in Pinehurst, N.C. Occupation: Physician, Surgeon

.... +Elizabeth Washington Fisher b: November 25, 1892 in Emmerton, Richmond, VA d: March 1982 in Greenville, N.C.

.... 8 Mary Pott b: Abt. 1922

.... 8 Elizabeth Hawks Pott b: March 22, 1924 d: December 17, 1992 in Surfside Beach, South Carolina

.... +Harold Milton Holcombe b: December 14, 1918 in Fayetteville, NC d: August 24, 1991 in Charleston, SC m: October 20, 1954

.... 9 Walter Stuart Young Holcombe b: October 16, 1947 in Geneva, NY

.... 9 Frank Lanman Holcombe b: December 9, 1955 in Greenville, NC

.... 7 Olivia Hawks Pott b: September 25, 1896 d: January 1969 in Roxbury, Conn. Occupation: Medic Dean's Secty, Columbia Univ

.... *2nd Wife of Francis Lister Hawks Pott:

.... +Emily Gwen Cooper b: March 10, 1863 d: in England m: June 12, 1919

.... 6 William Hawks Pott b: Abt. 1866 in NY? d: 1941 in NJ? Occupation: Clergyman

.... +Madeline Blythe b: July 14, 1889 in Wappingers Falls, Dutchess Co. NY d: October 1977 in NJ?

.... 7 Lister Pott

```
............ 7  William Hawks Pott, Jr.  b: December 11, 1917 in New York, NY  d: October 1979
............ 7  Joan Pott
.......... 6  Richard Malcolm Pott  b: Abt. 1868  d: 1948  Occupation: Publisher
............ +Louise Warhurst  d: 1953
............ 7  Katherine Pott
............ 7  Richard Moncrief Pott  b: November 28, 1895 in New York, NY  d: September 1970 in Tuckahoe, NY ?
............ +Lillian Churchill Frost
................ 8  Richard Moncrieff Pott  b: April 30, 1921 in New York, NY
............ 7  Louise Pott
.......... 5  Laura Hawks  b: September 7, 1835 in New York City
............ +G.W.C.Noble?  b: September 7, 1835
.......... 5  Edward Rutledge Hawks  b: June 1836 in New York City  d: July 10, 1837 in New York City  Event 1: July 10, 1837 Baptized in
             Extremis and died
........ 4  Julia Mary Hawks  b: October 25, 1800  d: October 13, 1821  Event 1: July 29, 1801 Baptized by Rev. Thomas Pitt Irving
........ 4  Frances Sarah Hawks  b: November 30, 1802  d: in New Bern, NC  Event 1: November 3, 1803 Baptized by Rev Thomas P. Irving
.......... +John Cameron  b: Abt. 1797
........ 4  Phoebe Rice Hawks  b: February 21, 1805 in New Bern, NC  d: April 17, 1881 in Pensacola, FL  Event 1: December 15, 1805
             Baptized by Doctor Halling
............ +Walker Anderson  b: July 29, 1801 in Petersburg, Dinwiddie Co, VA  d: January 18, 1857 in Pensacola, FL  Occupation: Chf
             Justice Fla Supreme Ct  m: July 29, 1822
.......... 5  Julia Anderson  b: Abt. 1825
.......... 5  Cameron Anderson  b: Abt. 1827
.......... 5  Walker Anderson  b: Abt. 1831
.......... 5  Mildred Anderson  b: Abt. 1833
.......... 5  [2] William Edward Anderson  b: November 20, 1833 in Hillsborough, Orange Co, NC  d: November 12, 1908 in Pensacola, FL.
             Event 1: Wrote "Tales of aGrandfather"
............ +[1] Anna Hawks  b: July 16, 1838 in New York City  d: July 19, 1908 in Pensacola, FL.  m: December 29, 1859  Event 1: May
             16, 1839 Baptism
............ 6  [3] Walker Anderson  b: September 8, 1864 in Baghdad, FL  d: July 14, 1920 in Vicksburg, MS
............ +[4] Elizabeth (Lillie) Maury  b: November 20, 1867 in Port Gibson, MS  d: January 30, 1923 in Greenville, SC  m: November
             20, 1889
............ 7  [5] Walker Anderson  b: February 12, 1893 in Mobile, AL  d: July 22, 1952 in Pittsburgh, Allegheny Co, PA
............ +[6] Katherine Gertrude McQuiston  b: January 30, 1900 in Jamestown, PA  d: August 10, 1984 in Glen Burnie, MD  m:
             June 9, 1923
................ 8  [7] Walker Anderson  b: February 12, 1928 in Wilkinsburg, PA  Occupation: Westinghouse Exec, Aero&Mech Engr
                  Event 1: Wrote "Handprints in the Clay"
............ +[8] Jane Lou Silliman  b: Abt. 1930  m: August 21, 1954
............ 9  [9] Susan Ashley Anderson  b: 1959 in Kansas City, MO
............ 9  [10] Walker Anderson  b: Abt. 1960 in Kansas City, MO
............ 9  [11] Amy Leigh Anderson  b: 1962 in Rockville, MD
............ 8  [12] Jane Maury Anderson  b: May 31, 1924
............ 8  [13] Bowden Anderson  b: April 27, 1935
.......... 5  Duncan Anderson  b: Abt. 1835
.......... 5  Hambrook Caldwalder(?) Anderson  b: Abt. 1837
........ 4  Samuel Cicero Hawks  b: March 1, 1807 in New Bern, NC  d: February 16, 1843 in Flushing, NY of TB  Occupation: Businessman,
             Educator  Event 1: August 8, 1809 Baptized by Rev. Thomas P. Irving
.......... +Caroline Post  b: April 7, 1812 in Perhaps 1815 in New York, NY  d: January 15, 1850 in New York, NY  m: October 6, 1829
.......... 5  John Hawks  b: Abt. 1830
.......... 5  Francis Lister Hawks  b: January 30, 1832 in New York City  d: August 10, 1897  Event 1: February 26, 1832 Baptism
.......... +Gertrude Richards Holmes  b: December 11, 1829  d: December 31, 1918  m: December 18, 1856  Marriage ending: 1869
............ 6  Ruth (Hawks) Holmes  b: July 28, 1862  d: December 28, 1932
............ +Edward Howe Wales  b: May 28, 1856 in New York, NY  d: October 31, 1922 in New York, NY  m: December 17, 1885
............ 7  Ruth Wales  b: June 10, 1889 in New York, NY  d: 1967 in Winterthur, DE
............ +Henry Francis du Pont  b: May 27, 1880 in Winterthur, DE  d: April 11, 1969 in Winterthur, DE  m: June 24, 1916
................ 8  Pauline Louise du Pont  b: 1918
............ +Alfred Craven Harrison  b: 1910  d: 1973
................ 8  Ruth Ellen du Pont  b: 1922
............ +George deForest Lord, Jr.  b: 1919
.......... 5  Julia Elizabeth (Miriam) Hawks  b: 1834 in New York City  Event 1: September 19, 1834 Baptism
```

```
..........5   Caroline Hawks  b: October 25, 1836 in New York City  Event 1: April 19, 1837 Baptism
..........5   [1] Anna Hawks  b: July 16, 1838 in New York City  d: July 19, 1908 in Pensacola, FL  Event 1: May 16, 1839 Baptism
...........  +[2] William Edward Anderson  b: November 20, 1833 in Hillsborough, Orange Co, NC  d: November 12, 1908 in Pensacola,
             FL. m: December 29, 1859  Event 1: Wrote "Tales of a Grandfather"
...............6   [3] Walker Anderson  b: September 8, 1864 in Baghdad, FL  d: July 14, 1920 in Vicksburg, MS
...............  +[4] Elizabeth (Lillie) Maury  b: November 20, 1867 in Port Gibson, MS  d: January 30, 1923 in Greenville, SC  m: November
                 20, 1889
...................7   [5] Walker Anderson  b: February 12, 1893 in Mobile, AL  d: July 22, 1952 in Pittsburgh, Allegheny Co, PA
.....................  +[6] Katherine Gertrude McQuiston  b: January 30, 1900 in Jamestown, PA  d: August 10, 1984 in Glen Burnie, MD  m:
                       June 9, 1923
.........................8   [7] Walker Anderson  b: February 12, 1928 in Wilkinsburg, PA  Occupation: Westinghouse Exec, Aero&Mech Engr
                             Event 1: Wrote " Handprints in the Clay"
...........................  +[8] Jane Lou Silliman  b: Abt. 1930  m: August 21, 1954
...............................9   [9] Susan Ashley Anderson  b: 1959 in Kansas City, MO
...............................9   [10] Walker Anderson  b: Abt. 1960 in Kansas City, MO
...............................9   [11] Amy Leigh Anderson  b: 1962 in Rockville, MD
.........................8   [12] Jane Maury Anderson  b: May 31, 1924
.........................8   [13] Bowden Anderson  b: April 27, 1935
..........4   William Nassau Hawks  b: March 4, 1809 in New Bern, NC  d: Abt. 1859 in Columbus, GA  Occupation: Episcopal Clergyman
             Event 1: August 8, 1809 Baptized by Mr. Irving
.............  +Sarah C. Coart  b: Abt. 1812  m: April 20, 1831
..........5   Elizabeth Coart Hawks  b: September 24, 1837
..........5   Cicero Lister Hawks  b: December 31, 1838
..........5   Julia Hawks  b: Abt. 1841
..........5   William Hawks  b: Abt. 1843
..........5   John Coart Hawks  b: Abt. 1847
..........4   Cicero Stephens Hawks  b: May 26, 1811 in New Bern, N.C.  d: April 19, 1868 in St Louis, MO  Occupation: 1st Episcopal Bishop
             of Missouri  Event 1: January 1, 1812 Baptized by Rev Thomas P. Irving
.............  +Ann Jones  b: in Hillsboro, N.C.  d: July 1855  m: February 19, 1835
..........5   Isabel Hawks  b: Abt. 1845  d: June 1864 in St. Louis, MO
..........  *2nd Wife of Cicero Stephens Hawks:
.............  +Ada Leonard  b: in Howard County, MO  m: Abt. 1857
..........5   Child #1
..........5   Child #2
..........4   Susannah Airy Hawks  b: April 2, 1813  d: September 3, 1864 in Columbus, GA  Event 1: May 8, 1814 Baptized by the Reverend
             W. Strebeck.
......  *2nd Wife of Francis Cicero Hawks:
...........  +Elizabeth Pugh Guion  b: September 10, 1778 in White Oak River, Onslow County  d: February 25, 1816 in New Bern, NC  m:
             December 8, 1814
......3   Samuel Hawks  b: Abt. 1771 in New Bern, NC  d: December 1804 in New Bern, NC
..........  +Ann Singleton  b: Abt. 1774  m: 1797
..........4   Samuel Hawks  b: Abt. 1798
..........4   Benjamin Blackledge Hawks  b: Abt. 1800  d: Abt. 1817
..........4   Evelina S. Hawks  b: Abt. 1802
.............  +Bryan Croom  b: Abt. 1799  m: 1826
..........4   Spyers Singleton Hawks  b: Abt. 1804
..  *2nd Wife of John Hawks:
......  +Mary Fisher  b: 1730 in St Andrew Penrith, Cumberland Co., England  Occupation: Questionable 2nd wife. Prob wife of Thos Hawks
        m: Abt. 1770
..2   Samuel Hawkes  b: January 21, 1736/37 in Shipston-upon-Stour, Warwick, England
..2   Anne Hawkes  b: February 1, 1738/39 in Shipston-upon-Stour, Warwick, England
..2   Elizabeth Hawkes  b: June 1, 1744 in Shipston-upon-Stour, Warwick, England
........  +William Clark  b: Abt. 1741 in Birmingham, England  m: August 12, 1773
..2   Sarah Hawkes  b: August 23, 1748 in Shipston-upon-Stour, Warwick, England
......  +Richard Tomes  b: March 1, 1744/45 in Bidford on Avon, Warwick, England  d: October 1, 1785 in Campden, Gloucester, England
        Occupation: Farmer & Sackmaker  m: February 28, 1774
......3   Charles Tomes  b: December 17, 1774 in Campden, Gloucester, England
......3   Elizabeth Tomes  b: May 30, 1776 in Campden, Gloucester, England
......3   Ann Tomes  b: May 19, 1778 in Campden, Gloucester, England
```

...... 3 Francis Tomes b: October 14, 1780 in Chipping Campden, Gloucester, England d: August 11, 1869 in Little Longstone, Derbyshire, England Occupation: Hardware Merchant, Import/Export

.... +Marin Roberts b: December 25, 1790 in Dolgelley, Merionethshire, North Wales d: January 17, 1869 in New York m: January 20, 1813

.... 4 Francis Tomes b: November 11, 1813 in Birmingham, England d: June 7, 1898

.... +Eleanor Hadden b: March 4, 1820 in New York City d: January 28, 1894 m: June 19, 1845

.... 4 Charles A. Tomes b: November 16, 1814 in Birmingham, England d: July 10, 1857 in Nashville, Tennessee Occupation: Episcopal priest

.... +Isbella Hadden b: 1815 in New York City d: 1844 in New York City m: October 6, 1838

.... *2nd Wife of Charles A. Tomes:

.... +Henrietta Otey b: July 7, 1826 in New York City d: February 22, 1887 in New York City m: November 26, 1846

.... 4 Robert Tomes b: March 27, 1817 in New York City d: August 28, 1882 Occupation: Doctor, Author, Publisher, Literary Patron

.... +Katherine Fasnet b: 1839 in Wiesbaden, Germany d: 1923 m: 1860

.... 5 Catherine Fasnet Tomes b: September 25, 1861 d: September 22, 1920

.... 5 Arthur Lloyd Tomes b: April 11, 1863 in Williamsburg d: August 17, 1922 in New York Occupation: Lawyer in Tomes, Sherk & Palmer

.... +Jenny Elizabeth Schauer

.... 5 William Austin Tomes b: February 14, 1865 in Williamsburg d: June 28, 1920 in Brooklyn Occupation: Doctor, Author, Publisher, Literary Patron

.... +Julia Hall b: 1870 in Brattleboro d: 1945 in Evanston, IL m: 1887 Marriage ending: 1908

.... 6 Yvonne Tomes b: Abt. 1888

.... 6 Valerie Tomes b: Abt. 1891

.... 6 William Austin Tomes, Jr b: July 26, 1894 in Brooklyn d: June 28, 1975 in CA but buried in Evanston

.... +Elizabeth Forrest Steel b: December 26, 1897 in Brooklyn d: April 27, 1957 in Evanston, IL m: 1926

.... 7 James Steel Tomes b: April 30, 1927 in Milwaukee, WI Occupation: Lawyer, Businessman, Publisher

.... +Joann Witmeyer Raymaley b: September 10, 1929 in Bridgeton, NJ Occupation: Fashion Consultant m: June 26, 1954

.... 8 Robert Steel Tomes b: September 14, 1960 in Chicago, IL Occupation: Lawyer, Newsprint Dealer

.... +Cynthia Zeltwanger b: May 30, 1960 in Morris, MN Occupation: Lawyer, Manager m: January 24, 1992

.... 8 Elizabeth Austin Tomes b: February 27, 1962 in Chicago, IL

.... +Scott Edwards Sandbo b: June 2, 1961 in Columbus, OH Occupation: Investment Banker m: October 25, 1986

.... 9 Elizabeth Austin Sandbo b: March 27, 1994 in Portland, OR

.... 9 John Douglas Sandbo b: August 23, 1996 in Portland, OR

.... 8 John Wilson Tomes b: February 27, 1962 in Chicago, IL Occupation: Investment Banker

.... +Jennifer Harrington b: February 9, 1966 in Boston, MA m: August 28, 1993

.... 9 Alexander Steel Tomes b: January 14, 1995 in Lake Forrest, IL

.... 9 Katherine Harrington Tomes b: October 28, 1996

.... 8 Julia Hall Tomes b: February 27, 1968 in Chicago, IL Occupation: Teacher in Portland, OR

.... 7 William Austin Tomes III b: December 24, 1929 in Milwaukee, WI

.... +Geraldine Slonaker b: 1929 m: 1951

.... 4 George Tomes b: 1819 in New York City d: December 27, 1851

.... +Maria L. b: 1830 in South America d: February 6, 1856 in New York

.... 5 Francis L. Tomes b: 1848 d: April 8, 1866

.... 4 Maria Tomes b: 1819 d: 1832 in New York City

.... 4 Richard Tomes b: 1823 in New York City d: Abt. 1827 in New York City

.... 4 Margaret Ann Tomes b: Abt. 1824 in New York City

.... +John A. Iselin b: Abt. 1821

.... 4 Benjamin Tomes b: Abt. 1826 d: June 1, 1895

.... 4 Mary Elizabeth Tomes b: 1828 in New York City

.... +Edward Burckhardt m: November 10, 1853

.... 5 Charlotte Louise Burckhardt b: Abt. 1854

...... 3 Benjamin Tomes b: January 2, 1783 in Campden, Gloucester, England

...... 3 Sarah Tomes b: October 16, 1785 in Campden, Gloucester, England d: Abt. 1851

As of July 5, 2003
POTTTREE:FTW